AMERICAN **MARKETING** ASSOCIATION

Future Marketing

Targeting Seniors, Boomers, and Generations X and Y

JOE MARCONI

NTC Business Books

NTC/Contemporary Publishing Group

273148 OCT 1 9 2002

Library of Congress Cataloging-in-Publication Data

Marconi, Joe.
      Future marketing : targeting seniors, boomers, and generations x and y / Joe Marconi.
         p.   cm. (American Marketing Association)
      Includes bibliographical references and index.
      ISBN 0-658-00138-8
      1. Target marketing.   I. Title.
    HF5415.127.M35   2000
    658.8—dc21   00-38000

For Todd and Kristin and Emily and for Karin

Portions of Chapter 4, "Targets Big Enough to Miss," first appeared in an article by the author in *American Demographics* magazine in October 1996. It is used here with permission of *American Demographics*.

Interior design by Precision Graphics

Published by NTC Business Books (in conjunction with the American Marketing Association)
A division of NTC/Contemporary Publishing Group, Inc.
4255 West Touhy Avenue, Lincolnwood (Chicago), Illinois 60712-1975 U.S.A.
Printed in the United States of America
International Standard Book Number: 0-658-00138-8

01 02 03 04 05 06 LB 20 19 18 17 16 15 14 13 12 11 10 9 8 7 6 5 4 3 2 1

Contents

Author's Note

THE MANUSCRIPT FOR this book was written by a baby boomer using fine writing instruments from Mont Blanc, Waterman, Pelikan, Parker, and Schaeffer's, and legal pads with the names Embassy and Ampad atop each binding strip. Another baby boomer typed the manuscript using Dell and Compaq computers and transferred the material to a disk, whereupon 325 pages or so of text were then slipped into the author's shirt pocket. Upon delivery to its publisher, the information was reviewed, modified, shaped, and polished by an editor and associates who are members of Generation X. This work, then, is a combination of the efforts of (at least) two generations, new technology, and old ways that still work. It's come to this.

Acknowledgments

THANKS TO THE NTC/Contemporary Publishing Group, John Nolan, Danielle Egan-Miller, Susan Moore-Kruse, and Denise Betts; the *marketing aces* at Joe Marconi Marketing Communications; Brennan Washburn and Mark de Souza at CommunicationsResource; Rich Girod, Lonny Bernardi, and Guy Kendler. Special thanks to Emily Gottschalk Marconi for the use of photo props and assistance and (again) to Karin Gottschalk Marconi for too many things to list.

Introduction

THE FUTURE. FOR DECADES THOSE words have carried images of things to come that promised to make the entire 20th century seem simple, even a bit backward. An often-cited reference is the classic film *2001: A Space Odyssey*, with its visions of automated intelligence that were both amazing and sometimes frightening in their sophistication. Everyday life would be pretty much computerized. While the word *future* still means "a time yet to come," the rapid rate of change has softened the word considerably. To many people, the future, with all its amazing possibilities, has arrived. As members of a certain generation might say, *technology rules!*

In any event, this technology, having touched virtually every part of the lives of most people in most of the world's developed countries, has brought about an exciting array of opportunities for people in the business of marketing.

Marketers have always had to be sensitive to changes in tastes and trends and have had to create or respond to whatever became "the next big thing"—a product, an event, a personality, or an issue that would strongly influence how people thought, lived, worked, and, quite significantly, made their purchasing decisions. Marketers have always had to keep an eye on the future and, in times of especially rapid change, be careful not to get poked in that eye.

The principles of effective marketing have not changed in decades, yet how these principles must be applied is seemingly ever-changing. Today's marketers know a lot more than their predecessors and have a variety of new and sophisticated tools available to them. The same can be said, however, of most of the public that the marketer must try to impress.

For a book on marketing to have any value, it must address and reflect the concerns of those people responsible for marketing, as well as the culture in which marketers must operate.

That is not to suggest that this book is a study in sociology. It's not.

It does, however, recognize that a strong marketing plan begins with the acceptance of certain principles that have been validated through research and juxtaposed against fads, trends, tastes, and geographical, ethnic, and cultural influences. Some readers may think that many of the conclusions arrived at in these chapters and, hence, the strategies, rely too much on pop culture and its reflections of (and influence on) the generations. That may be a fair critique. One defense is that overreliance on statistical analysis has often been said to remove the "soul" from a campaign aimed at touching an audience on an emotional level and hoping for a response. Marketing is not a one-way process—a lecture or presentation. If the marketer's efforts do not get a reaction or a response (a sale, a request for more information, a vote, a signature on a petition, a visit to the site, a referral . . .), then the efforts have fallen short of their objective.

"Future marketing" takes what is known and fits it to the curve of patterns of what has come before, considering seasons, cycles, what has succeeded, and, most important, what the market is saying it wants.

It is often asked whether marketing follows trends or creates trends. The answer depends on the trend and its participants, those persons who range from wanting the very newest, "cutting-edge" product to those who prefer familiarity, stability, simplicity, and a good name or reputation.

As we fully understand the factors that move our market, its needs, its desires, and what people not only are willing to accept but are willing to *pay for* as well, we can better create the products, services, programs, events, and messages that respond and even *extend* the limits.

Marketers and the management of companies large and small—and virtually every segment of the media—are again asking *What's next?* Whether their reasons for asking are practical, as in budgeting for tomorrow's needs, authorizing product research and development, or merely attempting to anticipate the next trend to satisfy a seemingly insatiable appetite for "new," it is a fair question. Competition is intense, and the cost of failure is high.

Consider the sheer numbers of persons affected by the aging of America. AARP (originally founded as the American Association of Retired Persons) claims a membership of more than 50 million. Older Americans are a powerful political and economic force, and many of them have made it clear that they are not planning to just sit on the porch and watch the sunset. These seniors want more out of life, and they represent a segment of the market that offers commercial opportunities from the simplest and most basic of products to the most luxurious recreational indulgences, from fur hats and cuff links to ocean cruises. Whether they are 55, 65, 75, or older, this market segment offers enormous opportunities for a wide range of products, services, and causes.

The baby boomers have another story. Now the largest segment of the U.S. population, they too want more—as in designer hair-care products, automobiles that reflect and convey distinctive personalities, thigh-masters, signed leather-bound first editions of bestselling books, and tax-free mutual funds. Of the estimated 75 million baby boomers, a significant percentage have considerable income and are eager for advice on what to do with it. Astute marketers are willing and eager to help.

Generation X is the name given to the market segment that follows the baby boomers in age. They want their own music, maintain their own often unique sense of fashion, and claim technology as their most visible form of expression. They are the Internet users and the MTV generation, comprising the largest market segment for the products of Microsoft and Calvin Klein, compact discs, and videos.

Generation Y follows X and is the newest emerging market segment, the children of the baby boomers. In their 20s and coming into their own, they want their place and space, literally and figuratively. Their tastes are varied but not simple. They represent a new and largely wide-open marketing opportunity.

The 21st century itself offers a platform for marketing as attention is focused to a greater degree than ever before on the *new*, the *next*, and the convergence of fashion, technology, finance, personal identity, and cultural evolution.

New wave, new age, new products.

Marketers have a unique opportunity to create, shape, or define what lies ahead. Whether building a rocket or jumping on board for the ride, the trip will be not only for the innovators but also for those who understand how to access emerging systems and commodities and adapt them to meet a variety of real or perceived needs.

Future marketing is about changes in mass marketing, mass media, and mass communications. A general audience is anything but general in its tastes, influence, or buying power. The mass market is made up of clearly defined segments; they can no longer be simply labeled as male and female; upper, middle, or lower income; liberal or conservative; northern or southern. Today's market includes so many unique and diverse elements that astute marketers can clearly define a target segment and address specific preferences quickly and more cost-effectively than ever before.

First, however, the marketer must understand the makeup and mood of those newly defined markets.

Consider the emergence of what's been characterized as *new media,* from interactive technology to changing ways to use the postal service, personal computers, cable TV, telemarketing, promotions, magazines, and "magalogs." Here they are examined for their respective efficiency as marketing vehicles.

An objective of this book is to serve as an outline or road map of the marketplace and address the myriad of target market segments. A new marketplace is unfolding, and to see it and sell it will take, quite literally, *Future Marketing.*

Part I

Meeting the Market

THE MORE THINGS change, the more they stay the same. Marketing seems to provide us with new examples of that adage every season.

Future marketing must be both an art and a science, in tune with the marketplace and all the innovations that convey its sights and sounds. Ideas and energy are the elements that keep the market alive.

Throughout the years, human nature has remained fairly constant. Hemlines and cowboy hats, SUVs and compacts come and go, but people's desires and aspirations remain largely what they've always been: success, happiness, the finer things, and the good life, however each person may choose to define it.

Principles of effective marketing have remained consistent as well. The new media overshadow the old, the Internet challenges traditional direct marketing, and a thriving and healthy economy produces more affluent consumers, or at least a significant enough percentage of people to make a market. Similarly, conditions such as fear, uncertainty, and hard times cause soft markets. People are still out there, one way or another, buying or looking for a cause to embrace, but how marketers respond must be finely tuned to reflect the pulse of the marketplace and the concerns of the consumers, businesses, the media, and the messengers.

From a perspective of some three decades of developing marketing programs for a diverse list of businesses, large and small, local and global, two truths have emerged amid all the talk of "a revolution in marketing." They are that good ideas are good ideas whether they are communicated on handbills or on the World Wide Web, and that trends and public tastes tend to come and go in cycles. Some of the most dazzling and inspired work in the 21st century will look a lot like some of the most successful work of the past. This is not because of a shortage of creativity (at least, not all of the time), but because the most effective methods for triggering emotional responses in the future will be no more revolutionary than the emotions themselves.

The message may sometimes be overshadowed by its dazzling delivery system, but it is still that message that will define what the marketer brings to the marketplace.

The diversity of the market makes the process more challenging, while opportunities have never been greater. All journeys start with a first step; this one starts on the next page.

1

Something for Everybody

Mass Marketing to the (Various) Masses

*Do unto others as you would have them do unto you.
Their tastes may not be the same.*
—George Bernard Shaw

MODERN COMMUNICATION METHODS make it possible for marketers to reach an enormous audience in only seconds. But is that what you really want to do? More important, is it the best way to market? The answer is a firm and unequivocal maybe and maybe not.

Marketing Is About Awareness and Perception

The very idea of marketing is centered on creating awareness and influencing perceptions on a particular subject, whether it is a product, a brand, a company, a service, a person, or a cause. The concept of *mass marketing* seems simple enough to understand and certainly cost-effective in its approach: present a message and a product or service to the largest possible audience at one time and, if only by the sheer force of numbers (or what used to be called the "law of averages"), the chances for success are maximized. Tell *everybody* what you've got, and the odds favor someone's (ideally, a *lot* of someones) caring.

There are enough documented instances of this theory to justify its continued employment as a primary strategy. One example involves the annual

Super Bowl games, to which companies have bragged about allocating their entire year's advertising budget in order to run a single television commercial for the largest assembled audience for any regularly scheduled event. For marketers lacking the six-figure sum for even that one buy, public relations may serve as an alternative. One well-publicized appearance on one highly rated TV program, with follow-up stories in the next day's print media, on talk radio, and on cable TV talk and news shows, can reach a mass audience and aim to be the story du jour—the subject about which everyone's talking.

For actors, political figures, CEOs, and others at the center of controversy, one appearance before a mass-media audience has successfully changed the way people think, literally overnight. A statement on the Dow Jones news wire by the chairman of the Federal Reserve, the chairman of Microsoft, or the head of IBM or Disney can make the stock market soar or plummet and affect the prices and inventory numbers immediately.

The whole world is watching, the old expression goes, and they're letting marketers (and everyone else) know immediately what they think.

Mass marketing has shown its impact on everyday consumers in more modest ways, but with just as great a relative impact. A common example when discussing advertising is toothpaste (replacing the other even more common example of selling soap). At the start of the last quarter of the 20th century, all the major brands of toothpaste could be gathered together and held in your hands. A good commercial spot presented on a popular national television program could create a spike in sales and propel a brand to market dominance, quickly establishing it as "America's favorite toothpaste" or, more noteworthy, "the toothpaste for the whole family."

That sort of thing doesn't happen much anymore. What happened to our *mass market*?

The Market Within

By the end of the century, it was not at all uncommon to find that every member of a family had his or her own toothpaste. One person may prefer a fluoride or a baking-soda-laced brand, while someone else likes one with "extra whiteness" or with a "tarter control" ingredient or one "specifically formulated to combat gingivitis." Or for sensitive gums. Or with a mouthwash or breath freshener added. Or a kids' version in a variety of fruity flavors. The challenge of providing something for everybody seemed a bit easier when "everybody" was defined as pretty much all of society. It may have been more *expensive*, but it was definitely easier. What has made it more difficult is, in part, the change in definition. A mass market today is not everyone in society, but everyone in a specific group *within* a society, and there can be many such groups. The overriding distinguishing characteristic, as far as marketers are concerned, is the fact that while all people in the mass may have common needs, the members of the various segments will have very different *wants*.

Marketing to the masses is now a process of marketing to *many* masses and not so much of aiming for an all-encompassing effect. Marketers no longer assume that, no matter how good the product or service is and how clever the marketing campaign, everybody is going to love or want what they have to offer at a given moment in time.

The distinctions that characterize the various masses have become even more dramatic, often serving not only as points of differentiation but also as overt statements of pride or identity. Lifestyle, ethnicity, age, gender, region, and income have evolved as more than demographic qualifiers. While often the members of one demographic group may have a great deal in common with members of another group, they may be unwilling to publicly concede as much. Each group embraces and sometimes flaunts what it perceives as its uniqueness. For marketers, this can be both a blessing and a curse. It can present opportunities, but it certainly represents another dimension to the challenge.

Applying the Principles of Marketing

To many professionals, marketing is both art and science, though not everyone agrees about what marketing encompasses. For purposes of this presentation, marketing is the *packaging, positioning, pricing, promotion, distribution,* and *selling* of a product or service. The principles extend as well to the marketing of an individual (as in an entertainer, a politician, or another type of public figure) or a cause.

While pricing, distribution, and selling can be fairly straightforward and specific, packaging, positioning, and promotion are elements that may elicit a strong emotional response. Often, this is what a marketer hopes to achieve. These factors change slightly or dramatically as a reflection of society's cultural shifts, tastes, and mood swings. An examination of a mass market— or of several mass markets—must consider certain known characteristics or, at least, reasonable assumptions. For example, people (whether they are customers, investors, shareholders, or supporters) want to feel valued on an individual level. While an audience, a database, or a target market may be viewed as a *mass* by marketers, all ads, scripts, and presentations must appear to be aimed at individuals. Each day, television spokespersons look directly into TV cameras and, their voices dripping with sincerity, tell 80 million or so people at once, "You are important to us. We care about your family, your health, your financial security, your business, your dreams. . . ."

Uh-huh. This total stranger on a soundstage somewhere in Hollywood or New York cares about an audience of total strangers. Do these guys really expect people to buy that?

Yes. Because they do every day.

Is this, then, an indictment of marketers as totally insincere in their concern, or even dishonest? Not at all. Research has told us that people like it when TV spokespersons appear to be speaking directly to them. They also like such personalization even when they know they are among millions of recipients of computer-generated form letters, as much as when they are part of a vast TV audience. Some people like to accept such familiarization and feel good about it, while others simply believe that it is a courtesy they deserve.

It is important for marketers to understand what members of the audience understand about the relationship between a presenter and the recipient of information, and not go overboard—overpromising and over-personalizing. A bad example is a speaker or performer who says, "You've been a wonderful audience, and I am grateful that you were here tonight" and then has security guards rebuff those who wish to shake his or her hand. Or the person who insists, "Your opinions matter to us, so write or call and tell me what you think" but does not accept or acknowledge the calls.

One Size Does Not Fit All

Credibility in marketing means delivering what is promised on a consistent basis. Some companies set up "customer service hot lines" that go unanswered or collect messages on a tape of calls that no one will ever hear. Some hot line.

These are cases of marketers failing to understand their relationship with the individuals who collectively make up their target market. Individual consumers do not consider themselves *mass* markets—or even parts of such a thing—and their individual relationships to a product, service, brand, company, candidate, or cause is a personal thing, if only on an unconscious level. A marketer who does not appreciate both the profile and the relationship of the consumer will not succeed in marketing to this person— alone *or* as a part of a mass.

Some articles of clothing are marked "one size fits all," and while that may be acceptable for a robe or a T-shirt, it is a bad approach to marketing. Diversity is often what gives a market its uniqueness and guides the marketer to develop specific value points that acknowledge this uniqueness. A marketing strategy developed with a faceless, featureless *mass* in mind is bound to be flawed.

Younger market segments are usually regarded as the most easily persuaded to support fads, trends, and abrupt shifts in styles in a wide range of categories. The cliché is "impressionable youth." A high school student wants the latest "tech vest" or backpack or shoe style or whatever is the first choice of most other high school students. At the same time, he or she wants to be thought of as unique and special. Research and casual observation tell us that this is not a characteristic exclusive to high school students or any particular age-group. Most people want to be accepted as a part of the mainstream and have their tastes and opinions validated and shared by others. They just don't want to be thought of as being "like everyone else."

A contradiction? Of course. It is one of many that marketers must balance as the desire for uniqueness and for community collide on a regular basis. Marketers who just aim for the big total numbers, as opposed to concentrating on methodically building market share, might simply say, "We consider our market to be everyone." They would probably be wrong. With what research can tell us, and has told us, we know that to approach a subject with a shotgun approach is silly and a sure way to waste both media impressions and marketing dollars. Everyone might be a prospect for toothpaste, but not everyone is a prospect for the same size or taste or formula of toothpaste, nor do all people agree on how much they are willing to pay and what they expect to get for their money.

Getting attention is the easy part. Any number of methods, from a huge advertising blitz to a pounding bass drum, will cause people to look and listen. But becoming an individual consumer's brand of choice and building brand loyalty and brand equity are the result of impressing the market with a sense of value, often one consumer at a time. The same is true of marketing a service, a person, or a cause. It is important to tell the public above all else *what's in it for them*. They might have no immediate choice but to take what you are offering, but without an understanding and acceptance of value, it's a good bet that they won't be back again. That you are the oldest and largest or are number one is lovely for you, but it holds nothing of value for the person you most want to impress and win over.

Applying the Research

Over time, marketers have learned that (1) trying to reach everybody at once with a something-for-everybody message is overkill and not the most efficient use of a marketing budget; (2) it is more effective to target only the most likely prospects and focus on growing market share; and (3) the traditional mass market that was once the coveted prize in marketing no longer exists.

Some research professionals contend that not only have the audiences become smaller, but they have also become fragmented. The addition of new competitors, products, brands, and line extensions to the marketplace means that hardly a product category remains in which sellers are not competing for dominance in comparatively small pools.

As a result, database marketing, niche marketing, one-on-one marketing, multilevel marketing, and a list of otherwise specialized approaches reflect a concession on the part of the industry that not everything is for everyone and that marketing to the masses needs to be a more defined and specific process.

For decades, the three major (and at times the *only*) television networks aggressively competed with one another to reach the largest possible audience in each day part. As soon as alternatives were operational—in the form of cable TV, satellite services, pay-per-view TV, home video, and the Internet—the networks watched their audience levels steadily erode. Many of the lost viewers did not desert mainstream TV in favor of the theater or a good book, but quietly shifted to special-interest channels and networks that offered only news, sports, comedy, movies, gardening, cooking, military history, children's shows, ethnic programming, or financial reporting. Large segments of the audience even turned to channels that programmed only old network reruns—the programs that ratings research indicated people were tired of watching. The audiences not only enjoyed seeing programs that were more than 30 years old but also enjoyed the nostalgia of the old commercials and indicated an eagerness to buy home videos, cups, shirts, watches, and other collectibles identified with material considered well past its prime.

While marketers pretty much insist that they have known all along about market segmentation, demographics, and psychographics and have understood how to interpret the data, their marketing plans would seem to defy all logic. The amount of advertising clutter continues to grow, even though marketers claim that jamming yet another ad into the clutter puts their message in an unfavorable environment. Despite the seemingly endless list of options, ads are still placed where they play to enormous audience and circulation waste, where the audience is made up of a large percentage of people who have absolutely no interest in the ad message.

TV commercial breaks have long been joked about as the signal to audiences to head for the refrigerator or the bathroom. More than 50 years after the first commercials hit the air, the ritual is still practiced. Audience numbers are larger overall, and the cost of producing a typical TV commercial is substantial. So, who stays to watch the ads, and who goes?

Market research could answer the questions, yet, even with the research available, the problem grows worse season after season.

Supply Versus Demand

Are clients receiving the research reports and simply not reading them? Maybe. But it is just as likely that the lure of "catching the brass ring"—of breaking through the clutter and playing to a huge audience, with soaring sales the result—is so seductive that marketers can't or won't let an opportunity go by.

It is a case of supply and demand. Business finds value in advertising and wants the time and space. The media want the revenue and are determined to squeeze every possible commercial second into a program. Buying ad time on the top-rated shows, leasing billboard space on the most-traveled highways, arranging appearances before a large gathering of people whenever and wherever possible, marketers continue, for all their amassed data and sophisticated skill at interpretation, to play a huge numbers game.

Sometimes it works. On a hot day, an appealing ad anywhere for Pepsi, which for years liked to differentiate itself from Coke by describing itself as the choice of a new generation, might well appeal to any generation. Or, it might not. But the same ad on a popular music video channel is far more likely to generate a good return on investment than it would if placed on a network news show.

This isn't rocket science; it is simply a reasoned approach to effective marketing. As obvious as the preceding example might seem, the agencies and marketers continue to favor being everywhere, playing the numbers and putting on a "blitz" to add to the clutter, while frequently and regularly overshooting the market.

Marketers must understand basic human nature. When people delight in saying that they were at the original Woodstock music festival or that they were in the middle of New York's Times Square on New Year's Eve, the listener pictures a huge mass of people, but the speaker is picturing only himself or herself at the center of it all—a *part* of it all, to be sure, but hardly a nameless, faceless mass. The marketer's goal (some may say *art*) is to reach the *person within the mass*. Keep before you the profile of the person to be reached—in this case, a person who likes the kind of music that typified Woodstock—and aim your message at that person, and not at everyone who likes music or has ever been to an outdoor concert or has ever been outdoors period. Accept that mass marketing is more effective when targeted to persons with specific, definable characteristics within a mass and not merely at the total mass.

Change Is the Lifeblood of Marketing

Few marketers would deny that the marketplace has changed and continues to change dramatically, whether they (or members of the public) like it or not. Efforts initiated to meet tomorrow's challenges may not be enough. Demographic and lifestyle shifts have altered traditional patterns in mass marketing and brand loyalty. In a multioption society, the individual consumer is in charge.

The distinction that the mass market has gone from meaning everyone to meaning everyone in a particular group represents a significant change in marketing.

Perhaps the most literally overused word in marketing is *change*. When Bob Dylan sang "The Times They Are A-Changin'" in the 1960s, a generation of then-young baby boomers listened in awe. They were struck by how profound the message seemed to be. The 21st century finds the same generation and others still awestruck at the power of change—economic, social, and cultural. The term *revolution* is applied liberally to describe developments in every category of fashion (the latest styles in clothes, shoes, haircuts), as well as breakthroughs in technology and a narrowing or broadening of standards of acceptability or tolerance toward once unconventional lifestyles.

Change has always been the lifeblood of marketing. It is what keeps business in business and creates new start-up opportunities. Experienced marketers know when it is time to "go for the face-lift"—update packaging, alter or dump a particular ad or campaign, retire a spokesperson or a slogan, reposition a brand or a brand extension.

This knowledge is neither magical nor a matter of luck, but a result of marketers' hearing the voice of the market and responding accordingly.

Listen and Learn

Increasingly, companies must listen and understand what the voices of the market are saying. What information may be obtained from customers, from dealers, and even from competitors must be considered in order to make the right decisions at the right time. Firms that stop listening to the market, or that ignore or misinterpret its signals, will be left behind in today's competitive environment.

Good marketers are good listeners. How information is acquired, processed, and applied is the difference between science and guessing. Market research will be discussed in some detail in a later chapter, but for now, beware of the fallacy of failing to distinguish among serious research, trend shop reports, and random statements of opinion. A CEO or another top gun who states empirically, "I know what works in my business, and I don't need research reports to tell me I'm right" displays a level of arrogance that may sound authoritative and impressive, but reflects an immaturity that could be costly in business.

Some marketing professionals, unwilling to concede that there could be information that they don't possess, will say that their great strength is having a feeling for the market, or a strong *sense* of the market. If in fact one is blessed with such talents or abilities, it should be counted as "value added." Listening to the voice of the market means hearing definitively what customers, clients, and the public need, want, and are willing to pay for, and having the data to back up those conclusions. It is not about waging a campaign to convince the public that you are smarter than the marketer—to say, "My job is to educate the public about our product (or company or cause), and once they become educated, they will be on our side."

Get real. Unless the product in question is something so vastly complex as to truly warrant education, this is arrogance masquerading as salesmanship disguised as marketing. People do not assign brand loyalty to something they had to be "persuaded" to buy, accept, or support. Instead of trying to change the minds of those who are *not* prospects for your message, devote attention, energy, and the marketing budget to true prospective customers or supporters. The marketplace rewards the listeners, those who respond by giving the public what it wants and needs. Good marketers don't need a sixth sense or any other psychic powers to succeed.

Keeping Up with the Times

For decades, two successful brands stood apart from their competitors as symbols of quality, tradition, status, and success: Brooks Brothers and the *Wall Street Journal*. An executive in a Brooks Brothers suit, reading a copy of the day's *Wall Street Journal*, projected an image that spoke volumes about that person's status and level of success—or, at least, the *appearance* of success (briefcase and eyeglasses optional).

As superficial as this reference might be, the perception was that when an executive wore Brooks Brothers and read the *Journal*, that person had *arrived*. Curiously, as perceptions go, the suit was relatively expensive and the paper was not, but the combination of the two conveyed the success image. If the suit were paired with *Sports Illustrated, National Geographic, Newsweek,* or *USA Today*, the image wasn't there. It was less. And a reader of the *Wall Street Journal* wearing any other attire, even pricey designer labels, was just a person reading a newspaper. The two brands together told the success story. As trends in fashion came and went, these two brands remained constant, seemingly oblivious to a need to keep pace with styles and trends.

Finally, seemingly without notice, both brands, having ridden out cycle after cycle, found change forced upon them in response to radical changes in the culture—specifically, the fragmenting of the mass market as it had been into several different masses. The overall perception of status was altered when there was no longer an overall authority on fashion or information or almost anything else. The "look of success" was no longer what it had been because the most successful figures in various professions and pursuits were revising all the old rules by breaking them.

Brooks Brothers and the *Wall Street Journal* both recognized that their need was less to be the arbiter of status than to be seen as a vital brand, in tune with the times and the market, not as much defining it anymore as reflecting it. Where once, both brands might have prided themselves on the public's perception that what they produced was not for everyone, economics, dramatic shifts in demographics, and a changing marketplace forced them to modify their time-honored characteristics and reposition to accommodate the preferences of the new mass markets or sacrifice not only reputation but also significant market share and the "currency" that was a historic part of each brand's name. The desire to remain viable prevailed. While neither came away with a powerful image comparable to what it had before, both remain respected, well-positioned brands.

As changes in retailing became more dramatic, one of the oldest and largest American retailers seemed so fully out-of-step that much of the marketplace could only look on in wonder, the way one can't resist gaping at an accident scene while passing it.

Sears, the giant department-store chain that once advertised itself as "where America shops," became the stores where only *some* of America shopped, and as the 20th century drew to a close, Sears seemed determined to see that number continue to shrink.

What happened?

A short answer might be that, in the face of change or in spite of it, Sears stopped listening to the voice of the market. It failed to take notice of the shift in how the new mass markets were constituted. Typical American consumers (although, such a generalization is certainly flawed) are more mobile and better informed as to both what they want and where it is available to them. Additionally, disposable income is no longer limited to only the wealthier segment of society, and the "local department store" is no longer the center of a family's shopping experience.

Malls, specialty stores, catalog shopping, home shopping networks, and E-commerce have all amassed considerable market share. Ethnicity, lifestyle, tastes, and the ability to both afford and project a desired image have become factors in buying decisions, where once only cost, convenience, and practicality ruled. Sears was mired in a corporate culture that no longer looked like the customers it served.

Building Brand Loyalty Isn't What It Used to Be

The public—the *masses*—have become better informed as to the wider range of choices available in products, services, and assorted trappings that help to define a lifestyle.

Brand marketing has loomed larger in the 21st century, primarily because of the cost of delivering new customers. The steadily rising prices of acquiring mailing lists, lead lists, telemarketing services, media advertising, direct mail, premiums and promotions, and research have driven up the cost that companies pay for every new customer. Sampling is fine, even loss leaders are still regarded as part of the cost of doing business, but every customer— from the detergent (and toothpaste) buyer to the ticket holder, cell phone user, magazine subscriber, and contributor to public television—is a costly customer to acquire. It is only through continued, repeat business, along with support and even referrals, that the marketer's enterprise stands to turn an investment into profit. Building brand loyalty is the only way to transform the first-time customer into the regular customer who becomes the revenue generator.

Changes in the marketing environment that work against brand loyalty have a lot to do with the multitude of choices available to consumers. Research indicates that consumers are willing to travel farther and pay more in order to acquire or associate themselves with certain image-rich brand names. Consumers have demonstrated that they are willing to pass dozens of places where a good cup of fresh-brewed coffee could be purchased at a lesser cost in order to buy a cup of premium-priced Starbucks coffee. For many consumers, just being seen carrying the easily identified paper cup with the Starbucks logo says much of what they want people to know about their ability to afford a premium product.

The consumers who choose luxury hotels and first-class travel accommodations are also willing to pay extra for image and the association with brands that "make a statement" about them. BMW, Mercedes-Benz, Tiffany, and Mont Blanc are only a few of the brands that hope to tap into this *mass* of status-conscious consumers. This group has long been regarded as highly discriminating, and in recent years, marketers have noted, they are much *younger*. The willingness of the members of this market segment to travel farther and pay more poses a serious brand-building challenge to, alas, lower-priced, closer-to-home products, services, companies, and brands that may be perceived as a less prestigious acquisition. This matter is of added concern, in that this target segment is one that can best afford to make such choices and show independent purchasing power.

In contrast to the brand-conscious, image-conscious big spender is the consumer who will drive for an hour to shop at an outlet mall where the

savings on any items purchased may be easily offset by the cost of traveling.
The perception is that the travel time and expense and perhaps even dealing with the dreaded crowds of fellow shoppers is all worth the effort in
order to get a deal and pay a lower price. Add to that the shopper's perception of having made the purchase on his or her own terms and you have a
satisfied, if somewhat impractical, customer.

Home shopping? Discount malls? High-status brands?

Fifty years ago and 50 years from now, the first rule of marketing remains
Know your market.

Changes Are Sometimes Simply Choices

Know what matters most to the customer, and market to that. Some people will never buy from a catalog or via computer. They won't give anyone
they can't see their home address or credit card number. These are the same
people who will never use an ATM (automatic teller machine) and might
insist on dealing directly with a bank teller or service representative. Others
will seize any opportunity to cut corners, save time, and limit travel expense.
Marketers know this. Again, it is a matter of listening to the voice of the
market.

To the companies, products, or brands with marketing plans built
around a positioning statement such as "We're number one" or "We are the
largest," consumers routinely respond, "So what?"

Such claims fail to tell *any* market segment or group why what the marketer has to sell should be the brand or company of choice. In an era of rapid
changes, the public has seen and heard so many different businesses deliver
so many variations on self-serving themes that they have largely begun to
"tune out" and, understandably, dismiss the message as meaningless. In any
market environment, claims that emphasize a subject's value to the customer are the ones the customer remembers.

Times do change, and listening to the market pays off. *Time* magazine's
reader research indicated that the gossipy "People" section was among the
most popular. So, *Time* spun off the section, expanded it into a magazine
all its own called *People*, and enjoyed one of the greatest successes in recent
publishing history. *Time* continued listening and heard that, while *People's*
feature stories on politics or human tragedy were read, it was the movie,
TV, and music pieces that most pleased the market. Because of this,

Entertainment Weekly was launched. After a shaky start and a bit of fine-tuning, the second spin-off also became a hit with readers and very profitable for its parent company. As if there were no end to how far the astute publisher was prepared to go, *Time* created a fourth-generation feature magazine with *In Style.*

Writing in its stylish competitor *The New Yorker,* Kurt Andersen noted of *In Style,* "A spin-off of *People,* the magazine is essentially a how-to manual for regular Americans who want the same haircut and wear the same boots, have the same curtains and eat the same salad as their favorite celebrities, except for the rich and famous part."

While not the runaway hit that *People* proved to be, *In Style* was nonetheless a success, mostly as a reflection of its readers and the times. Much of the public had moved from being "celebrity worshipers," as big fans were described, to believing that a bond existed between famous people and those who watched them, and that bond extended to sharing an insider's look at the celebrity's home and personal choices of designers, foods, and religious beliefs, from Buddhism to the Church of Scientology. These magazines, their TV counterparts *Entertainment Tonight, Inside Edition,* and *CNN NewsStand,* and a number of websites would once have been considered intrusive on a level with stalking. They now reflect the preferences of both marketers and the public.

Changing the Past

Changes are typically cyclical. Wait long enough and you'll see particular preferences in music, fashion, entertainment, foods, and even politics come and go and come around again. Bell-bottom slacks, long skirts, short skirts, sideburns, red meat, cigars, swing music, salad bars, rich desserts, cowboy hats, and compact cars are a few of the styles, trends, and indulgences that have passed in and out and in and out of favor over a span of decades, and the cycles appear to be getting shorter. Trends in marketing are often cyclical as well, with direct mail, market research, and consulting being the areas that seem to receive the greatest numbers of blessings and curses as the seasonal winds blow.

In terms of the work itself, many of the most successful marketing campaigns are resurrected on a fairly predictable cycle and relaunched. Spokespersons are brought back; sweepstakes are repeated; sometimes even the original TV and print ads are returned to center stage unaltered. That an approach has been used before doesn't mean it can't be done again (assuming that the something done was successful the first time out). Repeating successful campaigns might be justified as tapping into an appreciation by the target market group for nostalgia, or capitalizing on a trend toward *retro* advertising. The objective is a successful marketing effort, not a prize for originality. Even revivals get awards on Broadway, but usually only if a lot of tickets have been sold first. Don't be shy about using what works or has worked before.

Just make sure of your purpose.

In a late 1999 examination of the use of recycled advertising campaigns, the *New York Times* highlighted three golden oldies currently being reprised and asked prominent ad experts to assess the wisdom of such a move. Describing "Brand illusions—defunct advertising icons . . . being dusted off and spiffed up for today's market," the paper asked, "Will the nostalgia play work?"

Actually, several old campaigns came out of mothballs in 1999 in an apparent attempt to impress a new generation, but the trio the *Times* noted were the "Jolly Green Giant" (a longtime image used on behalf of Green Giant packaged foods), Charlie the Tuna (a cartoon spokesman for Star-Kist brand canned tuna), and Mr. Whipple (a fictional supermarket manager who policed store aisles looking for customers who seemed unable to resist squeezing rolls of Charmin bathroom tissue).

All these images were frivolous and would likely not be considered for introduction to the more sophisticated 21st-century audience. Yet, with their market share flat, these long-running (though long-retired) images, seemed worth a try.

It is easy to spot the differences between the earlier, successful versions of the ads and the newer, supposedly "revisited" versions. In the 1961 campaign using the Jolly Green Giant, the character was something of a caveman, later incarnations had him looking more like a toy action figure. The change doesn't work. The newer model is simply less interesting. The Green Giant of the 1940s was virtually a mythological figure, who has since evolved into a more Disney-like character, more suggestive of the hero of an animated action-figure movie. It may be colorful, but there is little reason to suspect that it is doing much to advance the product. Similarly, the revamped Charlie the Tuna is not the haplessly cool old Charlie that audiences remember; his features are enlarged, and he appears to be rubberized.

These somewhat recycled campaign icons meant to tap into baby-boomer nostalgia, but they lack the texture that made the characters (and by association, the products and brands) the subjects of likable, memorable ad campaigns. A more viable course might have been to show more respect for the aspects of the work that made it successful the first time. The new versions of the Green Giant and Charlie and, for that matter, Charmin's Mr. Whipple, are not the lovable old characters that baby boomers found endearing, nor are they appealing to a newer, younger audience, so why bother to bring them back?

If a brand marketer is recycling a previously successful campaign and hoping that lightning will strike twice, don't bring back a character and have him look like another character.

But, how risky would it have been to place the characters (particularly the cartoon characters) in the same context as their original versions? That is, in the case of both the Jolly Green Giant and Charlie the Tuna, as sophisticated as animation has become, would audience members of any age or demographic have responded favorably to the character's looking as it did in a 1960s animated version?

The overriding issue as it applies to the potential success of these three campaigns must be considered on two levels: (1) the fact that the original mass market for these ads is now a fragmented market and thus, perhaps different or distinct in its makeup, and (2) the question of whether marketers are trying to appeal to exactly the same audience to which they appealed some three decades earlier or to a whole new audience, and merely using a character that was used successfully before.

As for the second point, there's a big difference. In trying to appeal to a market segment on the basis of nostalgia, don't try to update or otherwise "tamper" with the symbol that you are asking people to recall. If, on the other hand, absent a great new idea, your approach is to "adapt" something that has worked in the past, then a more contemporary version fashioned to appeal to the tastes of the current market is totally appropriate. A "son of . . ." any of these characters could have given the marketers a stepping-off point and some familiarity to older audience members as well as a wide-open opportunity to interest new generations.

Whether the idea is old or new, what's key is knowing your market. If the market has changed and the idea has been presented before, the marketer must determine if the same idea would be viewed as fresh by a "new" market or whether it is the idea that needs to be *made* fresh.

Mass Communications Then and Now

Though it's true that the mass market has become a *group* of masses, the most efficient method of reaching the masses—separately or together—is still via mass communication. While it can be argued that there is no substitute for personal communication in bringing to bear the power to persuade, most marketers do not have the time, budget, or inclination to go door-to-door. Personal sales calls are certainly productive, and multilevel marketing programs (such as Amway or Avon) that concentrate on small group interaction work to meet recruiting objectives as much as market awareness and sales. Nevertheless, and despite the fragmentation of the mass market, most traditional means of mass communication are still quick and effective.

Where the members of the chorus sometime begin to go a bit off-key is in the definition of the term *mass communication*. Like so many other terms in marketing, this one carries definitions that are broad and varied, if not outright confusing.

Professor John R. Bittner of the University of North Carolina at Chapel Hill is an authority on the subject. He writes:

What is *Mass Communication*? It is the deadline of the investigative journalist, the creative artistry of documentaries, the bustle of the network newsroom, the silence of a computer, the hit record capturing the imagination of millions, the radio disc jockey and the advertising executive planning a campaign. It is radio, research, recordings, resonators, and ratings. It is television, teletext, telephones and tabloids. It is satellites, storyboards, systems and segues. It is all of these things and many more. It *is* dynamic and exciting, but it is not new. Let us go back for a moment to the dawn of civilization—more than two and a half million years ago.

The professor explains in detail how the term *mass communication* covers the very beginning of language, society's adapting a system of communication, print technology, papermaking, distribution, the invention of the telegraph by Morse, the telephone by Bell, and the radio by Marconi (no relation), evolving to the realities of sensory channels, personal and impersonal communication, and feedback.

With all due respect to Professor Bittner, what the marketer is looking for can probably be summed up in his declaration that "Essentially, then, *mass communication is messages communicated through a mass medium to a large number of people."*

Was the town crier of olden days engaging in an act of mass communication when he wandered the village streets ringing a bell, shouting, "Here ye, here ye..." and delivering what would be the modern equivalent of time, temperature, and headline news?

Yes.

And the Roman orator, speaking to the crowd gathered in the town square? The politician addressing a few dozen or a few hundred or a few thousand people at a campaign rally—is that also mass communication? Or the announcer with a microphone on opening day at the ballpark?

Yes to all of them.

But in a more practical sense, when marketers discuss mass communication, they are far less concerned with the fine early work of the cavemen in this area and are more concerned with what has been designated as the *mass media*—print, broadcast, cable, the Internet, and vehicles such as audio- and videotapes, CDs, and disks that can be distributed in large numbers to influence large numbers of people.

In the 21st century, how the breakdown of mass media will be ranked remains to be seen. In every era, the newest innovation has declared all previous forms of entertainment obsolete. Television was supposed to have signaled the end of movies and radio. The telephone was to have rendered mail—specifically greeting cards—unnecessary. Fax machines and Federal Express were triggers to more changes. Newspapers and magazines have been pronounced dead and buried and have come back again more times than Count Dracula. E-mail and the Internet marked only a later and more dramatic chapter in the history of mass communication, in no small part because the mass media declared the victors with the authority and a circulation and an audience reach more powerful than at any time in history.

Marketers can be justifiably both excited and frightened by what all of this means. In an industry driven by new, bigger, and better ideas and where *innovation* is a sacred word, the title of an old song resonates; "Everything old is new again."

Mass Media Exposed

A later chapter will lay out 21st-century media more specifically, but it is important at this juncture to make some distinctions between *media* and *mass media*. Again, definitions vary, as some people maintain that the term *mass media* is redundant—that all media are mass media. Considering each singular *medium*, doesn't print, even a low-circulation newspaper, address a *mass* of people? Of course it does. And the same is true of single TV stations, including the smallest cable-access channel.

It does seem to turn into a word game. One billboard in a carefully chosen location may be a finely targeted media buy. Yet, a billboard's only value is in its being seen by a mass of people.

In the interest of not getting tangled up in technicalities, let's agree that mass media are vehicles for reaching a significantly large segment of the market. An ad placed in a supermarket shopping cart or aisle display is point-of-sale advertising. It may be sold as out-of-home media, but it is not a *mass* media buy. Likewise, a marketer's participation in a closed-circuit television event or in the pages of a trade magazine is in media, but professionals would not consider it in the category of *mass* media.

An appearance or a mention on NBC's *Today Show* or CNN's *Larry King Live* is a mass-media exposure, partly because of the large audience these programs reach, and because such appearances are likely to have residual merchandising impact by being referenced in print and on other programs.

While it may be questioned whether or not limited-circulation or small-audience radio and TV exposures qualify as mass-media exposures, certain media leave little doubt as to their impact on the masses: these are the conglomerates. The growth that began seriously in this area in the third quarter of the 20th century, and kicked into high gear in the fourth quarter, will likely be continuing reality in the 21st century.

Time Warner, the Walt Disney Company, Viacom, News Corporation, General Electric, Bertelsmann, and Seagram continue to amass, consolidate, and cross-pollinate their interests in publishing, broadcasting, cable programming, movie and TV production, distribution, theme parks, lodging, and real estate.

More specifically, after years of fighting to maintain their control of television, every broadcast network surrendered to the power of cable and *added* a cable channel or network of its own. Some added many, such as General Electric's NBC, which added CNBC and later MSNBC, its joint venture with Microsoft. All networks also not only have Internet sites, but where once they would have discouraged their TV viewing audience from leaving them even momentarily to "check out our website," they now aggressively encourage such activity. On-air talent and production staff shift back and forth from the broadcast network to the cable channels and websites, as if moving from room to room in a house. Archival footage and current news and feature video are shared liberally. Presence and high visibility is a major objective with constant cross-promotion. The theory is that if the same organization has several channels, an audience may be lost to one and gained by another, rather than simply lost to a competitor.

Advertising is often sold as a "package," and news stories that offer marketers public relations or promotional opportunities can turn up on several channels.

Clearly, this is about as mass as media are likely to get.

So, when do you choose mass media versus point-of-sale, multilevel marketing, one-on-one relationship marketing, or telemarketing?

The answer is pure marketing: Clearly define your objective, and develop a strategy and tactics that will effectively achieve that objective within a specific budget and time line. Mass-marketing or mass-media exposures may be the course of choice, or they may not. Trade show participation or personal contact may be preferred.

For marketers, the fragmenting of the old mass markets into mass-market *groups* ultimately is both a budgeting advantage and a more target-market-specific plus, even if it does signal the end of a something-for-everybody-at-once era.

Summary Points

1. Marketing is centered on creating awareness and influencing perceptions.
2. Marketing to the masses has evolved to mean marketing to *many* masses or groups and not the sum total of everyone at once.
3. Diversity is often what gives a market its uniqueness and guides marketers to develop specific points that address this quality.
4. Younger market segments are usually regarded as the most easily influenced regarding fads, trends, and shifts in style.
5. Trying to reach everybody at once is overkill and is not the most effective use of your budget.
6. New strategies in marketing reflect a concession by marketers that not everything is for everybody.

7. Companies must be attuned to the voice of the market and listen. Firms that lose touch with the market and either ignore or misinterpret its signals will fail in a competitive environment.

8. Focus on giving the market what it wants, not what you want it to have.

9. Building brand loyalty is about turning first-time customers into longtime customers. Take seriously the idea of always emphasizing the value of your brand to your customer.

10. The fragmentation of the old mass markets into mass-market *groups* both creates a budgetary advantage and allows for a more target-specific marketing plan.

2

Segmenting the Market

*Understanding Demographics
and Psychographics*

The golden age is not in the past, but in the future.
—E. H. Chapin

IN THE FUTURE, will marketers leave a consumer alone in a crowd? How fragmented and finite can a market become before it technically no longer even qualifies as a market, but merely as a series of customized plans? The experience of dining out at such places as the Hard Rock Cafe, the Rainforest Cafe, or Planet Hollywood emphasizes that many restaurants no longer hope to appeal to everyone. And there are cigar bars, tearooms, and coffeehouses. Even the simple corner diner is likely to have a theme and be clear that its hope is to appeal to a special, like-minded customer. And when it comes to market segmentation, that word *special* takes on greater emphasis.

Mom and Pop Go Global

The late pop-culture artist Andy Warhol is reported to have said that in the future, everyone will be famous for 15 minutes. That was in 1968. People first laughed at the line, but today the expression "15 minutes of fame" is a part of the lexicon of everyday life. Perhaps most people don't really believe that, in America, anyone can grow up to be president, but people surely seem willing to believe that anyone can become a celebrity—or at least famous for 15 minutes.

And everyone's not *everyone* anymore. Marketers of automobiles, organizers on behalf of environmental issues, political candidates, and makers of candy bars know that the age of specialization has arrived. People don't want to be called "the market." If they must be categorized, the label must be special and worthy of notice: "yuppies" (young urban professionals), "puppies" (poor urban professionals), "skippies" (school kids with income and purchasing power), "woofs" (well-off older folks), "mobys" (older moms with babies), and the list keeps growing, as the population grows and the market goes up or down.

Year after year, the world's population continues to increase. To marketers, much like so many other occurrences, this represents an opportunity. Advances in technology and the creation of the "information superhighway" have elevated the idea of a global village. Borders are falling away, and the world is getting smaller. And for marketers, this can be viewed only as (ahem) a *world* of opportunity.

Hundreds of cable television channels, satellite transmissions, and, most especially, the explosive popularity of Internet communications have changed the dynamics of the marketplace. To treat the audience/public/target market as it was treated even a decade ago is not antiquated thinking; it's just stupid. Even the "mom-and-pop grocery store" so often referenced in examples now has E-mail and a website. These innovations have changed the way millions of people plan, work, shop, communicate, and live. Even the most successful businesses have had to reappraise how they relate to their public and how they market.

The previous chapter examined the concept of "something for everybody"—a single product that was deemed suitable for every person, regardless of age, gender, ethnicity, etc. In that scenario, the whole world would be considered as if everyone in it were one giant "market," and the fragmenting of that market into the smaller markets created masses nonetheless. The global marketplace brings the marketer not only more *people* but also more and different ways to market. As interests differ within families, age groups, and economic levels, the world market, viewed from virtually any perspective, affords a greater range of opportunities.

Even when the marketplace is viewed as *one world*, marketers must fully understand the inherent diversity and exploit the unique characteristics of the individuals, to the degree that is possible. This seeming contradiction—that everyone can be viewed as a group, yet separately—can be resolved by segmenting the market. Research is vital, and is the subject of the chapter that follows. *Knowing the market*—its size and shape and the likes and dislikes of those it comprises—is the first key to success.

Segmentation Basics

Segmenting the market simply means dividing a large population or group into smaller groups with the same or similar characteristics. The American Demographic Institute classifies the elements of segmentation in consumer marketing as geographic, demographic, and psychographic.

Geographics, as we learned in third grade, identify the position and characteristics of a particular area. In marketing, the term similarly relates to characteristics shared and geographic locations.

Demographics, the heart of market segmentation, are the characteristics about people that influence or relate to their behavior, such as age, ethnicity, lifestyle, income, family status, health, education, and gender.

Psychographics represent attitudes and values. After having defined target individuals or groups demographically, the next step is to understand what makes one individual or group act the same as or differently from another.

Such information would be important to marketers at any time, but the various options available for delivering one's message have become more immediate and often more expensive. Each communication channel has identified its audience in demographic terms and premium-priced it accordingly.

Relying on the Demographics

University of North Carolina professor John Bittner contends that "with a mass audience, it is often difficult to find certain segments of the population to which specific mass-media messages are to be directed. . . . As a result, media buyers must rely on demographics to categorize the population. Demographic characteristics are the basic statistical data. . . . They are used more often than any other method to pinpoint a certain mass audience and thus to determine such things as how much an advertiser will be charged for airing a commercial during a particular television program at a specified time."

Market segments include working mothers, young unmarried people, and even younger people who have just begun to drive cars and earn money—and are thinking about the first tastes of independence, with a bank ATM card and personal-care products at top of mind.

What about the middle-aged, overweight people with limited financial resources? This group is a prime target for low-cost or financed health-club memberships, weight-loss clinics, mail-order exercise equipment, books, videos, and referrals.

It is, and long has been, a youth-oriented culture. Marketers (and the media) are often criticized for celebrating the young and dismissing older people and those with special needs, unless of course the marketer's product line or service is aimed at those particular segments. What is true about the youth-marketing angle is that it is the higher-visibility (often louder and more graphic) marketing. Seasoned professionals recognize the fertile territory in each segment and leave nothing overlooked.

In the future, ratings and the other measurements of reach and influence will be increasingly more important in selling to segmented audiences, as well as in selling segmented audiences to advertisers.

Exploiting Opportunities

Demographic research has become a marketing device for exploitation in and of itself, in addition to being a tool used to define the composition of a particular audience. For example, a given radio program is number one in overall listenership: simply put, in raw numbers, it has the largest audience. However, unlike print, which can claim a shelf life for later reference and a pass-along potential, radio is there with its impact and then gone forever. This is often a negative, yet the *immediacy* of the medium is part of its attraction and its impact. To that end, having the largest audience is no minor claim. The station's advertising department certainly thinks so and is likely to issue a press release to that effect, and to run ads in the local and trade media to tout its success and, hopefully, convince more advertisers that the station with the largest audience is a good place to have one's message promoted.

Meanwhile, another radio station in the same market, while not having the most listeners overall, produces data to show that it has the most *women* listeners . . . and it plans to issue a press release and buy ad space to tout this fact. It plans to zero in on advertisers that have a particular interest in reaching women in large numbers.

Meanwhile (again), a third station in the market claims its audience is stronger than anyone else among male listeners 18 to 49 years of age, the group that is frequently referred to as the "all-important" demographic because it is a large segment and is made up of people with significant disposable income. More than any other target demo, this group also tends to recycle that disposable income in the marketplace. Big numbers for this group is very big news.

So . . . a press release? An ad? Some shouting from the rooftops by the station's ad director?

Bet on it.

Then there is the station that is number one among retired folks. While this segment, at first glance, may not seem to be the most sizzling target market, look again. Cruise lines, resorts and scenic destinations, historical sites, health insurance plans, and nutritional supplements love the older market and regard it as a highly valued target group.

Who Cares Who's on First?

So, it is possible for several radio stations in the same town to all be number one at something. Is it the best marketing strategy to take being number one as a positioning strategy and build on it? Not especially. Ads that claim the advertiser is supreme at something or other are largely dismissed as self-serving, grandstanding, or chest beating. Remember, customers and prospective customers like to believe that *they* are number one. They like to be reassured that their interests come first with you (even if they know it's not true). People who read ads, watch commercials, or listen to a telemarketer's pitch want to know how whatever the marketer's message is about affects *them*. That the advertiser is number one doesn't help the customer. That the candidate is leading in popular-opinion polls doesn't do anything for the voters.

Many marketers have run "we're number one" campaigns and have seen an increase in business. Logically, they can credit the ads and believe that such braggadocio works—that people rally around and want to be in proximity to someone singing "We Are the Champions!"

Well, maybe. But maybe not. One school of thought holds that it is not as much the "brag" ad that works as it is simply *advertising* that works. It is the visibility of advertising versus the invisibility of not advertising. It is not a coincidence that, under normal circumstances, companies that advertise get more business than companies that don't. Fund-raisers who run TV and print ads asking for support receive more contributions than the fund-raisers who do not advertise but somehow just expect people to find them.

Consider how much more effective an ad may be that, after—or instead of—bragging about how successful a company is, proceeded to list the benefits to the customer of doing business with good ol' number one. These may include free delivery, satisfaction guaranteed, discounts to frequent customers, coupons for discounts on related products and services, a private mailing of upcoming special sales or offers, reduced or zero financing, and the like.

Give the people who make up your target market a reason to choose you, a benefit statement that makes the product or brand worth buying.

If every ad or marketing effort does not win over the targeted market segment, it should at the very least not alienate it or any other market segments.

Media decisions are critical to successful marketing campaigns. Historically, a case could be made that television advertising, while arguably expensive when compared with other media, reached the largest and broadest audience and was therefore most effective. The importance of market segmentation altered that theory. Cable TV caused some marketers to reconsider the power of network buys, and the Internet dealt the networks yet another blow. The official death of TV networks and advertising seems to come up about once each week.

As every medium experiences some erosion, it tends to blame its competition and changing patterns of public taste, rather than its advertisers. Network TV viewership steadily declined throughout the 1990s, mostly due to the plethora of entertainment and information alternatives available.

Hundreds of cable channels and satellite choices, as well as the Internet, prerecorded video products, and a host of other options have made the half century of domination by NBC, ABC, and CBS seem like the days when their magazine forerunners *Look*, *Life*, and the *Saturday Evening Post* were as much fixtures in family homes as the family members themselves.

Each new medium (and each of its participants) has sought to define and sharpen its image by playing hard to the demographics group that it has or seeks. Along the way, a certain amount of stumbling is inevitable. In the 21st century, such competitive posturing will continue, some of it so aggressively as to appear almost desperate . . . and some of it, alas, out of desperation.

To Segment or Not to Segment

Some marketing professionals question whether market segmentation is the right strategy in certain cases. To determine the effectiveness of the course, a number of qualifying questions may first be considered, such as:

1. Can the market be identified and measured?
2. Is the segment large enough to be profitable?
3. Is the market reachable?
4. Is the segment responsive?
5. Is the segment expected not to change quickly?

By dividing the total target audience demographically and identifying the characteristics of each segment, media buying can be done more intelligently, certainly in terms of cost-effectiveness, with less audience waste. Shaping both the tone and focus of the marketing message along segment-specific demographic lines also points to a higher degree of effectiveness.

Nevertheless, astute marketers may well challenge a strategy that seems so obvious. Let's discuss the five qualifiers in order.

1. Questioning whether a particular market segment can be *identified and measured*, consider, for example, consumers whose vision is poor or whose scalps itch. While these are difficult, perhaps impossible, traits to measure, marketers of eyeglasses, contact lenses, and dandruff shampoos need such information at some level for proper product positioning. Would a survey or study of optometrists or optical shops and trade association research reveal how many people in a particular region, at a particular time, wear glasses or contact lenses; how many pairs of each are sold or prescribed annually; or the number or percentage of products sold from open racks in drugstores and bookshops versus prescription lenses sold through private practices and eye shops? Are there statistics on schoolchildren to whom vision tests are administered under state law?

    Do state departments of motor vehicles compile statistics on the numbers of drivers who wear or need corrective lenses? Do market research firms have any information derived from surveys or sampling that may be purchased or referenced?

    Itchy scalp? What about data on the sales of "dandruff shampoos" or medicated shampoos versus "regular formula" shampoo? Surveys of dermatologists? Barbers and hairstylists? The researchers' test groups?

    If such information cannot be amassed, the question may well have less to do with segmentation than whether or not a product should be brought to market at all, without a clear indication that a market for it exists.

2. The potential *profitability* of a particular segment is a function of several considerations, not the least of which is the manufacturer's and marketer's expectations. Using the previous example of a shampoo, obviously if research indicates that measurable interest is not there, perhaps the idea should remain only an idea for the time being. But if indicators are that a strong potential market exists, marketers need to take the next step.

   Suppose the research indicates that the marketplace wants the shampoo, but that only certain segments—such as younger women living in large metropolitan areas—are good prospects to purchase the companion conditioner as well. Given that only a limited number of the product's core customer base want the companion product, raising questions about the new product's potential to generate enough profit to justify an investment, does the company produce the conditioner in limited quantities and accept that it may never be profitable but is necessary to sell shampoo? Perhaps the marketer's goal is to sell an aftershave or a cologne or a bath soap, and the shampoo (with or without conditioner) will be factored into the cost of the core product, a premium-priced or designer-label brand.

   Questions such as these are a part of the exercise of bringing a product to market and have a decided impact on the market segmentation issue. Is it necessary to have every product be a runaway success, or is it acceptable to have modest sales, and possibly *no* profit on a product, but have a happy, loyal customer because you provide something extra? Another variable is the question of shelf space and warehouse space that retailers face (not always enthusiastically) when a new product extension is introduced.

3. Whether or not the market is *reachable* is less of a problem in the 21st century than perhaps at any other time. Regardless of the subject—a product, a service, a cause, an event, a candidate—the diversity of media for delivering a message anticipates virtually every challenge. Catalogs, direct mail, transit, malls, telemarketing, home shopping networks, community information boards, and the Internet have

made the ability of marketers to reach their targets widely diverse and broad enough to accommodate most every target segment.

4. A *response* is the goal of any marketing effort, including one-on-one marketing. That is, it's not a consideration that is exclusive to aiming for any particular market segment. If a product is a new entry to a mature or established category, the odds favor a quick market response. The audience is conditioned to react, often dramatically, to a challenge to established favorites. If the product is an absolute groundbreaker, virtually creating and defining a wholly new category, research and pretesting should have prepared marketers for what they can expect. Test marketing should have anticipated either rejection or acceptance but, in any case, also should have confirmed whether or not the market was "ripe" for such an entrant.

   If research indicates no real support for, or acceptance of, a product, idea, or message, the marketer must reconsider his or her priorities. Segmenting may not be the issue of the moment. The first decision is whether or not to proceed at all or to rethink the product or message. If the decision is to go ahead, the marketer must then mount a solid campaign to either demonstrate or create a need or a desire for what the marketer has to offer. Once that has been accomplished, the segmentation question can be tackled. Too many new entrants are provided only tentative support and modest budgets that limit the ability to establish a strong market presence. Many products fail not because the products weren't good or the market didn't want them, but because the market didn't know they were there.

5. *Changes* occurring within a segment or within the total marketplace are a given. How rapidly such changes occur in specific industries, products, or climates and cultures in general, relative to a marketer's investment, may be anticipated by examining cycles, past performance, and the public pulse. A company or a marketer who fears that the market may change too rapidly for a cost-effective response— whether the effort is segmented or not—is probably not ready to enter the marketplace. Such risks are fairly constant, as is change itself.

   One of marketing's most famous corporate missteps is Coca-Cola's introduction of a reformulated "New Coke" to a marketplace that was extremely satisfied with the product as it was. The company is reported to have believed it could retain its loyal consumers while appealing with the new product to the segment of the market that favored its main competitor, Pepsi-Cola. Observers will continue to debate whether the venture was an act of colossal stupidity or a deliberate ploy to reintroduce the original Coke product with the designation "classic" and the claim that it was brought back "by popular demand." While spokespersons for Coca-Cola say that was not the case, if it *had* been, it would better explain the move, rather than leaving the public (and the company's stockholders) with the impression that Coke's management was not listening to the voice of its market and, perhaps, didn't know what it was doing at all.

Other changes and trends, such as the marketplace's overwhelming approval shifting from fat to no-fat to fat again, may be, as with any ongoing issue in business, ascertained by regularly monitoring the pulse of the public, business, or industry. Phone calls, letters, faxes, E-mail messages, and surveys, as well as closely watching shifts and patterns in sales, adjusted for seasonal or cyclical variance, are among the least expensive ways that marketers can take the pulse of their own customers and be sensitive to change.

Changing quickly is also a relative factor that could refer to the course of a season or a decade. Good marketing plans, encompassing segmentation or not, are written to permit a flexibility that accommodates change without busting the budget or having to throw out the whole document.

The Standard Approach A fairly standard approach to developing a market segmentation plan includes first:

- Determining market boundaries
- Deciding which segmentation variables will be used
- Collecting and analyzing segmentation information
- Developing a profile of each segment
- Targeting the segments to be served
- Designing a marketing plan

While this is pretty much the basic model used in classroom exercises, it brings to mind the old knock at M.B.A. programs: Given a choice between spending a million dollars on marketing or a million dollars on a study to determine the feasibility of marketing, the M.B.A. will pick the study every time. There comes a time when, having studied the market, a marketer has to do something. The future is always a concern. It should not have come and gone without the marketing effort's ever getting out of the conference room.

A key to the success of any marketing effort is research—knowing all you can about your customers and your market. But too often, seasoned veterans of the profession criticize "the younger generation" for spending too much time thinking about marketing and talking about marketing and not enough time marketing. In fairness, many members of the younger generation say the same thing about the old guys.

The 21st-century marketer can almost be profiled into either of two distinct camps: One is the entrepreneur and is often the risk taker, eager to demonstrate boldness, a creative spirit, and a marketing campaign with an "edge"—irreverent, bold, and dramatic. A second group abuses the idea of research as a tool and makes it a shield, blanketing every aspect of a plan with data—much of it interpretive—as a means of covering his or her rear end in the event that any phase of the program falls short of success.

Of the six bullet points listed in the preceding outline, there is probably little of value to be gained by dedicating time and resources to *all* of them that cannot be realized by working out the fourth and sixth points alone. Developing a *profile* of a market segment is more than just a pro forma directive; it implies collecting and analyzing research data and whatever benefits and limitations such information provides. Designing a *marketing plan* uses all the amassed information to create a road map, showing how to get from the starting point to the finish line.

The Answer Should Be Clear When a marketer knows his or her market thoroughly, the decision on whether or not segmentation is the right course becomes obvious. In most instances, in light of what we know about profiling and target marketing, about affinity groups (such as membership organizations and trade organizations) and differentiated marketing (a sort of multisegment mix-and-match strategy, when it seems appropriate), we have become more aware of the strengths inherent in a marketing effort and what, if anything, will serve to counterbalance them. Given the costs involved, the argument seems to favor segmentation, in most cases, if for no stronger reason than trying to appeal to too large or diverse a mass in the current fragmented market is unrealistic.

The Psychographics Phenomenon

Studying psychographics—people's feelings and attitudes—in analyzing a target market has almost become redundant with demographic analysis. That is, as long as psychographic data had been amassed, the findings had been viewed as "lifestyle" data and considered in largely emotional terms. So much of this information, however, has taken on such weight in the current market climate that "emotional," "lifestyle" elements and characteristics are now every bit as influential as regionality, ethnicity, or education.

This is, for the most part, a contemporary cultural phenomenon that would not have been applicable or viable in the 1960s. Feelings, attitudes, and preferences that were once regarded as personal and private now serve not just as points of commonality but as the central or driving force within an entire community or market segment.

Examples include members of the gay community, religious activists, feminists, antifeminists, environmentalists, humanists, naturalists, survivalists, animal rights advocates, and members of various social and political movements. Increasingly—and with no end in sight—people's once private beliefs and sentiments are defining who they are as a community and as a market.

The psychographic approach to market segmentation has been described as looking at the entire constellation of a person's attitudes, beliefs, opinions, hopes, fears, prejudices, needs, desires, and aspirations that, taken together, govern how one behaves.

The levels of intensity in a community can cause a polarizing effect—for or against gun control, censorship, family planning, O. J. Simpson, the president, rap music, or conspiracy theories. These once seemingly personal concerns or opinions have become only a few of the touchstones around which industries have been created. Books, shirts, study courses, tours, newsletters, and a wide array of merchandise speak to the fact that one person's opinion is another person's marketing opportunity.

Summary Points

1. A global marketplace offers more opportunities to market to more people in different ways, extending the potential equity of every product, service, or message.

2. Segmentation is dividing a large population into small groups that share the same or similar characteristics. The elements of segmentation in consumer marketing are classified as geographic, demographic, and psychographic.

3. Geographic characteristics are those shared by people with the same interests and preferences because of regional or territorial influences.

4. Demographics are characteristics about people that influence their behavior, such as age, gender, ethnicity, income, family status, health, education, and lifestyle.

5. Psychographics consider people's attitudes and values and, in many instances, overlap demographic considerations.

6. A marketing campaign that excludes or offends any segment of the market is a bad campaign from the standpoint of a long-term marketing strategy.

7. The diversity of modern media allows a marketer to meet virtually any challenge in directly engaging the most finely targeted market segments.

8. Two essential steps in addressing a market segment are developing a profile of each segment and designing a marketing plan.

9. Psychographics measure emotions and feelings, while also defining the personality of the community and the environment.

3

Research and Technology

What Once Was R&D Is Now R&T

I believe the future is a wonderful place and I want to get as far into it as I can.
—Adrian Cronauer

They spend their time mostly looking forward to the past.
—John Osborne, from *Look Back in Anger*

MARKET RESEARCH HAS been the darling of the advertising and marketing industries so many times—and fallen from favor just as often—that research people must feel pretty insecure on an average day. In a conservative environment, when business leaders express "uncertainty," the call goes out to amass more research data and "learn all we can" about what the public wants and doesn't want.

But in strong economic times, when business is good, and when a more entrepreneurial spirit seems to be driving the market, its participants seem inclined to dismiss the need for research and simply follow their hearts, their guts, or whatever other body parts they might choose to listen to, rather than rely on surveys, studies, and statistical analysis. Besides, they are already supposed to know this stuff, right?

A Political Science Lesson

Political candidates hire research organizations and point to the sophisticated, scientific method employed by pollsters, when the poll results favor them or their positions. When the results provide conclusions that the politician does not want to hear, one of two responses is in order: (1) Claim that you never look at the polls and dismiss them as irrelevant, or (2) As with the advertising campaign that claims the advertiser is number one at *something* with *some* segment of the market, interpret the polling data in a positive way. The candidate is 10 points behind, so find a candidate in history that was *more than* 10 points behind and went on to win. Or claim the survey sample was skewed, so those comments or results were to be expected—and mean nothing.

The public is on to this, of course, but indulges the politician, seemingly thinking, "This one's going to lose anyway, so let him or her have this delusional moment of optimism." The culture itself encourages people being pummeled to maintain their dignity and confidence and not concede until the final blow has been struck. These are only two examples of the predictably hopeful and positive statements commonly made for the sake of image, even when defeat seems somewhere between overwhelming and inevitable. So, why bother? Why spend enormous amounts on research and then pray that it is wrong?

The Research Debate

Market research in business gets much the same treatment as those political polls. For decades, critics of the process have charged that research firms can produce studies or surveys that will provide whatever conclusion the customer wants.

There are various types of research, and debates over which forms or approaches yield the most reliable data are passionate, both inside and outside the research community. References to *aided and unaided awareness studies, on-site and on-line focus groups, telephone surveys, affinity studies,* and *random polling* describe only some of the researcher's options. In addition to providing specific data analysis, the process itself is constantly being improved, becoming more definitive or finite. For example:

- *Exploratory* research helps to identify marketing priorities, perhaps even determining if additional research is necessary.
- *Descriptive* research provides details into a specific area, such as a subject's image or reputation.
- *Causal* research is conducted to isolate predictive relationships between various demographic segments and sales relative to advertising or other marketing expenditures.

Want to launch a new product? How about relaunch a very old product? What does the research recommend? What do you *want* it to recommend?

Take the case of three once-popular chewing gums: Clove, Beemans, and Black Jack. The three defunct brands were revived "by popular demand" and because test groups said the timing was right for these long-ago favorites to make their return. The media and the public took notice as all three brands were relaunched at once in 1993, to great fanfare, a heavy ad schedule, and more than a hint of nostalgia. It was a beautiful moment, except for the fact that a few short months later, all three brands sank, this time probably permanently, into oblivion.

What happened? Did people lie to the researchers?

Maybe.

More likely, however, Warner-Lambert Company, never a huge force in the chewing gum business, just wanted to bring back these brands, possibly not noticing that they had failed earlier because the public simply wasn't interested in them. In a time when future campaigns are being constructed around brands of the past, hoping to capitalize on sentiment for "simpler times past," marketers must understand that just because a brand *existed* does not mean the public will embrace it.

A Story of Three Gums

Trends and cycles aren't about marketing campaigns alone. Sometimes they refer to the products themselves. In an attempt to capture perceived nostalgia for three brands of chewing gum that were popular in the 1950s, but since phased out, Warner-Lambert Company reintroduced Beemans, Black Jack, and Clove in 1993 and the response was great. A year later, however, the three brands had turned from nostalgia to novelty to no-interest. When the product could be found at all, it appeared more out-of-date than ever. (Photograph by Karin Gottschalk Marconi)

Rude Awakening

We also know that merely being "heavy" with research is no guarantee of success. What if market research as a science were put to the test and a television program were created *exactly* according to what the public told researchers it wanted? It's been tried—and it failed.

Before the ABC-TV network launched *Good Morning America*, its early-morning challenger to NBC's long-running *Today Show*, the network had a program that featured a host and hostess (Bill Beutel and Stephanie Edwards) who reflected the age, hair and eye color, and background that fit the profile that audiences said they wanted. The stage set was a mixture of soft blues and reds, with a large yellow painted sun and an electronic synthesizer playing a theme that sounded as if the sun would rise on cue to its strains.

The show was a disaster. Every moment seemed artificial and contrived. It was quickly replaced by the genial actor David Hartman, relaxing over a cup of morning coffee in what seemed like an understated breakfast nook.

A number of theories could account for what went wrong. One is that the heavily researched and tightly structured format was ultimately too rigid for a time of day when a more relaxed mood might have created a more welcoming, friendlier atmosphere. Another is that the tightly scripted format allowed no spontaneity or display of the personalities of the program's hosts. This created a barrier with the audience, who felt as if they did not really know these people who were coming into their homes.

Frequently, marketers will speak of research with a reverence, as if producing ads or programs according to what is known to be the public's specific tastes and preferences is akin to a spiritual experience. It's not. Marketing in the 21st century may well have the benefit of sophisticated polling and tracking, but it is still innovation and creativity, matched with the public's sensibilities, that will succeed, more than will simply replaying a familiar melody.

Technological Smoke and Mirrors

Consider how consistently a Republican spokesperson, on the one hand, will quote research that says the majority of the American people do not want legislation on a particular subject—gun control, for example—and on the other side, a Democratic counterpart will cite research that says just the opposite. Is one lying? Can two opposing positions both have research that scientifically supports opposite points of view?

Yes. If the test groups or focus groups or samples are loaded with people specifically chosen for views they are known to hold—based on the particular town or zip code, college, or religious group—the result will produce overwhelming sentiment for a certain position. The objective is to create a momentum and attract *more* like-minded people and to influence those who may be undecided by suggesting that one point of view is more dominant than another.

Think of how often a public figure declares that people overwhelmingly support something for which no real serious support ever seems to materialize. It is not research that is being quoted, but a *strategy* being represented as research. Such tactics are common, particularly with the use of technology to spread a message to a larger audience faster and with little or no scientific basis.

For example, a survey question is posted on the Internet, and its response is publicized as if it were a scientific sample. Of course, it is not. It is merely a reaction of people who happen to notice that site at that time, and often is part of an orchestrated effort to create an illusion of strong public sentiment. Such maneuvers, increasingly common in the age of new technology, are comparable to the "smoke-and-mirrors" techniques of another era.

Each day, MSNBC, CNN, and other cable networks will ask a number of questions within their various programs and news shows. Often the subjects have been suggested by public relations experts and range from fashion to child safety to airline experiences to automobile, lifestyle, sports, or food preferences to smoking in public places. Viewers are asked to "log on" and express their opinions. Newspapers likewise will pose a question of the day and ask readers to respond by phone or E-mail. The results of these exercises are often represented as reflective of public sentiment when, of course, they may be far from it. Yet, a published or announced report that "70 percent of our viewers (or readers) think that highway speed limits should be changed" or ". . . that the legal drinking age should be raised" or ". . . that smoking in public places should be permitted" will be represented as meaningful research. Perhaps the number of respondents represents only a handful of people (or maybe the same people voting several times). The result is the same: research that is both unscientific and somewhere between flawed and fake.

The theory is that Internet technology should make market research faster, easier, and less costly, but it clearly can present a highly nonrepresentative sampling of the market as well. Policing the Internet for fraud and abuse in all areas will be a challenge of the 21st century, and in no area may the effects of misuse be so far-reaching as in market research.

The Real Thing

Notwithstanding the abuses—both real and potential, from people lying to researchers, to people lying *about* research—the genuine value that market research has for business in virtually any market environment in this century cannot be stressed enough. The cost of doing business is constantly increasing, and the cost of marketing and promotion is significant. Anything that helps to better target the market and position the message is good for business, and market research, when conducted and applied correctly, is enormously beneficial.

Some industry professionals view market research as part of a more sophisticated process, that of gathering "business intelligence." Companies are realizing that timely and relevant information about competitors, customers, and suppliers is necessary for making good strategic business decisions.

The more sophisticated approaches to market research employ a combination of strategic planning and market research activities. Analytical processes convert raw data into relevant, accurate, and usable strategic knowledge. It is critical to amass information about a competitor's position, performance, capabilities, and intentions, along with other information about the forces or factors within the marketplace. Consider what information is necessary regarding specific products and technology. What are important factors external to the marketplace, such as economic, regulatory, political, and demographic influences?

Contrast this type of in-depth, serious research and analysis with a question or a series of questions posted on the Internet that is supposed to communicate to the marketer a sense of the market. Clearly, the former approach is considerably more costly, as well as more time and labor intensive than the more high-tech "shortcut." But the depth and quality of information is likely to contribute to a strategic marketing plan that will look and function like a real plan and not one fashioned from Cliff's Notes.

In the 1980s, research was often getting a watered-down treatment, with serious research organizations being passed over and upstaged by "trend shops." These boutique operations masquerading as researchers would assemble a report or a "box" of items that represented what was and what was *going to be* the hot new product that would shape tastes and styles. For this, large companies and seemingly bright people took as much as a million dollars per year from real research budgets. Once word got around that astrologers and fortune-tellers were about as accurate in forecasting market trends—and cost considerably less—trend shops seemed to diminish in their trendiness.

But the Internet has in some ways replaced them, in that it seems to offer a more "instant" type of research, and marketers tend to be impatient. When the media report that the Internet and the World Wide Web are positioned to provide fast, inexpensive access to the pulse of the market, it becomes increasingly difficult for marketers to authorize and indulge months (or more) of studies, surveys, and analysis.

Five Essentials of Market Research

Market research is about understanding customers. It means asking them questions and interpreting their answers through systematic, objective means that bear on specific, relevant marketing problems.

Research experts agree that the process should be systematic, objective, useful, specific, and decision oriented. It is exactly such a focused approach and attention to detail that has validated the place for market research in the total marketing process since it first became accepted practice in the 1920s. A significant distinction lies between these "essentials" of marketing research and the system of shortcuts common to the contemporary Internet approach.

First, a *systematic* approach, of the click-and-run variety, uses a personal computer's browsers to follow the trail of a key word or two. At least one problem with that method is that the best browsers find their way to only a fraction of the pages on the World Wide Web. That is like making use of a library and limiting yourself to the books on only one shelf.

Being *objective* is a large part of what research is about: specifically, finding value in conflicting pieces of data and reconciling the conflict. A bias brought to the process undermines its value, and an "electronic search" that limits the scope of data examined cannot ensure objectivity.

While stating that the approach should be *useful* may seem simplistic or obvious, often data are gathered that support a desired point of view—a crime that researchers are too often charged with committing—and fail to challenge a premise and advance the cause. This is especially important when you're reviewing the work of competitors and forming a useful (and objective) appraisal of both your own and your competitor's strengths and weaknesses, and applying your findings accordingly.

Being *specific* keeps the process on track, setting up a question to be answered by the research, or a premise to be validated, and dealing only with that before addressing peripheral matters.

Requiring that the approach be *decision oriented*, also imposes a discipline on the process. Whether the point of the research effort is to determine attitudes and awareness regarding a product or company (or your competition), perceptions of ethics (yours, competitors', and perhaps those of your entire industry), the research must have a reason for being and must generate information that has value to a marketing plan and solves a problem.

To the vast majority of marketers, research has become an increasingly valuable tool in intensely competitive times, and technology has provided new tools that can save both time and money. But recognizing the importance of accuracy as well as timeliness, marketers should employ such technology as *part* of the research, not as an alternative to it.

Not everyone is convinced of the value of research. Some marketers who prefer to create a plan based on instincts and their personal experience discourage allocating funds for research as a way of redirecting dollars elsewhere. A justification of their position is that Americans (and presumably others living in a free society) already suffer from "information overload"— that there is simply too much information being generated to be productively put to use.

Such an argument is pretty lame. To suggest that a marketing professional can have too much information is like saying that too much knowledge is bad for you. The amount of the budget allocated for research will vary from product to product and business to business, but anything that affords value should be worthy of a respectful funding consideration and not dismissed as a needless expense.

Looking back on the list of "essentials," if marketers can exert enough discipline, the same discipline applied to developing well-conceived creative work, perhaps the label "clutter" won't be applied to so much of what is advertising.

Technology Eclipses Development

Research can help marketers understand how and what the public thinks of them: their image, products, services, competition, industry at large, regulators, and shareholders, and the media that cover them (which should result in a better quality of media coverage) and carry their paid message.

For planning and budget purposes, research and development—R & D— have become virtually joined as one term. Presumably the assumption was that, upon completion of the research phase, a new or improved product or message would be developed and presented. Whether in product development or in the development of the marketing plan, research is a powerful tool.

In many respects, the explosive growth in interest in Internet technology, tied as it is to the start of a new century, has eclipsed and even negated much of the excitement typically lavished on the actual *development* phase of the research-and-development process. Have the advances in technology, with the proliferation of tens of thousands of new websites, made the electronic stage seem like an end in itself? Many people clearly see it that way, and research would be helpful to determine its potential impact.

Today's technology for acquiring information, performing quantitative analysis, and storing data is increasingly more sophisticated. A vast amount of information can be made available to branch offices or department managers on a variety of subjects.

Yet, some professionals argue that the technology for using data is underdeveloped. This is an especially important caveat, as significant competitive advantages go to those who understand how information is used, not merely to those who have it. There is a fundamental distinction between the technologies for doing research and those dedicated to improving its use.

As with Internet marketing itself, which is detailed in a later chapter, Internet access, search engines, and the ease and speed with which volumes of material appear can be truly amazing. But the medium should not be confused with its content and how the content is used.

People tend not to tell you if you're doing something wrong. Asking customers, clients, or prospects what they like and dislike about your product or service or message, and what they think could be better, can mean the difference between success and failure.

Weighing the Many Forms of Research

Research has proved to be a valuable component in the marketing process. The question is then, with the variety of tools and methods available, what is the most effective, cost-efficient means of conducting that research? To many marketers, nothing less than state-of-the-art, "21st-century" research methods will do. While that typically means technology in some form, it is important to remember that asking an assembled group of people to please raise their hands if they prefer the red background over the blue background is still effective and accurate research. In the future, marketers can expect that the boss or client will like to see something that looks at least a bit more scientific.

Computers are now as commonplace as telephones. As computers typically provide more information at faster speeds than most other forms of data gathering, incorporating the computer into the research phase for functions other than statistical tabulation seems logical.

Surveys? Focus groups? Opinion polls? In-person? By phone? On-line? The answer is *yes*.

The tools and methods for conducting market research are more easily accessible than ever before. Many researchers and firms are specializing in specific demographic segments, offering in-depth analysis of particular segments such as the teen market, seniors, and on-line services. The range of information they amass, process, and provide is not only more detailed but also more authoritative.

Marketers on modest budgets can turn to trade association studies, surveys, and reports—often available to members for little or no cost. Most major media entities, including *USA Today* and the *Wall Street Journal*, and larger business publications such as *Forbes, Business Week,* and *Fortune* magazines carry news and highlights from some study or survey in nearly every one of its issues. Additionally, the advertising departments of these and other media operations conduct reader research surveys that they are willing and eager to share with current or prospective advertisers. Much of the information includes exactly the data that marketers are looking for, data that reflect the pulse of the public on subjects both specific and general.

Publications such as *American Demographics* and *Brandweek* regularly report on trends and shifts in buying patterns or other changes in the marketplace. Most everything that is available from print media is also available on-line.

Computer Logic

Increasingly, marketers are finding that, when it comes to market research methods, there are no absolutes. Technology and demands have brought about more enhanced versions of even the most routine research functions.

Focus groups, for example, have gone beyond the one-way viewing window overlooking a conference table, to include teleconferencing and videoconferencing. Internet focus groups are easily assembled, relatively inexpensive, and much in fashion, though many research professionals insist that they fall short on several counts. For these sessions, an absolutely secure site is essential. Some researchers, while not wanting to seem unenthusiastic about the broad applications of the new technology, say an integral part of focus group research is the ability to note body language, facial expressions, eye contact, tone of voice, and the overall show of emotion. These observations cannot be applied with certainty to Internet focus groups.

Direct mailers glean demographic information and qualify media effectiveness by using coupons and response cards with tracking codes. More recently, computer users have become aware of "cookies"—coded signals planted usually without the recipients' knowledge or permission, the purpose of which is to provide information about website or chat room visitors, E-mail recipients, or other on-line consumers. The practice is controversial, with much of the criticism stemming from the interpretation of privacy laws. A solution has yet to be advanced that would simply disclose the existence of cookies and couple the disclosure with a request for permission to include such a tracking mechanism in the system to provide data that will help improve service and efficiency.

Observational research—essentially, having strategically placed cameras record the home or workplace environment to amass information that even participating subjects may tend to overlook—is another controversial, though serious form of research. The monitoring is designed as a potentially more accurate gauge of behavior than verbal reports, as critics debate whether people tend to answer researchers' questions truthfully or merely provide the responses that they think the researchers are looking for and will thus make participants "look smarter."

All in all, advances in technology have enabled electronic media and publishers of every stripe to make thousands of pages of data available instantly. Now all that's needed is for marketers to take time to study it.

A Study in Contradictions

In 1999, it was not uncommon for large professional research companies to characterize market segments into groups with catchy names such as: "strivers," "devouts," "altruists," "intimates," "fun seekers," and "creatives."

By identifying the segments in this way, ad copy writers and art directors are able to produce ads and marketing messages that evoke a favorable response. This is accomplished along the lines of classic differentiation between *touchy-feely* people and *cold-formal* people, along with identifying type A personalities, matching personalities to colors and seasons (dark colors are warm, autumn colors are moody), and the like. Some classifications break down liberals and conservatives. There are instances when this type of information is very useful, such as in trying to segment and target a group with a strong social conscience or a strong sense of national patriotism. It has its place, certainly.

However, a noteworthy conclusion of the Robert Starch study was that consumers around the globe are more similar than different and share certain attitudes and behaviors. This will shake the foundations of marketers who believed that the distinctions among people of the world were so specific that, say, a marketer could not write a marketing plan for Brazil without having first *worked* in Brazil.

It might be assumed that persons surveyed all profess a love of peace, country, children, God, music, and sunny days. Certainly ad writers have penned a word or two on those subjects. But if more distinct similarities or more distinct differences are revealed, the research will have provided considerable added value.

Objectives Dictate Choice

The best source and research method?

It is whatever a particular objective, time frame, and budget will allow. Research firms are accustomed to working within clients' budgets, and there too, the competition is intense. Electronic access has enabled firms to deliver more, faster and at a lower cost. Marketers must remember that research is the process of collecting and analyzing information. As the processes and formats for research gathering may become more sophisticated, the process should never be viewed as more relevant than the content.

But whatever the cost of market research, chances are it's a lot less than the cost of going into a new marketing program or ad campaign without the information that will maximize chances for success—and failing. Failures can be very, very expensive.

As the future unfolds, ever newer methods of gathering, processing, and interpreting market research—especially involving some new application of technology—are sure to emerge. A major thrust is likely to be providing more personalized service in response to a growing perception of an automated, impersonal environment.

Summary Points

1. Listen to the voice of the market, to what it is saying people like, don't like, and will support or buy.
2. Being "heavy into research" is no guarantee of success. Study and analyze data, then test your findings before committing all in anticipation of success.
3. Marketing in the 21st century has the benefit of sophisticated tracking and polling, but innovation and creativity, applied to responding to what the public says it wants, will prevail.
4. Marketers cite "overwhelming support" for a product, position, or message (based on a modest but representative sampling) and hope to create a momentum that will validate the position. This is not as much an application of research as it is a strategy.
5. Policing the Internet for fraud and abuse is a major challenge in the 21st century.
6. Market research is directed to understanding customers.
7. Marketers who create a plan based on their "instincts" and redirect research funds elsewhere are engaging in a highly risky maneuver.
8. Despite what some may perceive as major technological advances, research is still conducted through surveys, studies, focus groups, opinion polls, and in-person and phone interviews as well as on-line.
9. The advertising departments of most major media companies compile considerable amounts of research data that they are usually willing to share with current or prospective advertisers.
10. The best source and method is the one that best complements the marketing objective, time frame, and budget.

Part II

Marketing to the Generations

SEGMENTATION OF MARKETING targets identifies differences and distinctions, and rarely are such differences as dramatic as among the generations. It has been said, for example, that seniors resent baby boomers for their arrogance and for squandering the great opportunity that the prosperous times had given them. Certainly that is true for *some* seniors and boomers, greatly exaggerated regarding others, and likely not true at all for yet another group. This spectrum of applicability should always be kept in mind when you're segmenting any target group.

In recent times, a great deal has been written about the relationship between baby boomers and members of Generation X—that the boomers don't completely understand the younger generation and find themselves uncomfortable in the position of being the older generation—the one that, this time around, doesn't understand. It was, after all, baby boomers who embraced the term *generation gap* to describe how *their* elders didn't comprehend the sense of anger, frustration, or urgency that so many of them were feeling. Gen Xers, for their part, are said to resent the fact that the boomers had all the great milestones on their watch—major events of contemporary American history such as space exploration, the "Summer of

Love," the Vietnam War and draft resistance, the birth of the feminist movement, the sexual revolution, JFK, Elvis, rock 'n' roll, and Woodstock.

Marketers need to understand that, regardless of the target generation, there are those people who like who and where they are, and those who don't.

While segmentation by generation must be followed by still greater, more definitive segmentation within each generation, there are: older people who want to be younger; young people who want to be older; those who want a simpler life (with less technology and less crowding); those who wish for a more adventurous life of travel and a fuller schedule; those who are excited at the prospect of experiencing anything new and different; and those who prefer the familiarity, stability, and comfort of the known.

There are people of all generations who live with the *grass-is-always-greener-on-the-other-side* curse. They believe that their lives would be better if they drove a certain car, had a certain job title, took a particular trip, got a different haircut, or used a different mouthwash. The chapters in this section review the similarities and differences among the generations and explore how the distinctions represent opportunities. To marketers, those opportunities are virtually limitless.

4

Targets Big Enough
to Miss

The future is always a fairyland to the young.
—Sala

The future ain't what it used to be.
—Yogi Berra

TWENTY-FIRST-CENTURY marketing will be largely a process of segmentation, the marketer's idea of specialization. Demographics will be studied, and marketers will hone in on age, as well as gender, income, lifestyle, ethnicity, and regionality, but segmentation by age-groups will be the most overt. The following chapters examine how marketers are targeting baby boomers, Generation X, Generation Y, and seniors.

Marketing to Genders and Generations

Whether targeted by generations, regions, ethnicity, economics, or cultural traits, one truth remains: the target market segment will comprise men or women or both. That point, so simple and obvious, is enormously important in effective target marketing.

There have always been "women's pages" in newspapers and very successful "women's magazines" such as *Woman's Day* and *Ladies' Home Journal.* Men have had their macho-tinted "sports section." But at no time since marketers first decided that their field is a science has marketing to genders and generations been so blatantly their focus.

With all the tools available to make target marketing more efficient, it is still surprising how often marketers both overshoot and fall short of their targets.

Generalization Gap

Though, as described in earlier chapters, the concept of the mass market is dead, the inappropriate use of generalities to describe the market lives on. Consider, in the old model using the women's pages and women's magazines, where the target market (women) might seem to fall in relation to the four groups named—boomers, X, Y, and seniors. Of course, the theory holds, there are women in *each* of the groups.

Making generalizations can serve a purpose. When people complain about the influence of "the media," they could be talking about any number of media entities from Geraldo Rivera to the *Wall Street Journal*, from Rush Limbaugh to Larry King, C-SPAN, or *The Weekly Standard*. Complaints about "the government" might mean the Social Security Administration or the House Judiciary Committee or the meter maid who just slapped a parking ticket on the windshield. It is human nature to blame, and the objects of such gestures often tend to be a generalization. The practice also serves to create a certain empathy, as others who may have had or heard of similar experiences identify with a story and agree that the complaint has merit.

In marketing, however, broad generalizations can be expensive. Without the mass market of old, smaller mass markets have taken its place. Umbrella categories such as *baby boomers, the seniors market, Generation X,* and *Generation Y* are catchy, look great in the headlines, and may help to narrow the focus, but in target marketing, they can easily underestimate the range and diversity of the market by a long shot.

Virtually no generalization accurately encompasses an entire consumer group segment, and this is especially true of age-groups. Seniors can be wealthy or not, love the outdoors or not, be inclined to travel or just as easily hate to travel. They may live in a security-conscious high-rise apartment building or in a mobile home, be on a tight budget or travel frequently between vacation residences.

Attention to Detail

The importance of truly knowing all you can know about your market cannot be overemphasized. To plan a program or a campaign based on what you *think* is true can be costly, perhaps fatal. Doing it right doesn't mean simply distinguishing between old and young or rich and poor; it means defining a target with as much detail as circumstances allow.

The companies on the prestigious Fortune 500 list may have nothing more in common with each other than their immense size. Business-to-business marketers who claim their target audience is the Fortune 500 must consider whether companies as diverse as General Motors, IBM, Coca-Cola, and Disney are *truly* their target prospects. (Sometimes they are because part of the marketers' strategy is to enter into *some* type of relationship with them so that they can claim in their ads how many Fortune 500 companies they have. It is an attempt to create a "halo effect" and benefit from such an association.)

Companies that rank among the largest in the world didn't get there because they are pretty much the same as other big companies. They achieved their status in no small part by emphasizing their uniqueness. Market research should be used to create profiles of target customers by identifying the attributes they truly have in common. Or not. Pretty much every company likes to think it is different, or that it "does things a little differently." Perhaps marketers should create a whole new category for companies that are convinced they are like no others. When all is done, it would be a pretty short list. Cultures operate on commonality. Success comes from stepping enough outside of the "sameness" to get attention. That doesn't mean a company is not or is no longer part of the mainstream, but rather that it sits a bit higher *within* the mainstream.

There's No Substitute for Research

While shifts in the total market size, structure, and culture in the late 1990s resulted in virtually everyone's spending an increasing amount of his or her time in front of a personal computer, it is largely held that the market segment we commonly call Generation X is *the* computer generation. These folks grew up with video games and MTV and are thought to largely ignore most printed materials in favor of the electronic media. At the same time, dozens of new magazines have been launched to appeal specifically to Generation X (many have even adopted titles and typography suggestive of the computer). Not all of the publications will survive, of course. Some may fail for the very reason that, while they are bucking the stereotype that Xers don't read, they are also treating all Xers the same. Perhaps the most accurate generalization that people apply to Generation X is that it is one of the most difficult generations about which to generalize. Not all members are "cyberheads" and not all have tattoos and pierced navels.

Advertising Age published a widely referenced special report on Generation X as it began to emerge as a significant market force. The report noted: "They're hip, they're savvy, and they're worried . . . about AIDS, race relations, child abuse, abortion. . . . Brand loyalty is strong, but so is shopping for price."

While the report became a helpful guide for ad agencies across the United States and around the world, it should not be used as a substitute for timely market research. By virtue of age, social status, and economic power, this is still very much an evolving market segment. Figures vary, depending on how narrow or broad a sub-segment is being examined. Of the estimated 27 million people said to belong to this group, many reported that they considered themselves to be content, religious, and optimistic. A writer describing this segment may generalize about them, but marketers shouldn't.

At the other end of the age range, AARP (formerly the American Association of Retired Persons) is often regarded as the voice of older Americans when it comes to major concerns of consumerism, health care, and politics. For more than a decade it was said that the group, with its claim of more than 50 million members, was made up of people who were not necessarily Americans nor retired. Moreover, marketers found that to designate the target market for any product or service simply "the seniors market" said little about this market in terms of prospect potential.

Redefining a Generation

Sometimes, of course, overreaching is part of the strategy to expand the market, such as a campaign that designated everyone who was alive at a particular time as "the Pepsi Generation." But that was an advertising campaign and not a true positioning statement or an example of measurable target marketing. The brand was being pitched primarily to an audience of young people, but the ad campaign's overall message was in no way exclusionary. It appeared everywhere, and that's fine, as long as marketers don't confuse an ad campaign, a headline, a tag line, or a theme with targeted marketing.

The Gap retail clothier and private-label merchandiser takes a similar approach without actually renaming an entire generation. The retailer clearly conveys to its public an image that it sees itself as the brand of Generation X, yet some of its most memorable advertising has had broad crossover appeal, emphasizing style while suggesting that its target segment's parents would not be unwelcome in its stores. A particularly popular 1999 series of TV spots for the company featured a group of young people that could have passed for an entire senior class from a high school or college: clean and well dressed in The Gap's signature look of casual clothes, spread across an open stage against a stark backdrop, singing along and dancing to recordings both old and new, ranging from 1950s swing (Louis Prima's recording of "Jump, Jive, and Wail") to contemporary country music to 1990s pop-rock to scenes from Broadway's *West Side Story*. The spots appealed to a wide range as both entertainment and strong brand imagery.

Getting "Narrow" Minded

On occasion, marketers have attempted to narrowly define their targets, trying to achieve higher core-group identification and deeper market penetration with a campaign that suggests elitism or exclusivity. Some examples are Virginia Slims cigarettes (for women only); Mitchum deodorant (just for men); and *Ms.* magazine (for women who may have differing positions on a number of subjects but are theoretically joined in their desire to promote a "feminist" agenda).

Playboy magazine never remotely suggested that it was a product for every member of every market segment. As far back as the 1950s, its ads have been asking, "What sort of man reads *Playboy*?" Although the magazine had broad appeal to mostly males of several generations, from students to truckers to fast-food restaurant workers, the image conveyed that *Playboy* was for the smooth, sophisticated, upscale "playboy" who had a taste for the world's finer things. Again, this was the focus of an ad campaign, but it sought to position the brand as much as it tried to sell the product.

The careful, narrow focus of Virginia Slims and Mitchum allowed the companies to extend the brands and expand the market if and when the time seemed right. Such an approach is usually preferable to beginning from a too-broad baseline, which can send a message that, if not embraced by some market segments, will be more difficult to revise later. That is, a brand cannot start out as being suitable for anyone and later decide that it wants to be just for women or men. The public likely will already have developed its perceptions of the brand.

It may be fine for a toy company to initially target grandparents as a potential market, but it may make more sense to also target aunts, uncles, godparents, and others who may have an occasion to buy gifts for children who are not their own. The idea is to go narrow, yet nonexclusionary, whenever possible.

Culture Conflicts

A tendency or desire to be all-inclusive is both ambitious and expensive in today's market. The culture of the marketplace is often in conflict, as people like to think they lean away from preferring a product or brand that everyone else likes, yet they take comfort in knowing that their own choice is the market's most popular brand.

Amid efforts to reach the largest possible market segments, generalizations and stereotypes are sometimes treated as research. A story in the *New York Times* was of the tongue-in-cheek variety . . . or was it? It began, "Any traveler knows that people are different from country to country. Russians drink vodka, Germans drink beer, and the French drink wine. Americans are gregarious and overfed."

Humor and political correctness aside, when marketing to segments of any size, marketers must be aware of—and guard against offending—the particular sensitivities not only of the target market group but of any other group, however related, that has time on its hands and a strong desire to be mentioned on the evening news. Target marketing is about reaching an audience, not about provoking that (or any other) audience, however good-natured the pitch is intended to appear. Offering old vaudeville routines about lovable drunks and "morons" is not target marketing.

The culture has become more sensitized, and people seem to be more easily insulted when marketers try to impress one group at the expense of another. While many people are willing to accept that political correctness is appropriate, others believe that people should lighten up and let companies say what they want to say in their ads, as long as *their* sensitivities are not offended. The vast majority of those in most every market segment probably wish the entire subject would go away.

Marketers, however, have no such luxury. Despite a desire to be bold, memorable, and ever on the cutting edge, marketers are doing business—and usually with clients' or shareholders' money. There needs to be a disciplined and reasonable level of sensitivity. Achieving this without being dull and bland (as in playing it *too* safe), and still appeal to the well-targeted market, is what professional marketers do. Marketing and advertising do not have to come down to a choice between being offensive and being boring. The alternative is to be *creative*.

Shortcuts and Deep Holes

A common shortcut alternative to creativity is the use of a well-known spokesperson as a celebrity presenter, someone the target audience admires, perhaps even feels an empathy with. But again, as with the advertising focus noted earlier, sometimes the attempt to impress one market segment ends up alienating another. A couple of prominent examples illustrate the point:

Florida Citrus Growers became the subject of boycotts and organized protests because the association's celebrity spokesperson took very public positions that were insulting to gay men. That same gay community, along with several feminist and environmental groups, organized subsequent protests against the association for later hiring *another* celebrity spokesperson who was known for offering opinions that ranged from controversial to insulting.

But these were only the spokespersons—the celebrity presenters—not the *company*. Why should business take the heat for remarks offered by some celebrity? Because the spokesperson, to be effective, must be identified as the public face of the company or brand and represent how the front office wants people to think of it.

In another case, Sambo's, a family restaurant chain, found that some people were offended by its name, saying that it suggested an image demeaning to African Americans. The more the company protested that this was not its intention, the more it made the evening news, and people who'd never given it much thought . . . thought.

But where's the fairness? The restaurant name was not relevant to the company's service, pricing, quality, convenience, or any of the other functions people should care about.

Wrong again. A business's name tells the public how the business wants people to see it. By operating under a name that implied images of a time or place that some segments of the market found objectionable, the company put itself into a hole. Instead of marketing, its energies and budgets went for explaining, defending, and apologizing.

From a marketing perspective, it is simply more advisable to show sensitivity and a clear understanding of the market *before* a message or image is presented to the public. The alternative is to face the often difficult task of trying to change people's perceptions after the fact.

Reflections of the Times

Marketing is not something that takes place in a vacuum. People know more and believe less of what they see and hear from advertisers. Sensitivities are heightened. As the classic film *Network* suggested, much of the population wants to yell, "I'm mad as hell, and I'm not going to take it anymore."

The new century opened with new books, films, and studies on "road rage" and domestic violence. If this was a reflection of the times, people who make up the marketplace, individually or together, presented a bleak picture for marketers. Despite a healthy economy and strong evidence of "the good life," people don't trust their government, their employers, and perhaps most of all, the media. There are reasons why reliable market research looks at multiple factors such as age, gender, income, net worth, ethnicity, geography, lifestyle, and family status. It's fine to cite "families," for instance, as a potential description of a given market segment, as long as it isn't the synonym for the market itself. The customers for so-called family entertainment are not always families, or even the long-presumed families with children, but anyone interested in wholesome TV and movies or the safe thrills offered at Walt Disney World. Usually these attractions find their largest response among children, so "family entertainment" becomes synonymous with "entertainment for children."

Taking It One Group at a Time

Commentator and former presidential adviser George Stephanopolis has indicted the modern media for what he calls their preoccupation with "psychological reductionism in the information age." It's an interesting new euphemism to describe the process of reducing things to their simplest form. Generalizing can be clever at times, and it might even be necessary at times to make sense of the world and the variety of mixed messages coming and going at blinding speed. But the only generalities that are appropriate for a specific market are the ones that truly apply. In general, that is.

At the end of the day, as a '90s cliche goes, marketers need to be sure of who they are talking to and what they are saying. The folks described as seniors used to tell those called baby boomers that they could never understand their rock 'n' roll music. The boomers told Generation Xers that their heavy metal music wasn't really music at all. And . . . so on.

Taking one group at a time, and looking at the groups within the groups, may be a fussy, more time-consuming process, but it may also help to achieve this elusive "understanding."

At the very least, it should help anchor the marketing plan.

Summary Points

1. Umbrella terms such as *baby boomers, Generation X, Generation Y,* and the *seniors market* can easily underestimate the range and diversity of the market.

2. Virtually no generation accurately encompasses an entire consumer-group segment, and this is especially true of age-groups.

3. Perhaps the most accurate generalization about members of Generation X is that it is difficult to generalize about them. Yet, they have emerged as a significant market force.

4. Designating older, mature, or retired persons as simply "the seniors market" says little about who or what this group is as a marketing segment.

5. When marketing to segments, marketers must be aware not only of each group's sensitivities, but also those of attention-seeking groups waiting to protest anything even close to being "politically incorrect."

6. Much of the market believes that political correctness is appropriate, though others think the emphasis on it is overdone, and probably the majority wish the subject would go away.

7. "Psychological reductionism" describes a process of reducing subjects to their simplest form. As the media try to take this approach, marketers must be certain that their message is not adversely affected in the process.

5

Marketing to
Baby Boomers

There's no future like the present.
—American proverb

The '60s were revolutionary in every way.
—Mary Wells Lawrence, president,
  Wells, Rich, Green Advertising, 1990

IF BOB DYLAN thought the times they were a-changing when he wrote that famous line sometime around the early '60s, only a few years later there was enough large-scale change to provide him with at least a dozen additional verses. Others can debate whether the generation called the baby boomers cast a shadow that represented the cause or the effect of so much social, economic, political, and artistic change that was to occur from approximately 1963 forward. In all respects, though, their presence would be felt.

74 Million and Counting

The 1960s was an exciting decade by any measure, and the baby boomers were right in the middle of it. Here is a snapshot for marketers that may offer the ultimate "Kodak moment," a statistic warm enough to melt the most flash-frozen hearts: Baby boomers are the largest and most diverse segment of the market. Born in the years immediately following the end of World War II (roughly 1945 to 1964), they are more than 75 million in number, and it is not an exaggeration to say that they are pretty much running the world.

The start of the 21st century finds the older class of baby boomers entering middle age and heading governments, businesses, industries, and, most important perhaps for the purposes of this work, ad agencies, the media, and marketing programs. This group is important for the influence it exerts on other people and groups. The challenge for many marketers in relating to the baby boom generation is to keep their personal tastes and prejudices, which they assume to be the majority view, from clouding their professional judgment of what works best for the product, message, customer, or campaign.

Consider the influence of only a few prominent baby boomers on business and culture: Bill Clinton, Al Gore, and the leaders of the U.S. Congress; British Prime Minister Tony Blair and his predecessor John Major; Microsoft CEO Bill Gates; Disney CEO Michael Eisner; Apple Computer's Steve Jobs; ice cream moguls Ben and Jerry; and the heads of virtually every major film studio, record company, and TV network. These people have shaped the culture in ways that often have been radically different from those of their predecessors. People they have influenced or inspired have started cable channels, Internet businesses, telecommunications networks, and financial services companies.

Few would challenge that the 1960s—the time the boomers came of age—represented one of the most eventful and, as Mary Wells Lawrence described it, "revolutionary" periods in our history. Good economic times shaped boomers in a way that, apart from the Vietnam experience, provided a blank canvas to pursue seemingly unlimited opportunities. It is true that many who typified the generation were case studies in self-indulgence. Others created, contributed, and set a course for dramatic innovation in the arts and industry.

While the parents of the baby boomers took and held jobs for life, boomers were the first generation to follow the advice of one of their "spokesbands" Fleetwood Mac, to "go your own way." Even those entering the most prestigious professions, such as lawyers, doctors, and financiers, used their positions to leverage new businesses, franchises, and ventures worthy of lucrative licensing agreements.

But this chapter concerns baby boomers as the *object* of a marketing effort, not as the marketers themselves.

Masters of the Universe?

For all the diversity of the segment, it has largely come to be exemplified by its more visible and prominent members as generally brash, bright, and self-absorbed.

Tom Wolfe, in his 1987 bestseller *Bonfire of the Vanities*, showed as his central character a baby boomer who regarded himself as one of the "masters of the universe." The term stayed around to replace "yuppie" as a description of a certain type of successful, upscale baby boomer long after the book had been relegated to the sale tables.

The word *self* plays a big role in understanding baby boomers. Because they grew up as the first generation said to have been raised on television, they became more independent regarding learning and entertainment, with less emphasis on teams and groups than had previously been the case. Pop psychology in the form of est, transcendental meditation, Lifestream, Lifespring, and dozens of other enormously popular self-help, self-improvement programs contributed to baby boomers' inclination to focus inward. They were often described as the "Me Generation," the "Love Generation," and, the more free-spirited of them, as "Flower Children."

These were the most highly exposed examples and came to be regarded as the standard-bearers for the generation. Such characterizations, however, do not nearly represent reality. The overwhelming majority of baby boomers led (and continue to lead) normal lives by most mainstream standards. All the men are not Bill Clinton or Donald Trump, nor are the women Hillary Rodham Clinton or Jane Fonda. But as a generation, they qualify for many "firsts" of note to marketers, including being the first generation to use credit cards so freely in place of pocket cash and to use deficit financing for personal lifestyle advancement.

Platinum Bonds

By the late 1990s, consumption, credit, and the economy had caught up with them and left them with lessons about life and debt. The "masters of the universe," much like their parents before them, now worried about mortgages, the cost of their children's education, adequate health care, and their own quality of life and retirement options. Not many years before, the very word *retirement* seemed as near as the planet Jupiter, but by the start of the 21st century, those light-years of distance have become only a decade or so away.

The group whose lives had been shaped by Woodstock, Vietnam, the sizzling '60s, and the disco '70s are getting older and getting serious. Many of the credit cards are now designated "platinum" in a nod to both the creditworthiness of the individuals and the image to which they aspired.

Culturally aware marketers get their attention with the art of Monet, Magritte, and Andy Warhol and with the music of the Doors, James Brown, Etta James, the Beatles, and the Beach Boys, licensed for commercial use for disposable diapers, auto insurance, and more. Most boomers privately downplay embarrassing images of their days of "flower power." Much of their adult behavior reflects a sense that they would rather their children not have too great a picture of what they did in those great times in the '60s.

Some inherited money from trust funds; some were enriched by generous "golden parachutes" that opened when jobs disappeared, eliminated at newly merged or acquired businesses. But, alas, for the overwhelming majority, the spending power derived most likely from an increased limit on credit cards or refinancing of assets. In any case, baby boomers continue, in virtually every cycle of the economy, to be an overall highly desirable and responsive market segment, especially as they mature.

Nostalgia and Then Some

A news feature on "boomer consumers" noted that in less time than it takes to devour a Hostess Sno-ball, another American is turning 50. If the statistics are accurate, every 7.7 seconds, another baby boomer hits the half-century mark. Some who reach that milestone see it as a good reason to buy an expensive convertible. For others, thoughts turn to a diet, a prostate exam, or estrogen levels. Perhaps the most common thoughts are reflections of nostalgia and trivia.

It has been widely charged that baby boomers, as a group, take themselves and their role in history very seriously. For their parents, World War II was the defining event of the century. But boomers looked to the culture that had evolved—to rock 'n' roll, Elvis Presley, the Beatles, self-help groups, encounter groups, hair transplants, and introspective teachings of *The Prophet* and assorted mystics and gurus. As President Kennedy had said, "The torch has been passed to a new generation," taking stands against the power structure to protest war and believing they were largely responsible for two U.S. presidents' leaving office before they'd planned to go.

There were interesting, daring, and "fun" fashions and hairstyles, "open" relationships, and various drugs used without a prescription.

How much of what happened influenced the boomers versus how much the boomers influenced will be for sociologists and anthropologists to debate. Nevertheless, examples abound that baby boomers were a generation that made history, or at least a long list of memories to feed the nostalgia machine (and the cable TV shows that try to look like history). The poet-songwriter Paul Simon called it being "born at the right time."

Attention: Marketers

In marketing terms, it is worth repeating one of the most basic and important rules: Know your market—their likes, dislikes, and unique characterizations. The operative question to ask is *What are the things that are important to this market?*

In theory, pretty much every group should be able to answer: safety, security, happiness, wealth, peace, children, love, and perhaps a spiritual message as well. For baby boomers, all those points apply, but more so than other generations, boomers can recall defining moments that shaped who they are, who they may always have wanted to be, what they stand for . . . the notes and chords to which they respond. While nostalgia is a significant element in marketing generally, in the boomers' case, the times were so rich with significant events and people, virtually always with an accompanying musical score, that the word *nostalgia* hardly does it justice.

Go with the Flow

For decades to come, marketers would do well to try getting the attention of the baby boomer segment by offering images of the persons, places, and things that shaped their consciousness. That list may include:

American Bandstand
Barbie
The Beach Boys
The Beatles
Camelot
College sit-ins, love-ins, be-ins
Consciousness-raising groups
Elvis
"Flower power" (love beads, tie-dye, headbands)
Folk music
"Hands Across America"

I Love Lucy
James Bond
James Brown
James Dean
Live concerts (and live concert albums)
The Mickey Mouse Club
"Mrs. Robinson"
Playboy
Political correctness
President Kennedy (and Mrs. Kennedy)
President Ronald Reagan
Saturday Night Fever
Simon and Garfunkel
Soul Train
Star Trek
Support groups
Surfing
Television
10
Toga parties
Urban Cowboy
Vietnam
The women's movement
Woodstock

From this "starter list," comments should begin to flow—quotes and memories—on which to build an ad or a campaign or a parody. This is, after all, the generation that ran the gamut from JFK's Peace Corps to Ronald Reagan's new appreciation of the capitalist system.

Packaging Impact

The 1977 film *Saturday Night Fever* had a dynamic impact on both a generation and a culture. Virtually overnight, it changed the prevailing fashions in both clothing and popular music, as well as generating a phenomenal return on its investment. When a movie can register such a reaction, not only altering styles but also forcing other styles into the background, marketers should be studying it for clues.

In addition, the film's soundtrack album, with some 20 million copies sold, and a string of hit songs individually dominating the pop music chart redefined the music of the rock 'n' roll age.

Oklahoma!, South Pacific, Camelot, Hello, Dolly!, and *The Sound of Music* were all enormously successful Broadway musicals and all became enormously successful Hollywood films with hit cast and soundtrack albums. Yet none of these great and timeless hits came close to altering the public's tastes, wardrobes, or lifestyle.

Take a Tip

The first lesson for marketers to understand is that such an enormous impact was even *possible*. Second, note that the market was ripe (or perhaps overripe) for such a hard cultural kick on the dance floor, and how marketing played such a pivotal role in influencing a marketplace that didn't know what hit it.

Marketers were packaging fantasy and escapism and continue to repackage it decades later as the image-inducing backdrop in commercials, ads, and entire trade show presentations.

As noted, baby boomers grew up with TV as a teacher, baby-sitter, and companion, which offers yet another lesson: TV operates on a format basis, on a *theme* approach; a successful marketing effort will offer a format and a theme, with the clothes, the look, and the driving beat to carry it along.

Radical It's Not

Marketers understand that the public needs and wants products and services, but give people a *whole package* that drives them and helps them find a rhythm and tempo that can change the beat of their lives, and they will follow, wrapping themselves in the clothes, the personality, and the music.

This may be a bit over-the-top to sell toothpaste, shampoo, bathroom tissue, or a roller-ball pen, but creating a mood as a backdrop to sell product is not a radical concept. Many ads reflect a theme that is suggestive of a film, a TV show, or popular escapist fare. Practically every program on television—from sitcom to drama to the evening news—has a CD for sale featuring its music and, often, a fashion line tied to a character who goes with the music and the program.

The public wants to move to the same music, while copying Jennifer Aniston's haircut, Jerry Seinfeld's gestures, and the one-liners from *Saturday Night Live*, and stay tuned to the closing credits to see who designed and fitted Tom Brokaw's suit and who furnished Diane Sawyer's wardrobe and jewelry. Anchorman Dan Rather received more attention for incorporating a sweater into his regular evening newscasts than for reading the news.

Urban Legends

Baby boomers respond well to the overall look and sound, the format and theme, the package. Concrete evidence of this statement is another film that launched a major shift in fashion, musical tastes, and lifestyle, packaged and marketed to create a cultural icon. In 1980, *Urban Cowboy* sent city slickers on a whirlwind shopping spree for western clothing, boots, hats, scarves, and *trucks*, all to the accompaniment of a soundtrack album.

What may have been a lot like any other day in Dallas or Houston was a phenomenon coast to coast as baby boomers headed for the in restaurants, banks, law offices, ad agencies, brokerage firms, schools, and stock exchanges looking and acting as if they would be much more at home on the range, even if they'd never been west of the nearest shopping mall.

Thousands of "personal trucks," jeeps, and "sport utility vehicles" replaced BMWs and Volvos in the family driveway, not as symbols of status or success, but as signs of being "with the times." Sales of Willie Nelson albums soared, purchased by people who had ignored his music for 30 years or so.

"Mamas, Don't Let Your Babies Grow Up to Be Cowboys" was a sad lament, sung along with by people who could understand the loneliness and pain of the cowboy's life, even if they lived in New Jersey, Wisconsin, Florida, or Chicago.

Cowboys? No, *image.*

The film, the book, the music, the clothes, the theme song . . . Baby boomers, again, didn't just want to go to a movie; they wanted to live the story, if only vicariously, if only in daydreams. This is a generation that hears music and wants a soundtrack to everyday life.

Disney recognized the power of this total marketing approach in the 1950s, when it wasn't enough to enjoy the Davy Crockett TV films; a kid had to have the coonskin cap, record, coloring book, and pajamas that went with it. Those kids were the young baby boomers, and they haven't changed in 50 years.

While many movies have launched fads and trends, to which baby boomers, more than most other market segments, seemed poised to respond, *American Graffiti, Animal House, The Graduate, Saturday Night Fever*, and *Urban Cowboy* stand out as still fresh in boomers' minds decades later, partly thanks to the marketing boost from TV and the local video store. They offer images of times filled with memories . . . and with product placements.

The More Things Change . . .

As tempting as it is for marketers to try a revival, the charge is still to come up with *new* ideas. But drawing from entries on the list of what baby boomers remember is a good place to start. The media and the marketplace are waiting and watching for "the next big thing"—that big idea that will have the cultural impact of the images of the '60s.

In *Megatrends 2000*, John Naisbitt and Patricia Aburdene point out characteristics of baby boomers relative to their jobs and careers that are equally true in other contexts. Baby boomers, the authors contend, "thought loyalty was important, but never as important as personal growth." They add, "'Have skills, will travel' seems to be the motto of the job-jumping baby boom generation, confirming the stereotype of the selfish yuppie. On the other hand, the fast pace of social and technological change has forced (them) to adapt and change."

Sometimes such changes are brought about by the boomers themselves, and sometimes they are forced upon them. Either way, as much as they may have to change with the times, they will always be subject to symbols that left a deep impression upon them in their most formative years.

A Defining Moment of Opportunity

Until the baby boomers, no generation had struggled so hard to "find" itself—or wanted to. The hunger for that identification continues. For marketers, it is a rich opportunity.

Many boomers saw themselves as idealists. Theirs was the generation with a mission. They spoke and wrote songs about peace, love, freedom, changing the world. They spoke openly and publicly about their feelings, about alienation, and about how much they were not like their parents and grandparents.

So, it's not all cowboy hats and rock 'n' roll. Boomers saw both their responsibility and the opportunity to change the world in a list of empowerment programs aimed at hunger, poverty, and literacy. From the Peace Corps to saving the rain forests, boomers stepped forward.

Factors other than social, political, and artistic set boomers apart from their elders. They are what some term a "sandwiched" generation, dealing with concerns and needs of their aging parents and grandparents as well as with the needs of their children. They also are the first generation to come of age at a time when the national divorce rate shifted from 50 percent to a projected two couples out of three. Many married later in life, divorced more often, had children later, and often have split families—that is, their own children from different marriages as well as stepchildren in remarriages.

Some kept the fashions and idealism of their youth, while others contemplated the effects of the Cold War and whether or not the Social Security system would be bankrupt and unable to help them survive in their later years. The sheer size of the boomer market prompted insurance companies and brokerage firms to develop or repackage retirement benefit programs for a generation that not long before had a difficult time fathoming that *retirement* could ever apply to them.

Common History, Diverse Concerns

Data such as the foregoing confirm that boomers, as a group, have little more than the history of their generation in common. Having lived through the same years, they heard the same music and witnessed war, assassinations, the dividing of the country across no clear-cut lines, healing, coming together, prosperity, and middle age. The context notwithstanding, a baby boomer couple is as likely to have a 4-year-old child as a 14-year-old or a child of 24. The changing nature of the American family allows for concerns about education, the environment, and quality of life to be revisited again and again, as boomers repeat themselves, having children, emptying the nest, and refilling it.

It is important that marketers understand and reflect this diversity of concerns—from aging to environment.

Thus, a boomer who has to be thinking about retirement may also be thinking about education costs and having to plan for both simultaneously.

It is not only the boomer *segment* that is rich in diversity; the same may be said of individual boomers themselves.

A boomer woman who is caring for not only children but parents and/or grandparents may also be single and/or a working mother. Such a picture would appear to contradict that of the selfish yuppie of the Me Generation and illustrates the significant problem marketers have in drawing a profile of boomers based on information that they are only self-absorbed stereotypes.

Unwieldy Influence

Life magazine devoted a special issue to baby boomers turning 50 and listed its "50 Most Influential Boomers." Without question, the individuals on the roster *are* influential. In addition to President and Mrs. Clinton, it includes such prominent persons as filmmakers Steven Spielberg and Spike Lee; Michaels Jackson, Jordan, and Milken; David Letterman; O. J. Simpson; Donna Karan; Karen Silkwood; Supreme Court Justice Clarence Thomas; Howard Stern; Oprah Winfrey; and Madonna.

As a target group for marketers, these personages would appear to have little more in common than their fame or celebrity. Would they all stop to hear a commercial that featured music from their younger years and spoke to them about "their time"?

Perhaps.

But a serious demographer may suggest that a marketer not try to reach Justice Thomas and Howard Stern with the same message (or the same song). The *Know your market* rule covers more than age.

Look at each of the "influencers" to see in what ways their stories made a difference. In advertising terms, their *USP*—unique selling proposition— provided seed material for a marketing plan, a message, or a campaign that would likely get the attention of baby boomers and be entertaining in ways that celebrities are entertaining.

So, What's the Good Word?

In a very large way, the word for baby boomers is *image*. It is reaching for an emotionally gratifying response. Any kind of marketing or advertising effort must emphasize benefits to the consumer, but in the boomers' case, facts alone will take you only part of the way there. However persuasive "low monthly financing" or "great mileage" or "best discount prices" may be, the balance will be tipped by image—how what you are showing or saying will make the baby boomer look and feel, if only in his or her own eyes.

The secondary message: one word—*packaging* (not, as in the classic baby boomer film *The Graduate*, "plastics"). If a film is good, boomers want to read the book, get the video, buy the soundtrack album, repeat the most memorable lines to friends, copy the wardrobe, and try recreating the meals served in the film. It used to be called "art imitating life" or "life imitating art." Now it's simply the way things are. The lines are so blurred that both schoolchildren and their parents barely make it through conversations without echoing lines from favorite TV shows *and* popular commercials.

Miami Vice was a mediocre TV detective series, but it was a marketing bonanza. The *look* of the show set off the season's style, with the clothes and music selling, even if the show itself was easy to forget. And Miami tourism benefited, despite headlines detailing serious local crime problems.

The bestselling book *Midnight in the Garden of Good and Evil* received the now routine movie and soundtrack album treatment, but more newsworthy was what the book did for tourism in its setting, Savannah, Georgia. Regularly scheduled tour groups have often overwhelmed the little town. Merchandising is going well.

Nearly every major news event (and many minor ones) is immediately followed by its principals' negotiating a book-film-rights deal, with a schedule of media interviews and appearances, lectures, and national promotions—whether that principal was an astronaut, a ski instructor, a cashier, or a homeless person. The news is as much an audition tape as a source of information. And marketers are watching the news to get a sense of what the public is thinking and doing. It is not always pretty, but it is often marketable.

Work, Relationship, Family

Psychologists point out that, while each lifestyle emphasizes different priorities, life for the majority of boomers is made up of three interconnected elements: work, personal relationships, and family. Unlike generations before them, boomers tend to refuse to present different images of themselves in their professional and their personal lives. This is the generation that publicly embraced the notion of being themselves at all times. They are also the first generation to not only allow for, but expect, work to also be satisfying to the degree of even being fun.

While marketers understand the risks of generalizing, these considerations appear applicable as each market segment is further segmented based on high or low income, male or female, city or rural, degree of ethnicity, and religious and social concerns.

Sidestepping the Feminist Shift

Baby boomers also represent the generation or market segment from which women came into their own in a meaningful way. The feminist movement, or women's liberation, led to consciousness-raising and political correctness. To marketers, this means a shift in attitudes regarding marketing to women.

Some women prefer to be addressed as women have for a century, in traditional terms, such as homemakers, wives, and mothers, with an emphasis on domestic considerations. But a significant percentage of women resent being regarded as only "the lady of the house" and want the respect that reflects their right to be taken more seriously.

So, how does the marketer walk this fine line? The marketer doesn't.

Women Are People First Instead of wasting time trying to decide how *feminine* an ad or a press release, the packaging, or an event sponsorship can be before it becomes offensive to feminist sensibilities, simply market to women as *customers*. Learn what the women in your target group are looking for in a product, service, or issue, and *address that*.

By addressing the needs and concerns of the *market* and the *marketplace*, you can avert the gender trap for the time being.

Working women, working mothers, and professional women represent a market that has matured. Of course, it may always need some fine-tuning, since particular segments of the market are more aggressive or militant in matters as basic as how they choose to be referred to. Remember that, in an era in which political correctness is the order of the day for some and detested by others, passions run high. As one example, many women object to feminists' (or anyone else) speaking on their behalf on the basis that the speakers are not inherently reflecting their concerns. Marketers who want the attention and support of women as a targeted segment can either exploit this opportunity or step into the trap. Some marketers believe that quick-sand is a fair analogy, asserting that in areas of political or social "touchi-ness," a situation that begins with a presumption of a stereotype and proceeds on that premise can only get worse.

Recognizing Women's Place Working women of the baby boomer gen-eration have a statistically higher income level than both their predeces-sors and younger consumers and, accordingly, a higher level of buying power. While many women are responsible for most or all of the house-hold purchases, from food to health and cleaning products, some share that responsibility with husbands or other partners. What's more relevant is that increasingly, women are making or sharing major purchase decisions as well.

In some situations, there is no partner or husband, and the professional working woman makes *all* decisions on her own—cars, condos, houses, other real estate, and investments. In any event, in no other generation is the decision sharing as distinguishable as among baby boomers, the gener-ation that was in the forefront of the campaign for "equal rights."

Statistically, women live longer than men. They are also credited, gen-erally, with having a keener eye for detail and excellent organizational skills.

As we know, many members of groups do not appreciate being treated as merely part of a crowd, and that is decidedly true of the segment that has been called the Me Generation, especially the large number of women within this segment who have pressed hard for recognition and believe they deserve it. Marketers must be sensitive to this fact and remember that, if their message does not specifically speak to certain segments within a mar-ket, they should at least be conscious not to offend or exclude a segment that may openly resent the slight.

Simply put, that means, when in doubt, speak to *the market*, not to men or women.

Value Added

The last word on the subject must always be *benefit*. Whether the marketing effort is highlighted by a PR campaign, advertising, a trade show booth, or a website, if the message to the target audience lacks a sense of value and ben-efit to the consumer, the product or the message needs to be reconsidered.

But once a marketer segments the market, demonstrates the benefit, value, and unique selling propositions within the message, and takes careful aim, the interesting process of actually marketing is free to take place.

Modern Maturity Marketing

Statistically, Americans appear to make more conservative choices as they grow older, from clothing and personal-care products to automobiles and investments. Something this generation has in common with older generations is an appreciation of nostalgia, images that remind them of times they may consider simpler when compared with responsibilities or vulnerabilities of the present, and a feeling about the future that runs from uncertainty to outright fear. This gives marketers a lot to work with, presenting messages that tap sentimental notes of the most powerful images from baby boomers' youth, framing positive images of satisfaction in the present, and invoking visions of times both exciting and secure ahead. In the final analysis, the "hot buttons" are the same for most every generation; it is a matter of *when they are most important to a particular generation* that marketers need to determine and exploit.

In the future, baby boomers' vanity will tend to drive behavior as maturing yields to the more visible signs of aging. Hair loss, weight gain, stronger prescriptions for eyeglasses, and the need for a skosh more material in the rear end of those jeans will be on the minds of boomers in segments that marketers will want to reach. So will the environment and the ability to remain true to the social concerns that many boomers believe they "fought for" in their way.

Marketers often take the concepts of campaigns and media flights too literally and create messages that are defined narrowly, abruptly, even jerkily. Images are black or white, old or young, cool or very *un*cool. Though the Electronic Age rapidly became the Internet Revolution, the faces and players didn't change, nor did those touchstones that were most important to a generation. Marketing to a generation does not need to be focused on time in increments of hours, months, or this year's marketing budget.

As the attention of this population shifts more to investment products and more serious purchase decisions (as in more certificate of deposit CDs and fewer compact disc CDs), marketers have a huge opportunity to build a bridge from an exciting and memorable past to a promising future where dreams can be fully realized. Defining images of today and tomorrow as the *evolution* of the best of times provides a broad stage on which to work.

Summary Points

1. Baby boomers are the largest, most diverse segment of the total market.
2. While their parents often took and held jobs for life, baby boomers are less inclined to do so.
3. Baby boomers are both widely known and regarded as the Me Generation.
4. Many baby boomers grew up with television as a constant companion, teacher, baby-sitter, and friend.
5. Many baby boomers are idealists who see their mission as "changing the world." They are highly concerned with social issues and causes.
6. Baby boomers married later, divorced more often, had children later, and often have families that live together only part of the time.
7. A marketer targeting a message to the baby boomer segment should bridge images of a rich past, positive images of today, and visions of what can be, without alienating other market segments or promoting an exclusionary message along the way.

6

Marketing to Generation X

What is future will grow out of what has already passed or is passing.
—G. B. Cheever

WHILE THE OBJECTIVE of this book is to advance future marketing strategies, not to incite controversy, the very mention of Generation X causes some people to become defensive, even argumentative. As a market segment, this group is widely diversified, encompassing some of the brightest minds in the United States—people who have made an indelible mark in a number of fields, including technology, film, and music, and inspired countless others to aim high. The group also includes people who have been among the most reluctant to leave the security of the family nest. But to suggest that there is diversity within the segment can be said of any segment. For marketers, it is the common characteristics that contribute to a profile that in turn shapes a target for which marketing programs must aim.

Problems from the Get-Go

From the beginning, it looked as if there would be at least two problems with Generation X. The first is that applying the most fitting label—"enigmatic"—would have been to describe it without a description. Yet, that is the sort of circular profiling this group inspires. The second problem is what seems to be overt tension (even hostility) between Xers and baby boomers. This is not simply a case of the old generation gap being resurrected, as when in the 1960s, parents and their children agreed that they did not understand each other's points of view and were content to regard each other as simply wrong about most things. In the matter of Xers and boomers, the younger generation seems angry with boomers for having lived during what seemed like the most dramatic, interesting, and defining moments in American history in at least a century.

Of course, Generation X is not alone in being problematic. Marketers have to pause over the fact that the highly regarded process of market segmentation designates the baby boomer generation as covering persons born between 1945 and 1964. Doesn't, in fact, an age span of nearly 20 years qualify for listing as *two* separate generations? Isn't someone turning 35 subject to different concerns from those of someone turning 50?

One explanation offered is that the post–World War II boom in births continued for a period of nearly two decades, which means that all the boomers born to the same families over those years are siblings, hence the same generation. The same generation or not, 20 years is 20 years. The boomer designation has survived intact for this long because, quite simply, it works for pundits to describe the commonality of those who, in full, came to symbolize the '60s, its energy, and its excesses.

Another reason may be that through well-managed market segmentation, marketers are able to appropriately define groups by decade, lifestyle, and enough common characteristics as to be manageable. Once the target group's profile is fixed, whether it is composed of 30-year-olds or people in their 50s, the categorical distinction is less relevant. As the parameters have been set, it sometimes looks as if parents and children are falling within the same generation. A 20-year gap can do that. Marketers might best target 30-year-olds without worrying about which generation they represent.

Living in the Shadows

Generation X most certainly appears to be a group lacking in dominant, distinguishing characteristics. Researchers say a common trait is its vagueness.

Xers followed the baby boomers, thus making them the next generation. Yet, a person of 23 or 24 is hardly distinguishable as of a different generation from someone of 36 (the age of younger baby boomers). They are virtual contemporaries. Boomers born in the 1940s, however, fit the profile of the older generation. In the most superficial sense, this reflects a problem with Generation X, particularly in its relationship with baby boomers. Members of Gen X have demonstrated enough of an "attitude" to get the attention of researchers, who, while acknowledging the overgeneralization, find Generation X so vaguely defined as to put it strongly and squarely in the shadow of the baby boomers . . . and not liking it at all.

Some put it simply, insisting that the 1960s and the generation that emerged from it were a hard act to follow, so why even try? It was this no-win position that won members of Generation X the sobriquet of *slackers*.

Whatchamacallit

Frequent attempts to position the segment somewhat more upscale by calling it "20-somethings" never quite caught on. An early casual designation, the "MTV Generation" was less of an inclusive or encompassing name as an attempt to qualify the segment by common interests. The inference was that Xers not only were excessive television viewers to the extent of being characterized by it but also limited themselves to a single channel. So, it was with some reluctance that the group accepted the designation of Generation X—or Xers—a designation that itself arrives with some baggage. To many people, it suggests a generation without a name, like *Brand X*, advertising's traditional label for "the other guy." In this case, however, it is not so much a question of not *choosing* to call it what it is, but rather still trying to identify and understand what it is.

Clues from the Chroniclers

Marketers can look for clues by turning to those who chronicle the moves and motives of the target group. Douglas Coupland writes well of the generation and pop culture. In his satirical novel *Generation X: Tales for an Accelerated Culture*, a sampling of his chapter titles offers some insight into its content and concerns. While it is a work of fiction and fun, its references closely track the conclusions of researchers studying the group from a non-fiction perspective. Consider what this array says about Generation X and what its members are thinking:

> The Sun Is Your Enemy
> Our Parents Had More
> Quit Recycling the Past
> I Am Not a Target Market
> Dead at 30, Buried at 70
> It Can't Last
> Shopping Is Not Creating
> Purchased Experiences Don't Count

Why Am I Poor?
I Am Not Jealous
Define Normal
Adventure Without Risk Is Disneyland
Await Lightning

Whether they are intended to be fictional or funny or both or not, the references in fact reflect the cynical, angry, expressed indifference that researchers have used to characterize members of Generation X.

Ages vary and numbers disagree depending on who's doing the counting. In any case, the market is huge. Karen Ritchie, a Detroit-based marketing and media expert, points out: "*Sixty-five million* adult Xers came of age in a world radically different from the one that baby boomers inherited. The decline of the economy and the upsurge in divorce had made Xers more sober and cynical, yet more flexible and less ideological, about the definition of 'family.' Although jaded by the materialistic '80s, they are on the whole much more comfortable with interactivity and other sophisticated technology than boomers. Although disillusioned by the boomer swing from activism in the '60s to status in the '80s, they are more tolerant of diversity and experiment than their forebears."

Whoa! Sober? Cynical? Less ideological? Jaded? Disillusioned? More tolerant?

While again it can be subject to charges of overgeneralizing, as a capsule description of what research has managed to tell us over many pages about Generation X, this comes pretty close.

Walt Would Be Proud

How does one market to sober, disillusioned, and jaded? A glib answer may be "very carefully."

Another answer may be to recall the theory of marketing that says people will come over to your side if you not only make your case in a positive, persuasive way but also make them feel good about themselves, emphasizing the value and benefits to *them* in what you are offering.

Walt Disney is reported to have claimed that a secret to his success was that everything he produced had to both educate and entertain. While Xers may not, in their cynicism, appreciate being marketed to according to rules set down by the man who brought you *Snow White and the Seven Dwarfs*, there's something to be said for the approach—and his very successful track record.

Putting rubber to the road, the Swedish automaker Volvo, for its first big ad campaign of the 21st century, did two things that might have surprised market observers: (1) It chose Generation X as its target market, and (2) It chose the Internet—Generation X's medium of choice—as the venue for its message.

A new character, named Lars, was created for the occasion, and it was as if he had sprung from the minds that create the quirky sitcom characters who populate Thursday-night television. Lars is a funny, hip Generation Xer who rides a mountain bike, windsurfs, and cares about the environment. He is also a sailor who likes to attend the Volvo Ocean Race, likes to talk about his love of the environment, and is interested in the Biosphere in Tucson, Arizona, where, just coincidentally, Volvo is sponsor of a study program.

Mr. Disney would have been proud. While the verdict on Lars and Volvo's Internet strategy is still not in, ultimately it almost cannot fail. By running an exclusively Internet campaign, the company clearly hopes to target and cultivate this market segment. Additionally, if the profile of Generation X as it has been drawn is anywhere near accurate, the pairing of Xers and Swedish Volvo would seem to be a good fit. Both are viewed as outside the establishment mainstream. Lars would fit the profile as well, with his interest in environmental matters, which can be interpreted as a not-so-subtle swipe by Generation X at previous generations' abuse of all the good things nature gave them to start with.

A Cable-Ready Read on the Market

Consider again the description of the Xers as the MTV Generation—the target segment that marketers have sought to define by its strong support of and identification with a cable television channel built around nonstop music videos. Journalist Tom McGrath observed: "Indeed the term 'MTV-like'—a synonym for fast-moving images set to loud music—had entered the language. Some even argued that the channel and its visual style had started to change the very way young people's minds worked. . . . You couldn't deny that the influence was great. As the *Washington Post* had put it . . . 'MTV was perhaps the most influential single cultural product of the decade.'"

MTV captured the interest of its target generation with its music videos, wildly overshadowing Top 40 radio, if not all radio, as the last word on popular music. Record companies quickly learned that a music video delivered to MTV was as important as—or more important than—copies of a new disc sent to major radio stations, or even promotional tours.

Top motion-picture directors, many of whom said they would never work in the less artistic medium of television, were being recruited to work in music videos. Unlike radio, music videos not only allowed the audience to see the performer but also showcased the music in a cultural context, immediately creating an image for the performer, promoting the music— the song, the album of which it was a part, or both—and giving additional life to the product by creating a *video* product that could be marketed simultaneously or at a later date. The result was an enormous new lucrative and powerful industry, the music video for rental or sale.

And the music video and MTV, through both the video format and its presentation, connected with a generation seeking desperately to define itself.

While many pop stars stake their fame and success on MTV, many others have shrewdly managed their exposure to generate huge contracts for outside commercial relationships (sponsored tours, advertising connections) and other media appearances, extending their MTV exposure to other networks and films.

Hail to the Chief

Expanding its own image and influence, MTV launched featured programming beyond just music videos and generationally focused news. One of its singularly successful promotions, recognizing the importance of America's voting age having been lowered from 21 to 18, was the "Rock the Vote" campaign. The promotion featured pop stars who were definitely not considered to be a part of "the political system" stressing to the young audience how great an impact they could have on the process by voting in the upcoming presidential election. In many ways, it was like the story line from the '60s cult movie *Wild in the Streets*, in which teenagers provide the deciding vote and elect a rock star president.

Candidate Bill Clinton, then the governor of Arkansas and credited with being both an astute politician and perhaps the most media-savvy contender the process had ever seen, felt MTV was worth his coming in for an exclusive interview and sitting for questions from members of its youthful audience. A generation earlier, it would have been difficult to conceive of the president of the United States making a serious campaign appearance on, say, *American Bandstand*, or to imagine such an invitation's ever being extended.

But politics was changing. The media had changed. And the marketing of a candidate, as with any other "product," held that the market be targeted and addressed in as nonexclusionary a way as possible to add depth and texture and enhance the message.

MTV and its audience were maturing together. As its audience grew older, it added a companion cable channel, VH-1, as part of an effort to both hold its faithful core constituency and adapt to embrace the younger audience just coming of age to embody the MTV Generation.

Acknowledging the impact of the "Rock the Vote" campaign and the importance of MTV and its audience to his election victory, on the evening of his inauguration, President Clinton, with his wife and daughter, attended an MTV-sponsored party. He told the cheering young crowd, "I think everybody here knows MTV had a lot to do with the Clinton-Gore victory. And Tab (MTV reporter Tabitha Soren) brought me on the show and let all the young people ask me questions. . . . And one of the things that I'm proudest of is that so many young voters turned out in record numbers. I want you to know that I still believe in 'Rock the Vote.'"

Not many TV networks, newspapers, or other media have received such public endorsements from a president of the United States. As the President and Mrs. Clinton left to put in appearances at the evening's other inaugural celebrations, their teenage daughter chose to remain at the MTV party.

It is at such times that members of Generation X have been able to bask in the reflection of something big, a characteristic they strongly resented about their baby boomer counterparts, who they felt had all the really great events happen in *their* time.

Ye of Little Faith

MTV, for all its ultimate power and influence over a generation, had a shaky beginning financially. American advertisers were slow to come forward with support. According to Tom McGrath, that reticence was hard to understand even then.

"Why," he posed, "weren't American companies ready to kill each other for the opportunity to send their commercials down the musical pipeline and into the homes, hearts, and minds of the country's youth? Partly it was the ad community's attitude toward cable. Not only did cable still reach a limited number of people—by the spring of 1981, fewer than 25 percent of the country's homes had cable—but more than that, the ad community, like the broadcast networks and the record industry, simply didn't like change. Ad agencies didn't like to take a chance on an experiment—which was what cable was to them."

MTV eventually succeeded in winning both an infusion of cash and solid advertising support. It was popular with its audience, and as marketers have both proved and watched happen again and again, if something is permitted to stay in one place long enough, it will likely find acceptance, as MTV did with Generation X—whether its members had cable TV or not. And that generation was brash and irreverent, though not in the same way that could be said of the baby boomers.

Bag the Identity Crisis

Researchers described Gen Xers as angry. The Xers' baggy, shapeless clothes contributed to their shapeless image, as if they wanted an identity—to be recognized in their own right—but not to be *defined*.

This was a problem for marketers, who require a profile of a typical consumer to market against. Thus, marketers did not embrace or court Gen X as they had so aggressively, even shamelessly, courted generations before them. Here was an enormous market segment, a large percentage of whom were moderately affluent young people, and advertisers were almost overtly having to categorize it as an opportunity missed.

In a fascinating account titled *The Conquest of Cool*, reporter Thomas Frank offers an analysis of the problem:

> How dark things must have seemed on Madison Avenue in 1992. . . . How fervently the diviners of the American public mind must have wished for some new mass-cultural dispensation, some array of symbols and celebrities that would make them seem relevant again. . . .
>
> And how they must have rejoiced when the leading minds of the cultural industry announced the discovery of an all-new angry generation, the "20-somethings," complete with a panoply of musical styles, hairdos, and verbal signifiers ready-made to rejuvenate advertising's sagging credibility. Armed with quickly produced books and informative cover stories in

Advertising Age, Business Week, U.S. News, and *Newsweek,* admen were eager to take on the inscrutable "Generation X."

They were very savvy consumers . . . far more knowledgeable about and suspicious of advertising than earlier generations passing through their 20s. . . . They are media savvy but are said to feel alienated from the mainstream culture. . . . Exactly like the boomers, Xers are said to respond well to "honest" advertising. . . .

Most important of all, the 20-somethings really go for "irreverence."

Irreverence—*finally* something marketers could wrap themselves in— like the humor of the long-running TV hit *Saturday Night Live* or late-night comedian David Letterman, a personality built on coolness, sarcasm, putdowns, and a serious disdain for authority.

At least here is something marketers could embrace as being *close* to a profile of Generation X: affluent outsiders, similar in many ways to baby boomers, yet eager to establish their own identity and agenda.

Boomers had planned to change the world, and the world had in fact changed dramatically in their time. Whether it was the kind of change they'd had in mind and how much credit they deserve may be topics for discussion. Still, Gen Xers came of age in a much different environment from the one that the baby boomers had encountered.

The most dramatic change is clearly in the area of technology, and for all the talk of a cynical, disillusioned, disconnected generation, Gen Xers are extremely well prepared.

Marketing's Technological Breakthrough

The MTV Generation did not spend *all* of its time watching television. Their introduction to, and preparation for, cyberspace and the information superhighway came by way of years of Nintendo, Game Boy, the Super Mario Brothers, MYST, and other assorted beeping, flashing computer games and videos.

Baby boomers (and their elders) are all too frequently exasperated in their encounters with technology, only to have Xers step forward and, with relative calm, resolve the problem, all the while casually muttering terms that seem left over from a *Star Trek* script.

While boomers considered their schools' replacing the faithful old "projectors" from the AV department with videotape players and monitors to be a leap into the future, Gen Xers found computers in their classrooms—computers similar to the ones many of them already knew how to use, the result of home PCs and computer games.

"Surfing" the Internet was a common enough form of home entertainment, and applying what they knew to real life and the real world gives Xers an edge over many older, more experienced professionals. The *new media* are, in many respects, about them.

And for marketers, the means to reach Gen Xers and to market to them are as vast as space, or at least cyberspace.

Media executive Karen Ritchie notes: "Xers use technology to personalize and humanize everything they touch, demanding only that hype and communication be kept in check. They will be the first generation to realize the potential marriage between television and the computer. They are already heavily immersed in communication through computer networks, they understand being 'wired,' and because of Xers, interactive television is just around the corner."

Though boomers and seniors may be running the world, many admit they are somewhere between clueless and slow-to-catch-on when it comes to matters of technology.

Personal computers are commonplace, and cellular phones are in the pockets, purses, and backpacks of everyone from sales rep to high schooler. Call forwarding, E-mail, voice mail, chat rooms, teleconferencing, and a virtual yellow pages of "dot-com" services have made E-commerce the norm, and Gen Xers are the first market segment to relate to this as a way of life, not as an event. Whether it started with Pac-man or movie phone, Xers respond to technology as their primary means of receiving the most routine forms of information and for communicating.

How and What

For marketers, the two major questions regarding Generation X are (1) How do we get to them? and (2) What do we say?

First, Incorporate

While the way to reach Gen X would seem to be electronically—via the Internet, cell phone, and MTV—indications are that no medium, new or old, is off limits. Consider that the members of this group, long dismissed as nonreaders, have been the primary targets of more than two dozen new magazines. The language, layout, graphics, and subject matter are heavy with "inside" references and "attitude" that consciously exclude the older generations.

Many of these new publications have succeeded very well, and while they all carry the obligatory prompt "Check out our website," they continue to hawk subscriptions to printed matter with a reasonable success rate. CDs and audiocassettes are also viable, as are toll-free numbers for providing information or transacting business. And while the U.S. Postal Service is derided as "snail mail," it is still ever present in the form of coupons, samples, personal letters, catalogs, and "magalogs" (the combination magazine and catalog).

So, while PCs and the Internet are getting all the publicity and being hailed as the future, the traditional "old media" of print and mail are still very much alive. It may be significant to count the increasing number of tech-oriented print vehicles and ask if the publishers of these magazines know something about their targeted market. It may be reasonable to believe that research exists somewhere that says the "generation that wasn't interested in print or reading" would be receptive to new magazines aimed at them.

Retailers do well with customized, logo-imprinted music CDs. Each week, tens of thousands of computer disks and CDs offering samples of great new products and services are distributed—by mail.

Communicating and marketing via the Internet can be a dramatic and exciting opportunity, but it doesn't have to mean that a new medium discovered thus signals the end of all other media. Future marketing should *incorporate* new media, not replace it if it still works.

Uncoupling Xers

What do marketers say to trigger a response from Gen Xers?

In the words of Barry Manilow, try saying, "This one's for you."

The enormous success of MTV validated the notion that Xers, believing that all the good stuff already fell to the baby boomers, were ready and willing to support something pitched just for them. A candidate who presented a message punctuated with a request for Xers' support got it. Marketers, however, must appreciate that Xers are more media savvy in many respects than "older generations." They have a good "BS detector" and

Add Some Music to . . .

Dove ice cream, Starbucks, Williams-Sonoma, Lee Jeans, Blockbuster Video, and Hard Rock Cafe are only a few brands that provide music to accompany the use of their products. The theory is that the demographic groups for all of these products have a heavy interest and appreciation in carefully selected music that somehow reflects the images of the brands. CDs are offered free or below retail cost as a way of keeping the brand's logo in front of consumers, even when the product is not. (Photograph by Karin Gottschalk Marconi)

can see when they are being exploited and patronized. Literally dozens of expensive Hollywood films aimed at Xers' restless, angry, disillusioned spirit have gone directly (or quickly) to home video and languished, never finding an audience.

Principles of good marketing demand that the marketer *know the market* and its concerns. Gen Xers who are cynical or in transition *are* "the market" nonetheless.

Identify their needs, and meet them. Know too that they are as interested in T-shirts, caps, jackets, and other assorted logo-imprinted merchandise as are the generations that came before and after them.

Generalizations have been made about Xers regarding sex, dating practices, the environment, nutrition, and spirituality. Marketers should conduct or analyze research carefully. Attitudes relative to all of those points

A Look at the Designer's Best Work?

Perry Ellis is a successful designer brand in both clothing and fragrance. This attempt to bring the brand to the public's attention will certainly prove attention-getting and make people notice the Perry Ellis name, but if it will create a brand identification with clothes or fragrance products (ahem) remains to be seen. Even a great looking ad should not upstage the product if the brand is to be remembered. (Copyright 1999 Perry Ellis) are not all-encompassing. Different age-groups in different communities and regions will differ dramatically. Gen Xers are the first generation to routinely engage in "group dating," in which a group of friends or invited guests go out or stay in together, not necessarily "pairing" or even gathering in even numbers. This is a significant point, as so much of advertising and marketing is based on assumptions of couples or traditional relationships. That dynamic is not a requirement of this segment.

It Doesn't Seem Like Old Times

Gen Xers are better informed about health and diseases and appear to be somewhat more conservative than boomers or seniors.

As much as they (and seemingly every generation) have certain issues with other generations, advertising messages such as "This is not your father's Oldsmobile" or MSNBC's ad for its evening news show, "It's not your father's news," have been met with a big *So what?* Saying "This one's for you" does require that you say *why* and be a bit more specific.

If marketers want to reach this generation, simply taking their side and taking shots at the other generations won't cut it. As sketchy as the profile of the Xers is, it would be a mistake to assume that all members of the generation (or any generation) are in agreement about everything, including MTV and the Internet, and that all are marching in the same direction. Keep media options open, and don't risk excluding the people who may be your best market in the future.

The foods, films, clothes, and music targeted to members of Generation X came to their attention via media that played to them, but the successes, as with other solid marketing messages, were largely nonexclusionary. Future marketing does not have to take either one road or another to reach the target market when all roads can lead to the same place.

Summary Points

1. Generation X lacks dominant, distinguishing characteristics but is generally described as cynical, angry, disconnected, and somewhat resentful of the baby boomer generation.

2. Gen Xers seem to have a high degree of concern for the environment but are not singularly identified with a particular social cause or unifying issue.

3. Xers are, on the whole, more comfortable with technology than are other generations.
4. The "MTV Generation" seemed a fitting description of the Gen Xers who have indicated an appreciation of loud music and fast-moving images.
5. Personal computers and cell phones are common examples of Xers' links to technology.
6. Xers respond well to messages pitched specifically to them but are sensitive to messages that exploit or patronize them.

7

Marketing to Generation Y

We are always looking to the future; the present does not satisfy us. Our ideal, whatever it may be, lies further on.
—Gillett

MARKETING PEOPLE ARE among the most creative people in the arts and business. Each year, they are called upon to name products and companies and assign titles to many and sundry projects, programs, and brand extensions. So, it is noteworthy that the identifier that marketers selected to define a totally new and emerging market segment is as descriptive and colorful as, say, the wind. It is called Generation Y, or to some, the Millennium Generation (the M Generation). Its members are also called the *Echo Boomers*, as well as *teenagers* or simply *kids*. They've got big numbers and some big bucks to spend and are a very important group.

The Generation Y age span—representing people born between 1978 and 1994—again, as with the two generations preceding, is wide enough to cause marketers to be concerned over generalizing about common motivators.

Obviously, this situation represents an exciting new opportunity for marketers. In truth, seasoned marketers tend to view virtually everything, definable or not, as an opportunity, and they may be right.

Why the name? Why the fuss? Who *are* these people? Good questions.

"Y" as in "Yet to Come"?

They are called Generation Y either because *Y* follows *X* and they are the market segment that follows Generation X in age, or because *Y* is the first letter of *young*, which they are, compared with boomers and Xers. They are basically younger people coming of age at the start of the 21st century. Demographers place their birth between 1978 and 1994. They are the children of the younger baby boomers or of the older baby boomers who started late or started again after divorces, remarriage, or a simple desire to have more kids, albeit later in their lives. Or they are the children of the upper reaches of Generation X.

And they are an estimated 60 million in number—some three times the size of Generation X by some measures, slightly smaller by others. In either case, it's a very large market. Mention the phrase *a market segment of 60 million* to a marketer and little more need be said.

So, where does the headache come in? Let's compare. Once we put the words *angry, cynical,* and *disillusioned* on the blackboard under Generation X, we concede that this is a market that has yet to fully mature, and it is reasonable to hope that with maturity, some or all of these negative emotions will be overcome or outgrown. Generation Y, coming up behind the Xers, are even *less* defined in the sense that they have so many stages ahead of them—college, jobs, marriage, going out on their own—that they provide marketers a very fast moving target.

Because all of Generation Y is not *yet,* there is much that is not known about it. That's the bad news from a marketing standpoint. The good news is that marketers do know some things about Generation Y in the current market environment, and smart marketers see a chance to follow this group through life, being there for every ceremony and status change, with a plethora of products and services to celebrate, enhance, and help shape the buying habits at the various stages of their lives.

In that respect, almost everything known about this segment represents both the marketing challenge of the moment and the tremendous potential *ahead.*

What Every Marketer Hopes For

According to *Business Week,* "Though the echo boom rivals its parent's generation in size, in almost every other way, it is very different. This generation is more racially diverse: One in three is not Caucasian. One in four lives in a single-parent household. Three in four have working mothers. While boomers are still mastering Microsoft 98, their kids are tapping away at computers in nursery school."

This information should come as no surprise to experienced marketers because, to quote the expression so popular during the Clinton administration, it looks like America. Racial diversity and a family profile that offers distinctive characteristics is what every marketer hopes for. It reflects the reality that everyone of the same age is not generic and has interests and needs that should respond to well-crafted marketing efforts.

Statistics Will Matter

Of the nearly one-third of the Generation Y members who are "not Caucasian," what percentage are of Hispanic, Asian, African American, or other ethnic or racial heritage, and to what degree may that be a factor in positioning products, services, and messages?

What is the ratio of male to female, and how significant is that?

In all likelihood, these statistics will matter a great deal, as will the economic circumstances of each segment of the group. The reason telemarketers call specific area codes, and mailing-list services break out lists by specific zip codes, is to capitalize on economic demographics, defined in large part (though not totally) by community.

While political correctness (and federal antidiscrimination laws) would discourage the use of demographic data as related to race or ethnicity, the simple truth is that specific communities have a larger population of people of one race or ethnic group or another—a fact that will not come as a bolt to the people of that community—and for marketers to address this consideration in terms of products, services, or businesses is not inherently bad.

The pendulum having swung from a passionate crusade for integration to a strong movement on behalf of a type of community separatism that promotes ethnic and racial pride, Generation Y is in the unique position of being able to lean in either direction. Once again, this is good news for marketers.

He Who Pays . . .

Another variable is to what degree the income or estimated net worth of a parent or head of household, based on zip codes, is reflected in either the interests or economics of the young person (or people) in that household. Some teenagers at 18 have their own cars, jobs, and income; others don't. Marketers need to qualify prospects in this market segment as in any other.

Household economics is especially important relative to a youthful market segment because it has an impact on brand marketing. For example, the "house" brand or other moderately priced pair of jeans, such as Gap, Old Navy, or Sears, may sell for one-half or one-third the price of designer-label jeans. In a normal discussion of brand marketing, the matter of "who pays" is rarely a component. But in a youth-segment market, it's a basic.

If the parent is buying the clothing, to what extent is the decision based on the young person's choice or powers of persuasion, and how much is it a matter of the marketer's speaking beyond the consumer of the product and targeting the message to parents or other purchasers? Market research can provide the data to make targeting more efficient.

Brand-Preference Roulette

Parental participation and economic considerations notwithstanding, the matter of brand preference is another area in which Generation Y has chosen to move in its own direction and is worthy of some market analysis.

Research indicates that members of Generation Y are neither as cynical nor as angry as the members of Generation X. They are, however, very media savvy, and this applies strongly to advertising and marketing. Generation X was the first group to be born into a world of brand consciousness, one that baby boomers shaped. Generation Y is, depending on a variety of parameters, either the second generation or the first full generation to arrive at a time when the practice of identifying brand preferences early on was a given.

Business Week reported, "Asked what brands are cool, these teens (Generation Y) rattled off a list their parents blank on. Mudd. Paris Blues. In Vitro. Cement. What's over? Now the names are familiar: Levi's. Converse. Nike."

Once again, this should not be a revelation to seasoned marketers, if for no other reason than, historically, each generation seeks to somehow distinguish and distance itself from its parents, and an obvious way is through its choices of branded merchandise.

What is notable in the *Business Week* article is that this news seemed to surprise the companies that were not the brands of choice. That a brand such as Nike, for example, which markets so aggressively to a specific target (and seems to have considerable insight regarding its core customers) would assume that the *children* of its core customers would also automatically make Nike *their* brand of choice is hopelessly naive.

Even more dramatic was Pepsi's highly unsuccessful introduction of Pepsi Next, which was visibly rejected by members of Generation Y. How much research was conducted before such an approach was made? The answer seems to be *not enough*. A brand such as Pepsi, as huge and powerful and knowledgeable a source of market information that it is, and as entrenched a force as it is within the soft drink market, must be especially creative in marketing to Generation Y (or anyone else) and not take its position in the market for granted.

Pepsi aggressively courted baby boomers and Generation X over a period of some three decades, with advertising campaigns such as "Pepsi, for those who think young" and "You're in the Pepsi Generation." In light of these messages, to which Gen Y people had been exposed since prenatal days, why would this audience assume that the new product was aimed at them? The Pepsi Next effort fell well short of conveying the necessary targeted message.

Similarly, Nike spent a fortune on celebrity endorsers, many of whom had retired by the time the members of Gen Y had the price of a pair of Nikes in hand.

A shortcut might have been simply for the long-established brand to hire a celebrity endorser-spokesperson who would connect with Gen Y and, hopefully, connect the *brand* with Gen Y.

Or turn again to the research, determine what are the concerns and interests of Gen Y, and speak to those points.

Fountain of Youth Obsession

That one generation should feel a bit of uneasiness about a younger group's assuming a greater role is not uncommon. Some feel more strongly than others. *Advertising Age* editor in chief Rance Crain, for example, believes that advertisers who place an excessive emphasis on youth are doing a disservice:

"The obsession to reach younger people at the expense of all others is killing network television, and it's killing advertising," he asserts. "It's a vicious spiral that is out of control: Marketers, convinced brand habits are set in stone once consumers near 35, demand TV shows that attract young, impressionable audiences; the networks churn out programs featuring young people that drive away older viewers; the ad people produce commercials aimed at the younger audiences and unfathomable to everyone else; ad agencies, as if to confirm the wisdom of buying shows for a limited audience and crafting ads that nobody gets, pay more and more for less and less; CEOs, repelled by excessive costs and TV spots they don't understand, step up their devaluation of advertising in their marketing efforts; and finally, great old brands hit the skids, based at least partly on all of the above. . . .

"Top executives are seeing for themselves every night on TV that too many ads have a distorted notion of how people live, work, and play. There is a growing disconnect here."

While he begins with a solid premise and constructs a logical argument, alas, some marketers would say that this same argument could have been made with equal conviction at almost any point in time since, perhaps, the 1970s.

The Desperate Hours

Marketers and ad agencies have almost always been accused of "playing too heavily to the youth market." Back in the 1950s, popular young-audience programs such as *American Bandstand,* and in the '60s, *Shindig* and *Hullabaloo,* were showcases for ads and products that were a fit for the market that these shows reflected: Beechnut gum, Clearasil and Stridex acne medication, Coke and Pepsi. The lines were more clearly drawn. One rarely found an acne cream ad on *Gunsmoke* or *Playhouse 90.*

By the late 1990s, the period that Crain singled out, those lines had blurred, as so much of prime-time network viewing was aimed at a younger audience—at least intellectually—with the Olsen twins, *Sabrina the Teenage Witch, Boy Meets World, Moesha,* and *Sister Sister.* As ratings for these shows held strong, more programs like them appeared. Older audiences sought (and were rewarded with a raft of) news "magazine" shows, trying to repeat the success of such hits as *60 Minutes, Dateline,* and *20/20,* each broadcast several times per week and packed with ads that the research said fit their demographics: ads for cars, airlines, hair-care products, and the latest Hollywood films.

While some marketers can seem almost desperate or pathetic in their attempts to capture a younger market or broaden their reach, a case can be made that this has always been true of some businesses to some degree.

When a TV news program redesigns its set and ends up looking like the bridge of a spaceship and opens with a "futuristic" high-tech-sounding theme played on a synthesizer, is that any less pathetic in its way?

Or the long-running program that dumps its host in favor of a younger, "fresher" face?

Cable channels, such as MTV and VH-1, have been built around an adults-need-not-apply image, and both the programming and the commercials reflect that cultural representation—and exploit it—for better or worse.

At the same time, *CNN NewsStand, CNBC, MSNBC,* and *Fox News* cable channels, among other offerings are packed wall-to-wall with ads for mortgage lenders and computer day-trading brokerage services that aren't pretending to appeal to Generation Y.

Agencies and marketers can often be faulted for appearing "desperate" in their attempts to seem cool, but that is simply bad advertising and certainly doomed to fail. Any advertiser that so blatantly plays to one generation while offending another also is guilty of bad advertising and doubtless will feel the effects of such strategic missteps over both the short term and the long run.

Obeying the Law of Evolution

As an example of the tastes of Gen Y, *Business Week* magazine developed a list that contrasted its products or subjects and its ideas of "What's hot" with those of baby boomers on the same day. The boomer list included such entries as Estée Lauder, L. L. Bean, Super Bowl ads, Nikes, and political activism.

The Generation Y list included:

Jeep Wrangler
Skateboard Triple Crown
Delia's
Dawson's Creek
Lilith Fair sponsorship
Hard Candy
The North Face
Motorola Flex pagers
The WB Network
Volunteerism
Spice Girls
Mountain Dew
Jenny McCarthy

What is noteworthy about the list is the fact that less than six months after its publication, at least three of the entries were largely regarded as "over." This reflects both the still-evolving character of Generation Y, the hyper pace and brief life cycles of trends, and the riskiness for marketers of tying too tightly with celebrities, fads, and moments in pop culture.

Think of it as a variation on the law of evolution: Members of the baby boom generation have strong ties to the birth of rock 'n' roll and the music of Elvis, the films of James Dean, and a time when dining out meant cheeseburgers at drive-in restaurants. As they grew to be adults (and parents of teenagers), many boomers not only still enjoyed all those same things—often nostalgically and passionately—but also had grown to appreciate classical music and jazz, the films of Harrison Ford and Meryl Streep, and fine dining at pricey restaurants, such as the chain created by fellow boomer Wolfgang Puck.

Likewise, Gen Xers began building the compact disc or cassette collection with Aerosmith and Nirvana and entered the 21st century buying bigband swing albums and the music of Tony Bennett.

Generation Y, like those who came before them, will keep some of what influenced them and gave them joy, and then move on to enjoy what may be called "more mature interests." The marketer's challenge is to develop a feel for what stays, what goes, and what's to come. The highly evolved method of doing this is to *ask*. Research proves to be less expensive and more reliable than guessing almost every time.

Is all this simply a very predictable matter of changing tastes? Of growing up? Or of the lists of *what's hot and what's not?*

It may be any and all of that, but it is the job of the marketer to take the pulse of the market, segment by segment, and put that information to best advantage, tapping all the considerable experience and resources that can be brought to bear.

Mark Your Calendars

It is also important to look at your own calendar and to note the time at which you are putting this information to use. Certainly a book like this will be more useful at some times than others. Trends and fads come and go—some coming, alas, after a book has gone to press. Every effort has been made to create a useful volume with recommendations that have worked in the past and are not particularly time sensitive. They can be adapted to work again and again in a variety of market environments.

With that noted, within a decade of this material's first appearance, baby boomers will qualify for senior status; members of Generation X will have taken the places of boomers as heads of state, studio moguls, publishers, artists, bankers, and other leaders; and the Generation Y people will move up a notch in seniority as well. Marketers need to understand the fact that, just as they can market to boomers with the music of Elvis or Cole Porter, the Beach Boys or Yo Yo Ma, Generation Y will evolve and move on to embrace some of the concerns and pleasures of their elders, while defining totally new ones for themselves.

Still, there is every reason for marketers to think that skateboarding will be to Gen Y what surfing was to boomers (and in both cases, they didn't actually have to *do it* in order to love it), that *Dawson's Creek* will be that generation's *Seinfeld, Hill Street Blues,* or *Melrose Place*, a connection with the passions and pains of the times.

Kahn Job

And Delia's catalog likely will still be remembered as the one that *really* spoke to Gen Y girls. The company has a website, as the Internet has clearly emerged as the group's medium of choice, but it is the catalog that gets the gather-around/pass-it-around treatment at high schools across America.

Think Generation Y doesn't read? Show these girls a Delia's catalog and you've found the good book they're eager to curl up with. Overall, parents seem to hate Delia's styles, but then again, what parent was thrilled to get the news about body piercing?

Stephen Kahn, a Delia's founder, told *Business Week* that he envisions the company going beyond its hot line of clothes and accessories for teenage girls' bedrooms to the time they get their first credit card, first car, even their first mortgage.

"We'll follow them and broaden our offerings," he says, adding that a male version of the Delia's catalog would do for the young men of Generation Y what the original Delia's has done for young ladies.

Mag Wheels

All the rush to E-commerce notwithstanding, catalogs and, more recently, "magalogs" (magazine-catalog combinations) maintain a large and loyal audience.

Meanwhile, newer emerging magazines have followed the marketing plan, done the research, and launched titles designed to appeal to that young audience's concerns. Periodicals such as *ESPN the Magazine*, to a young person, make the great *Sports Illustrated* seem creaky with age in comparison.

Fads get to cover all the bases. Collectors of Beanie Babies, small, inexpensive beanbag toys—a huge '90s promotion in which an artificial "collectors market" was created to drive up prices of older inventory—are surrounded by *Beanie World, Bean Bag World,* and *Beanie Mania,* among a dozen or so similar titles. Virtually all report on the "collectors" market, and all have the look of being done with a desktop publishing computer program and a home press.

XY is a magazine exclusively targeted to gay members of Generation Y.

Starbucks, Sony, and Benetton are only three of many companies that have launched colorful, costly monthly magazines aimed at identifying their brands with a younger audience and encouraging the Y market members to believe that the offerings are only for them. The magazines are sold onsite at the various company stores and at large retailers and bookstores, which tend to attract more upscale demographics.

Cue the Walking Billboards

Marketers can take a great deal of credit for initially convincing the general public to *buy* caps, shirts, jackets, backpacks, and a huge menu of products bearing the marketers' logo and signature. Earlier generations received these items free, and they were called promotions or premiums. Perhaps going on the assumption that their customers believed "you get what you pay for," marketers started pricing logo merchandise and positioning it as collectible, coveted, elitist, and, most important for several reasons, *worth paying for.*

Do consumers perceive greater value in something they buy versus something that is given to them and, presumably, to countless others?

Of course they do. And a consumer who chooses to wear clothing and accessories with a manufacturer or designer name and logo displayed colorfully and prominently is a virtual walking billboard—a distinction that the customer has paid to have. Some may say this comes under the heading of "ultimate tributes to American capitalism."

It may be in the blood, as Generation Y parents (baby boomers) exhibited this same type of status consciousness throughout their own emerging years. Their brands of choice displayed Izod alligators, Adidas logos, and Members Only labels in the '70s, and all through the '90s, the names Polo,

Tommy Hilfiger, and Calvin Klein, among others, were more prominent than school colors.

For them, an important element of how an article of clothing fit was that the entire name or logo was visible, not just a portion of it. The names and call letters of favorite radio stations were on bumper stickers, gym bags, book covers, backpacks, and baby strollers. It was into this environment that the members of Generation Y were born.

Corporations may still invest enormous amounts of money in promotional items such as pens, caps, and key rings with the company logo, but it is quite a different marketing dynamic when the target prospect can be induced to *buy* the merchandise.

A CBS coffee mug given to an ad agency's media buyer by the CBS rep is a nice item. But a coffee mug imprinted with David Letterman's name and photo, or the logo from *Touched by an Angel*, or a picture of Howard Stern, purchased either at the CBS store, through a catalog, over the Internet, or from another retail outlet, is an even more prized possession . . . with the CBS logo shown just as prominently.

A Proud Tradition

Marketers have been wise to this type of promotional merchandising since at least the 1950s, when stores could not stock enough of the fast-selling Howdy Doody lunch boxes, Roy Rogers pajamas, Little Orphan Annie dresses, or Davy Crockett coonskin caps. Disney was more astute than most companies in marketing products that cross-promoted its films, TV programs, books, records, and theme park. The baby boomer generation of marketers took note of the delight consumers experienced in purchasing such merchandise and that it was something they didn't outgrow.

In the year 2000, the public could buy Elvis cigars and bathroom tissue, and neckties with the name of conservative talk-show host and political pundit Rush Limbaugh on the label.

Generation Y accepted such marketing ventures as a given. They grew up in a culture that had blatantly come to treat most occurrences as marketing events, from celebrity addictions and anniversaries of public monuments to murders, kidnappings, and presidential assassinations. To marketers, the year 2000 was not so much the millennium as it was an event for merchandising, and the first such big event in which Generation Y was old enough to participate (which is a marketing euphemism for *buy*).

Publishing as Tactical Advancement

Magazines are each brands in their own right, seeking to distinguish them-selves in content, positioning, and presentation from competing magazines. Companies best known for nonpublishing products entering the magazine-publishing business is another overt cross-sell strategy. It is a serious tacti-cal advancement both for brands per se and for magazine publishing.

Starbuck's *Joe* magazine, *Sony Style*, Benetton's *Colors*, *ESPN the Magazine*, *Yahoo! Internet Life*, and a variety of product-branded magazines from toy companies and software firms are increasingly becoming part of the marketing mix. They are, in most cases, high-quality (Starbuck's *Joe* was a private-label product created for the coffee purveyor by no less a brand name than Time, Inc.) vehicles intended to advance the product-brand's marketing effort.

The Generation Y crowd understands all this—the companies basically having thrown subtlety into the recycling bin—and as long as they are get-ting what they want from the magazines, which is news about their favorite products and people, they seem to have no problem paying out a few dol-lars each month for the latest on Beanie Babies, coffees, and search engines.

No Pledge of Allegiance

Taking notice of the direction of marketing to this segment, the *New York Times* reported: "Even traditional companies like Levi Straus & Company are revamping their offerings and shifting their focus away from the baby boom generation that grew up on jeans. . . . Companies are making a big bet on one of the ficklest groups of consumers—as Nike and Reebok have learned—who have shown their ability to hurt a brand by turning away from style or dismissing poor products.

". . . And, of course, as always, it helps if parents are befuddled by the music and the message and maybe even a little wary as well. That is why it is all the harder for brands popular with baby boomers to win allegiance of their children."

Again, this development should not be a shock to experienced marketers. Particularly in music and clothing, each generation has displayed a hunger for its own. This trait has added greatly to the frustration of Generation X, members of which seemed so noticeably desperate for icons to distinguish themselves from the highly romanticized baby boomers. The result of that exercise is repeated references to a generation that tends to fix blame for what it didn't have, rather than going after something to have.

Jettison the Baggage

It's unfair to Gen X to have to carry the baggage of such a reputation because clearly there are those of that generation—in business, sports, and the arts—who have accomplished much. But the opportunities for *marketing* that generation to the public, and to history, have told of a potential not yet realized.

Generation Y is still so fully evolving and emerging that the story is yet to play out, much less be told.

The potential is enormous. The millennium celebration in the United States is a time of economic growth and prosperity. While so much attention is trained on the Internet and other technology and the launches of new cyberbusinesses, it is also a time of new brands, retail outlets, and business services.

The consensus seems to be that Generation Y has officially rejected the established, mainstream brands in favor of new names. Their choices include products from the likes of Delia's catalog, Mecca, FUBU, Enyce, P.N.B. Nation, and Phat Farm. While many members of the group are still too young to hold full-time jobs, their disposable income is (as they might say) awesome. From baby-sitting, part-time work, and allowances, they manage to pull together enough to indulge themselves with compact discs, designer clothes, and movie and concert tickets totaling billions of dollars annually. Their favorite performers are names that their older brothers and sisters don't recognize, much less their parents.

Meanwhile, Pepsi, Nike, The Gap, and others are being dismissed by commentators as brands left to history.

Not so fast.

Don't Assume; Strategize

The history of marketing includes brands that were considered past their prime, only to rise again. In marketing, it is not necessary to be a phoenix, only to have a good strategy. If a product, whether it is a soft drink, running shoe, or brand of jeans, is a good product, it can be repackaged, repositioned, and marketed to success. The fact that some brands—from Tommy Hilfiger to Honda—are strong among members of four generations is proof that it is possible to market a product without encountering an automatic, impenetrable wall of generational resistance.

Whether the subject is a new launch, a struggling brand, or a message that must be reedited for a new generation, the task may be daunting, but it is not impossible.

Identify the strongest market for your message and the strongest media to reach that market. Don't assume that tremendous success with one generation provides either an advantage or a disadvantage when trying to connect with another generation. Just as it is sometimes advisable to create distinctive messages for outdoor displays as opposed to magazines or for radio rather than TV, and to customize some messages to more effectively target women or Southerners or foreign audiences, you can tailor the message to Generation Y to maximize its impact.

Perhaps to reach a new generation as a market segment, it is even necessary that there be a new generation of the product, service, or message—a *Lite* or a *II* or a wholly new something ". . . from the people who brought you. . . ."

It is extremely rare in a 21st-century market environment that one product will be the choice of everyone. That's rarely the case *within* a generation with regard to even the most popular brands.

A possible course is a brand extension, such as Coke has done so successfully with Classic Coke, Diet Coke, Cherry Coke, Caffeine-Free Coke, and so on. Then again, when Coke's rival Pepsi launched the lamentable Pepsi Next campaign aimed at Generation Y, treating it as a millennium version of its "Pepsi Generation" idea, the overhype and pseudohipness were not well received.

Three Choices

It is not necessary to market to one generation by trashing another. Despite some chroniclers' suggesting that a position such as "If it was my parent's choice, it's not right for me" be accepted as the mantra of generational rivalry, that is not necessarily the case. Gen Y loves sarcastic, put-down humor and an "attitude." Marketers who try seriously to translate this insight into advertising or PR campaigns should understand that sometimes such an "attitude" can be carried to excess, and members of the target audience are left unimpressed. Principles of good marketing demand that you *know your market*, its prejudices, likes, and dislikes.

If the product is not a good fit as is for the current market, the choices are: (1) Introduce a spin-off product or brand extension to respond to the specific concerns of Generation Y members; (2) Accept a *share* of the market rather than holding out to totally dominate it; or (3) Listen to what the voice of the market says it wants. It is possible to show value, stress benefits to the consumer, wrap the message in a creative package, and stay alive.

Marketers who precipitously try to be hip and appealing, without a sense of how such an approach shows benefits to the audience, are not framing the message that shows the product to its best advantage. It is not enough to simply *say* you're cool.

Before leaving any examination of Generation Y, these points must be made as they represent important contradictions marketers must be aware of:

- Generation Y is both media- and marketing-savvy and claims to know when it is being manipulated. Yet, it wants its own identity and will eagerly embrace what's new and hot.
- Regulators love to claim they are "protecting" young people and are quick to criticize overtly manipulative ad campaigns that try to create trends and fashions—while supporting a free market system with fewer controls.
- The next generation is coming up fast.

Summary Points

1. Some estimate there are 60 million members of Generation Y. They are younger than Generation X, and they are the children of the baby boomers or the upper reaches of Generation X.
2. Statistically different from other generations, they are more than two-thirds Caucasian, 25 percent live in single-parent households, 75 percent have working mothers, and they are the most computer-literate, media-savvy younger generation in history.
3. They prefer their own brands, ones identified so far only with them—names such as Mudd, Enyce, Phat Farm, Paris Blue, and In Vitro, rather than Nike or The Gap, which are identified with those who came before them.

4. Generation Y's medium of choice is the Internet, yet they have made innovative catalogs, such as Delia's, enormously popular and successful.

5. Despite the fact that they understand merchandising and exploitation very well, members of Generation Y enjoy logo-imprinted clothing and accessories from favorite films, shows, and brands.

6. Though not as overtly cynical or angry as Generation X, the Y crowd wants its own icons, music, and clothing styles rather than to live in the shadow of their baby boomer parents. This seeming act of rebellion is commonly understood by marketers to be pretty much the pattern of most generations coming of age. It can be developed and used in a marketing strategy.

8

Marketing to Seniors

*. . . And if you should survive to 105, look at all you'll derive out
of being alive.*
—from "Young at Heart" by Carolyn Leigh and Johnny
Richards

THE ITEM ON the news described them as the largest,
most active and influential block of voters in America. That meant power.
The candidates in the upcoming election knew this and courted them
openly, shamelessly. They fought in World War II—the Big War—the War
to End All Wars. But when it came to the marketplace, as the comedian
Rodney Dangerfield was known to complain, they seemed to "get no
respect." Although there are certainly those in some quarters who recognize
the importance of senior citizens and the highly lucrative market they represent, it is widely felt that they have not really been given their due—and
that this makes little sense.

The Market That Just Won't Quit

Statistically, women live longer than men, and everyone lives longer than
people used to live. For wealthy, aging people, this is regarded as good news.
For marketing people, the news is even better.

Whether they are described as *old folks*, *seniors*, or the *mature market*,
there are at least 60 million of them. Unlike the groups referenced earlier,
the seniors market is constantly being replenished. One day, there will be
no more baby boomers, Generation X, or Generation Y. There will, however, always be older people—the seniors market—and the variety of interests and diversity within the category is expanding.

Many older folks strive to squeeze the most they can out of every
moment of their lives. They want to be active, independent, involved, busy,

on the scene, on-line, traveling, dancing, experiencing, and discovering all forms of entertainment.

And many don't.

Their ideal life is to be left alone. They believe that they have earned a break, a rest, some time to themselves. They don't want to talk to salespeople or hear from telemarketers. And yet, they want to enjoy "what's out there."

For marketers, the opportunities represented here are almost limitless, from supplying comfortable chairs and great books to booking great and comfortable cruises, trips, and accommodations, with a world of choices in between.

Marketer's Dream Job

The marketer's first step—and a critical one—is to check the research. It is not enough to "feel" you know this category and act on common assumptions about older people. Such assumptions are often drawn on stereotypes that may be wrong in the current environment, if they were ever right to begin with. The research should identify the specific characteristics the marketer needs to do the job effectively.

At any given time, regardless of how it compares with other markets in size, the seniors market is likely to be vastly more diverse. Some will be retired and living on pensions, income from assets, or Social Security payments. Others will be running businesses, continuing in careers or professions they have developed over decades. And increasingly, postretirement seniors are pursuing *new* careers or educational degrees or starting businesses—all things they may have dreamed of doing but didn't have the time or resources to go after earlier in their lives.

Marketing and advertising often allude to dreams—specifically, to bringing about a way that dreams can come true, whether through a purchase, a service, or participation in an effort that will bring happiness or satisfaction. In marketing to seniors, this message can be especially powerful. The challenge is to identify ways that what the marketer has to offer can provide a sense of satisfaction. Since almost anything—a good book, a power mower, cologne, breath freshener, or a boat ride that affords a perfect view of the sunset—can evoke that type of feeling, the goal seems attainable.

Like other market segments, seniors comprise both men and women, are all over the world, with various levels of wealth. They are subject to regional and ethnic, religious and societal influences. But there are distinctions unique to seniors as well.

The Age-Old Image Thing

Some cultures revere their elders as the wisest among them and worthy of deep respect. Other cultures lean heavily in the opposite direction and, as the song goes, not only believe "the children are our future" but also become known as "a culture that worships youth."

Even a simple and sentimental song such as the old standard "Young at Heart" speaks to the purity of a heart that is young. What is one to make of lines that declare "For as rich as you are, it's much better by far, to be young at heart"?

Dr. Ken Dychtwald, author of the bestselling book *Age Wave*, suggests that "At least in part, our images of aging are negative because of our glorification of youth. The image of youth so vigorous and powerful and sexy has as its shadow an image of older people as incompetent, inflexible, wedded to the past, desexed, uncreative, poor, sick, and slow.

"When we ascribe to youth much of what is good about life and to age every trauma and sorrow, we create the image of a descending slope from one another."

Without question, the image many people have of seniors is synonymous with people who are not only very old but also feeble and infirm. That image comes to exist largely because of the lack of a strong counterimage offered by those who are supposed to represent the good aspects of getting older.

Most TV commercials showing seniors present them as doddering and nearly helpless, in fear of losing their health insurance or fighting valiantly to win the battle against irregularity. Or it's a silver-haired couple spinning (slowly) around a dance floor and laughing. Marketers need to make it clear to the advertising department that older people do more than dodder and dance. It is amazing that the advertising industry has permitted this image to be perpetuated.

While it is true that older people are more concerned about health than younger people usually are, to continually portray seniors as involved only to the limited degree that creaky old bones permit is to foreclose the wide array of marketing opportunities.

Roll Out the Role Models

Former *Cosmopolitan* magazine editor Helen Gurley Brown, in *The Late Show: A Semi-Wild but Practical Survival Plan for Women over 50*, notes, "We are so hard on ourselves. . . . Older is what we *get*. And it's OK. It even has its seriously great moments."

In a youth-obsessed society, it is easy to overlook the long list of writers, actors, artists, and politicians, as well as business leaders, who are in the news every day, are over 60, and are active, superb role models.

If the marketer's job is to sell Depends adult diapers or Metamucil to seniors, as with any product, the best marketing sells the benefits of the product to the consumer. In these cases, the details are less necessary than the fact that life can be active, less stressful, and less restrictive with what these products offer.

But what about the ads for local supermarkets? A typical spot features a June Cleaver look-alike with a little Tommy and Susie in tow. So much for cutting-edge marketing. Older people shop for groceries and not just to assume the role of nosy neighbor. Marketers have all too often relegated seniors in ads to products that are stereotypical of older people—denture adhesive, antacid tablets, arthritis pain formula. Yet, seniors buy Hondas and Toyotas, deodorants and coffee. They swim, purchase health club memberships, and buy furniture and clothes. A TV viewer on a typical day would get the impression that anyone over 60 is a potential customer only for Colonial Penn mail-order insurance or is preoccupied with a need to write members of Congress and vote no on whatever bill is coming up.

And that TV viewer, during many day parts, is a senior—who would respond positively to a portrayal of seniors as something other than the slightly hard-of-hearing oldster being set straight by a 10-year-old on the amount of nutrients in breakfast cereal.

50-50 Propositions

AARP, the largest advocate group for seniors, begins soliciting potential members at age 50—a point in life when few people like to be reminded that they are now on the declining side of the age slope. Not many people are receiving retirement benefits at 50 or are even eligible for the seniors' discount at the movies or on public transportation. The inclusion of younger people among an older segment is one more reason to portray the people who make up this group as active and involved.

Marketers have found that mileage programs, frequent-diner programs, and discounts on certain designated days work well as business builders for all age groups. Including seniors in this group without singling them out— merely treating them as *valued customers*—may well be more effective than singling them out for "seniors's discounts" that often have the effect of being a demoralizing, dispiriting, charitable subsidy. If marketers hope to tap into the highly lucrative seniors market, it is necessary to tailor the message along lines that historically reflect the essence of effective marketing: be irresistible . . . or at least very welcoming.

A Clear Lack of Understanding

Intelligent marketers stopped the insensitive and insulting practice of bombarding women with images of fresh-faced 17-year-old models in TV and print ads long ago. It took a while for them to check the research and find that women age 45 and older are buying more than the occasional shampoo and lipstick at the supermarket.

Members of the mature market can be said to reflect all of society in their group composition. Some are at or near the edge of poverty; some are comfortable but nervous about the possibility of outliving their savings and being forced to lead a less comfortable life than they have known; some are still upwardly mobile. But the seniors group has by far the greatest percentage of those who have achieved financial and professional success and who can stop at a clothing or department store, cosmetic boutique, or fine jewelry counter and buy without guilt and without compromising the family budget.

To market successfully to seniors, it is necessary to understand them. If that seems obvious, consider how much the current and recent marketing to seniors reflects a clear *lack* of understanding. It is as if some marketers are addressing the seniors market they see depicted in TV sitcoms—kindly, curmudgeonly, loud, unsophisticated, ill-informed—such as the parents on *Seinfeld*, *Mad About You*, and *Everybody Loves Raymond*. As each of these popular shows ends its run on network TV, it moves into the syndication market, where it will be seen—and continue to perpetuate these images—

for decades to come. There's no doubt some of these wacky TV parents exist, but they are not the market or typical of the market.

Sometimes Funny Is a Matter of Opinion

Robert S. Menchin, Chicago-based authority on the mature market, asks, "Why is so much general advertising clever, imaginative, and effective, while advertising aimed at the older generation continues to be dull, stereotype ridden, and ineffective?"

He adds, "There is more art than science in creating good advertising, and there are certainly no absolutes in creating advertising to attract the attention—and the dollars—of older Americans. . . . Mature adults don't want to be segregated in a world of age peers. Ads and commercials are most effective when they portray interaction between the sexes and between generations."

In that regard, people do not like to see someone who is supposed to be representing them (or their generation) portrayed as a cartoon character or a buffoon. It is reasonable to conclude that ads, TV spots, brochures, or other presentations that show older people in an unflattering way were not conceived or written by older people. A creative director or copywriter who believes effective marketing involves ridiculing people has lost sight of—if he or she ever understood—what marketing is supposed to do.

Humor is very subjective. Mention the name Jim Carrey, or Joan Rivers, Eddie Murphy, Mel Brooks, Whoopi Goldberg, Howie Mandel, Howard Stern, or any number of other successful comedic performers, and the response is sure to run the full gamut of love and hate. These performers, in attempting to build their images and careers, are fully prepared—even *hoping*, in some cases—to shock and turn off some segments of the public.

That is not the objective of marketing. People laugh at so many different things, and older people are popular targets in comedy bits, especially in spoofs of ads and TV commercials. The TV spot that depicted an elderly woman calling out, "I've fallen and I can't get up" was a serious ad with a message that was no joke to the many older people who have been in such situations. Yet, the spot and that one line were used over and over again in parodies and skits for years.

Great residual exposure for the product?

Hardly. The product is barely remembered, and even the people who thought the spot was funny thought it depicted seniors as feeble, dependent, and troublesome.

The Distinguished Senator

Viagra is one of the more successful product launches of the 1990s and one with life-changing effects. Some might think Viagra's manufacturer, Pfizer, in hiring former U.S. senator and presidential candidate Bob Dole as the product's TV spokesman, made a truly inspired choice. The print ads and TV spots featured a serious subject, serious product, serious guy.

Alas, the campaign came at a time when Dole had spent more than a year doing guest appearances with David Letterman, Jay Leno, and other TV personalities, trying to soften his image as the sometimes mean-spirited, angry man. The resulting, artfully created TV spots presented a distinguished 75-year-old gentleman in a dark suit—a gentleman who only months before had sought the job of leader of the free world—discussing erectile dysfunction. The ads distracted from the seriousness of the subject in the same way they drew attention. That is, the person doing the ads was given greater emphasis than the content. The prescription product was in fact an instant success from the day it reached doctors' offices and drugstores, well before the advertising began to appear. Early press releases, news coverage, physicians' recommendations, and word of mouth caused a sensation. TV and every major national publication carried at least one headline story. It appeared as though Viagra was the talk of the media and the nation. Some people suggested that not only were the ads, especially the costly television spots, unnecessary to ensure the product's success, but that the presence of Dole as the spokesman also created a problem by giving late-night comics a supply of new snickering gags—at the expense of the former senator and other older people, though not to the detriment of the product.

An inspired marketing campaign? Maybe. And maybe not. If the company's aim was to call attention to the *condition* so that it could promote the product as the treatment, a series of ads in newspapers or other national media recommending that people ask their doctors for information on a highly effective new product to treat impotence would have been far less costly and probably quite effective, and would have inspired a lot fewer gags about older people.

It's Called Discrimination

The two preceding examples are of ad campaigns that were not intended to be humorous, yet became the butt of ongoing jokes. The intentionally humorous ads, usually with a youngster setting the oldster straight, likewise compromise the dignity of seniors.

Some marketers may say to lighten up, that older folks would do better if they did not take themselves so seriously, if they joined in and laughed at themselves.

Wrong.

As a matter of course, not taking one's self too seriously is probably good advice. As a marketing methodology, it is better left aside. Political correctness about possibly offending ethnic, racial, or religious groups is a serious consideration in planning any campaign directed to the public. Seniors should be shown the same sensitivity, having as they do to confront many of the same forms of discrimination.

Spotlight, Please

Some seniors—Helen Gurley Brown, for example—have declined to passively accept the role typically assigned to older people, that of a generation in the background, past their prime; they have aggressively sought the spotlight. Brown lists broadcast journalist Barbara Walters, publishing executive Katharine Graham, and business executive Lillian Vernon among the role models for active seniors, involved, worthy of notice, and successful.

Countless teachers, doctors, nurses, limo drivers, and retail clerks are over 60, attractive, and energetic. Marketers depicting these types of seniors in ads and commercials might well find a huge audience that connects with, responds to, and supports such representations over the geezer stumbling around looking for the bran flakes.

As marketers look to break the old patterns with future marketing, they would do well to present older people in scenes that routinely might have depicted someone of 35. There is a huge market waiting for astute marketers to notice the opportunity before their eyes.

The Pretend World

Ken Dychtwald quotes this remark from successful, gray-haired, middle-aged, beautiful fashion model Kaylan Pickford: "The fashion industry lives in a world of pretend. In advertising terms, it pretends there is no woman in the country over 30 or 35. But the facts are different. The midlife woman is the major clothes buyer today, and she spends the most money. Her dollar has four times the buying power of that of the young, and that amount is increasing every year."

Dychtwald adds, "Already, one in four of us is gray, and the silver look is becoming very popular in fashion circles."

Statistics continue to roll in regarding the raw numbers of seniors and their significant buying power. The question then becomes rather simple: With such a huge and fertile market all around us, why do so many marketers ignore them, dismiss them, or market to them only with the figurative gun to their head?

One media executive had a ready answer. He said that he knew all about the huge audience that reads *Modern Maturity* magazine and that supported *Murder, She Wrote*; *Diagnosis: Murder*; and *Matlock*, three popular 1990s TV series that had large, passionately loyal audiences of mostly seniors. The executive added that it wasn't *just* the numbers; it was the people behind them. "Advertisers want the 18–34 market, who they see as long-term prospects worth cultivating. They will spend now and later. They are not old now; they will grow old with the product. And those people want to see younger, prettier people in the ads. If you want to keep those advertisers, you give them what they want."

A Common Sense Tack

Given a mind set in such a position, a serious marketer would do well not to waste time trying to change it, but simply move on. *Other* advertisers want to see those numbers, and for all the debate over "ageism" and political correctness, common sense should prevail. If the seniors market is not a prime target market for the product, service, or message, no sensible professional should broach it.

If seniors *are* the right target market, the pros should stop trying to talk themselves out of accepting that because pitching boomers, Xers, and Generation Y seems sexier. It is not, after all, as if future sales are guaranteed.

And what of the customers? Isn't there a happy medium for media planners and account execs between bikini wax and Geritol? Between *Baywatch* and reruns of *The Lawrence Welk Show*?

Of course there is.

An ad that appeals to seniors and sells product has done its job—and that's just about as good a sale as one to the 18–34 age-group.

Mixed and Missing Signals

Clearly seniors have been known to send out mixed signals, as the expression goes. While insisting they should be respected and taken seriously for who and what they are (usually a sound approach), they are as much a product or victim of a youth-obsessed culture as anyone.

Respected marketing authority Regis McKenna notes: "Markets and customers operate like light and energy. In fact, like light, the customer is more than one thing at the same time. Sometimes customers behave as part of a group, fitting neatly into social and psychographic classifications. Other times, the consumer breaks loose and is iconoclastic. Customers make and break patterns: the senior citizen market is filled with older people who intensely wish to act youthful, and the upscale market must contend with wealthy people who hide their money behind the most utilitarian purchase."

Actress Linda Evans was a favorite of many seniors for her ability to retain her beauty and grace into middle age. Many were disappointed that she made a series of department store appearances around the United States, helping to promote *Rejuvenique Facial Treatment System*. Ads hyping her appearances at New York's Macy's, for example, carried the headline "Meet Linda Evans as She Unveils the Modern Age Answer to the Fountain of Youth."

Unveils . . . the Fountain of Youth?

This example illustrates a problem with marketing to seniors: Some really *do* want to sit on the porch and watch the sunset, and some want to travel as they couldn't in their younger years, what with caring for small children, holding down outside jobs, or both. But there are those who, late in life, really are looking for that fountain of youth. At the very least, they are just not happy about all the years that have gone by. Into this situation comes the marketer who must relate to the mix of feeling that causes seniors to send out those mixed messages.

Did the still beautiful woman of 50 or 60 buy that great sexy dress because she looked terrific in it or because she wanted to look younger? Did he buy that sporty, low-to-the-ground convertible because it gets good mileage, did he need to fuel his image as still very cool, or was he simply being middle-age crazy?

The answer may be *yes* to all the above. It is helpful if marketers know the answers, but it is crucial that they at least know the questions.

First Why, Then How

Why people buy is a subject that is studied endlessly because the answer(s) will determine how we market. Remember that people often buy and choose for more than one reason. The more reasons they can be given to justify their decisions, the more likely they will buy, be satisfied, and buy again and again.

According to Robert Menchin, in *The Mature Market*: "Creative marketing to the older population starts with recognition of the shared interests and common needs, as well as the differences and diversity of lifestyles, within the 50-and-over age segment. Understanding the great range of interests and lifestyles within today's older population is key to success in marketing to the mature. In many categories of goods and services, such as mainstream food and packaged goods, the need for a special marketing approach may not be necessary. There are, however, highly personal categories like fashion, clothing, personal care, health care, and travel, where sensitivity to mature preferences, and possible physical limitations, are crucial to success."

So, again, it becomes a matter of knowing your market—knowing how seniors, in this case, are both unique and not so unique—and when your best chance to influence them is through an ad or a press release, *Modern Maturity* or *USA Today*, or any number of special interest newsletters.

Healthy? Wealthy? Wise?

It should surprise no one that a major concern of seniors is health: health care, disease prevention, and health maintenance programs. This concern cuts across all lines and applies to male and female and all economic levels and geographic regions. Politicians have exploited this concern for years with positions emphasizing the protection of Social Security benefits and Medicare. Without question, this is a major "hot button" issue. It is almost universally agreed that (1) health care and health maintenance are costly (most people believe *too* costly) and (2) most seniors expect these costs to keep going up, and this increases their concern and anxiety.

Marketers for pharmaceutical interests are almost constantly on the defensive, as are hospitals, doctors, and most insurance plan providers. In the 21st century, HMOs (health maintenance organizations) have replaced Satan as another name for the devil.

In an environment that is reality based, let's accept everything in the preceding paragraph as undeniable fact. Let's also assume that, regardless of how the company or providers justify the costs, they are what they are and are not likely to decline.

Now what?

Reaching Out Brings Far-Reaching Results

First, develop a marketing plan that is aggressive but not defensive. Lead with a *positioning statement* such as "(your company or practice name here) thinks health care costs too much!"

This creates a position that puts you on the same side as the consumer. Then, be helpful. After *very briefly* stating that *your* costs are skyrocketing too, offer some "offsets" in the form of free or inexpensive subscriptions to health-related newsletters or other publications (which, if you don't have the capability to produce on your own, may be purchased and "branded" with your name from a variety of services).

Offer discounts where possible, and partner with companies or individuals willing to offer discounts to your constituents. Potential partners include any business that delivers—restaurants, drugstore chains, limo and taxi services, housekeeping services, optical suppliers, lawn care services—anything that seniors want but may not be able to easily afford.

Provide a list of hot-line numbers that are useful in times of emergency or that, in nonemergency cases, are just helpful to seniors. Offer free literature. Just about every business interested in reaching seniors has literature, videos, and websites. Help to facilitate dissemination of this information to the appropriate markets, particularly where free trials or discounts are involved, and you have performed a valuable service.

If regionality and facilities permit, schedule on-site events of interest to seniors. Underscore your sense of community and service.

Be responsive, and reach out.

Very often, marketers as well as sales and service professionals find interactions with seniors frustrating. While some seniors are mellow and easygoing, many are impatient, angry, and fed up with those who appear to take them for granted or show no respect. As tempting as it may be to react in kind, promoting a caring, service-oriented image instead can yield far-reaching results.

Checking the Pulse of the Market

This is a generation that attaches a premium to loyalty and service *and tells people about it.* They write letters to their friends, to government agencies, and to editors. They call radio talk shows, C-SPAN, and MSNBC. They speak with implied authority on who and what is reliable and who or what is not. On the whole, they actively participate in the debate on the lives and times of seniors, and nothing gets them as motivated as health-related subjects.

For this reason, marketers need to be cognizant of "elder care" issues and play to them with sensitivity.

Repeat After Me . . .

Herschell Gordon Lewis, noted direct-marketing expert, believes there are certain "trigger words" that have a particularly strong appeal to seniors. Among the words and phrases he identifies are:

- Discount
- Buy direct
- Have a problem with . . . ?
- Do you remember how (whatever) used to be . . . ?

He adds, "No one familiar with marketing to seniors has to explain that word *Discount.*" Seniors firmly believe they've earned the right to get a better price. Restaurants have "early-bird" dinner prices aimed at seniors. Many department stores set aside Tuesday or Wednesday as days on which seniors who belong to the "buyers' club" can get a 10 percent discount on any purchase.

The other entries on the list of "trigger words" can be effectively applied to any target, but seniors, in general, are both less patient and less tolerant with poor or indifferent service. A phrase such as *Buy direct* implies not only a cost savings but also an opportunity to bypass the clerks and sales functionaries who tend to try one's patience.

The ability to buy direct suggests the conferring of a certain privilege or status on the customer, along with importance and, thus, *respect,* which is a priority to a market that believes it is underappreciated.

Asking if customers *remember* or *have a problem with* a service or product recognizes the problem of inefficient or frustrating salesclerks or bad customer-service practices and implies an offer of a way to get around such people and systems. It is an invitation to the senior to do business with someone who identifies with his or her complaints and frustrations and wants to help find a better way.

It All Comes Down to Respect

Seniors are concerned with value, safety, security, and quality. They don't want to be taken for granted in a "youth culture." Of course, the same can be cited about the other target market segments, and that is, in no small way, the point. If you as a marketer have what adman George Lois termed "the Big Idea" for a uniquely creative way to address seniors as a special segment, do it. Otherwise, treat the seniors market as all prospective customers should be treated, *with respect* and appreciation for their support.

Stress the benefits of what you are offering and the qualities that distinguish your product, service, or message. If you follow the rule to avoid being *exclusionary* in your message, seniors will respond without pausing to ask whether or not you are talking to them. Is this a rather formulaic approach to marketing to seniors and lacking in "futurist" hooks? Perhaps. The recommendations are direct and grounded in logic, much like the audience the approach seeks to impress.

What these recommendations do is reject the stereotypical images of doddering oldsters and accept that seniors may want to work in their later years, or play, or dedicate their efforts to causes that will bring them satisfaction more than financial gain. The marketer's job is to identify which groups within the segment respond to which messages. If the lowest percentage of Internet users are seniors, it is not a good idea to concentrate energy on Internet marketing for now. But *the lowest percentage* is not the same as *no percentage*. Creating innovative ways to both package and present a marketing message to a marketplace that is made up of nontechnicians in a technical environment is challenging. But it is also what marketers do.

Summary Points

1. Senior citizens have been described as one of the largest, most active, and most influential blocks of voters in America.

2. The seniors market affords a limitless range of opportunities, as some seniors want activities and involvement, while others want rest and relaxation. In between lies everyone else.

3. Define the target market carefully; some seniors may be on a pension, fixed-income, or tight budget, while others may have substantial investments, resources, and disposable income.

4. Some cultures revere their elders; others dismiss older people and "worship youth." Marketers need to be sensitive to such characteristics and work within or against perceptions, depending on the impression that is to be created.

5. Humorous ads that treat seniors as feeble or bumbling cartoon types may get laughs, but they will offend a large part of the audience. Marketers must ask if humor *advances* or *distracts* from the messages the ad is supposed to convey.

6. Seniors should be shown the same sensitivity as any other respected core group of customers.

7. Often seniors themselves send mixed signals—wanting to be respected and acknowledged for their years of service, yet struggling with the realities of aging.

8. Phrases such as *discount, buy direct,* and asking if consumers *remember when* or *have a problem with* something are "trigger words" with added appeal to the seniors market.

9. "Early-bird specials" and "buyers' club days" engage seniors, who perceive that they are being offered unique recognition.

10. Absent the "Big Idea" for a uniquely creative approach to marketing to seniors, simply stress the benefits of your message, and avoid discriminating against or distinguishing segments of the audience.

Part III

Marketing Then and Now

IN MARKETING TERMS, profound adages such as "The more things change, the more they stay the same" and "Everything old is new again" are simply called *cycles*. Future marketing is (and will be), in most instances, a continuation of these cycles, with perhaps a few new twists and turns and terms. Does this mean that there will be nothing new in future marketing? Not at all. It means, however, that the arrival of "the next big thing" whenever it occurs, triggering a new wave of excitement and energy, will not require unlearning the skills that have so far taken marketers successfully to the 21st century.

Principles of good marketing don't change, and some very good ideas deserve to be revisited. Whether they become formula ideas that can be adapted to circumstances or are nostalgia that is recycled for another presentation to a once appreciative audience or exposed to a new generation, they are nonetheless worthy. Some people may suggest that a really good marketing program doesn't need to change with the times so much as, like a great old house, it just needs some periodic freshening up.

Future marketing will apply these principles and adapt successful formulas or great campaigns to new technology and new audiences, building from what's worked well in the past.

9

Cycles, Trends, and Just Good Ideas

So all my best is dressing old words new,
Spending again what is already spent.
—Shakespeare

THE TERM *MARKETING* has a long history of being misapplied. In the highest offices, people have been heard to say they need to work on their marketing, when what they meant was that they needed to change their *image*, to change public or industry perceptions about their company, their product, their message, or themselves. That would be a public relations matter, and while PR is normally a part of the marketing mix, it isn't marketing.

Others have spoken of needing to strengthen their marketing efforts, when they were really talking about their *sales* program. Still others use the terms *marketing* and *promotion* interchangeably—and incorrectly.

This is not to be picky, but to convey a point that needs to be registered strongly: Before millions of dollars of a budget and many people's jobs and careers are put on the line, it is important to know that all parties to the process are speaking the same language or, at least, that each person can understand what others are saying.

What Are We Talking About Here?

There is a story about a marketing ace who was invited to speak to a trade group on *creating a marketing plan*. Days before the event, the group's program chairman called to confirm arrangements and said, "I'm so pleased you'll be speaking to us on creating a business plan."

"No," the marketing ace replied, "I'm a marketing guy. I'll be speaking on creating a *marketing* plan."

After an awkward pause, the program chairman responded, "Aren't they the same thing?"

The answer is no, they're not. And the person who was confused was a mature, sophisticated, intelligent owner of a successful business. Was this man the only bright person in the business community whose bulb had gone dim on this subject? Probably not.

Is this still a good example if this individual was in fact vastly less knowledgeable than most other businesspeople?

Yes, because it illustrates that people have differing ideas about what something is—in this case, *marketing*.

For purposes of this book, keep in mind that *marketing* is the term that covers packaging, positioning, pricing, promotion, distribution, sales, advertising, public relations, and, perhaps, even research. Anything can be marketed. Typically, a marketing text uses such categories as *products, services,* or *businesses,* but it's important to always consider how broadly these terms can be applied. Some of the most aggressive marketing in the 20th century— some of which was the work of people who came somewhat late to the party—was done on behalf of trade associations, religious denominations, political candidates, professional services, diseases (for fund-raising and research), branches of government, and even entire countries. As various trade associations lobby (or market to) government, so governments and departments of commerce of countries market to other countries in order to receive loans, trade agreements, lower taxes, treaties, or tourism.

Form Follows Function—out the Door

For many years, there were those who believed that any form of marketing for professional services was obscene. Lawyers and doctors disdainfully compared the promoting of their services to "selling soap" and deemed it, at the very least, undignified. Today, they recognize the value and legitimacy of marketing, although in many circles they still insist on using euphemisms, such as *practice building* or *business development.* That's OK, but . . .

It's marketing.

And it takes a number of forms, such as *direct marketing, database marketing, telemarketing, on-line marketing,* and *multilevel marketing.* Much of it is cyclical and tied to economic conditions, forecasts, and the boss having a bad-hair day. Marketing budgets get slashed or eliminated altogether for no sensible reason or because a new CEO doesn't exactly understand what marketing means to a company.

Lawyers write books, and doctors create diets. They go on TV and give interviews to promote them and, not incidently, their practices. That's all marketing.

Advertising's Tobacco Road

Four centuries ago—1660 to be a bit more precise—the word *advertising* is said to have appeared on posters nailed to post office and courthouse walls. It is reasonable to assume that people debated even then if their presence was appropriate.

In the early days of television, one of the most familiar sights was a cavalier—his sword drawn, his plume smartly set on his large hat—coming to life and stepping down off the package of Cavalier cigarettes. Elsewhere a hotel bellboy named Johnny put his hand to the side of his mouth and, in a shrill voice, shouted in the manner that hotel bellboys and pages used to call guests to the telephone. "Call for Philip Morris!" he said, as he flashed a pack of Philip Morris cigarettes. Smokers could also save the cost of fancy "status" cigarette cases by buying a pack of Paxton, the menthol cigarette in the green and white molded plastic "sports pack."

Cigarette advertising on television has been banned in the United States for decades, although that is not the case in other parts of the world, where despite health warnings, sales flourish. The brands just mentioned don't benefit from it though, as they are all defunct. They fell victim in part to changing public attitudes about smoking, but mostly they were victims of bad marketing.

Numerous cigarette brands survive and continue to enjoy healthy sales (no pun intended). Marlboro, Camel, Winston, Virginia Slims, and several other brands are hugely successful because they do not market defensively, nor do they preach or push. They research what are the important "life moments" of the people in their target market, and they create magazine and billboard ads showing people in those situations . . . smoking cigarettes. They reinforce the consumer's choice, affirm the smoker's judgment, and avoid concerns of guilt, health, or liability.

In the 21st century, tobacco company budgets are heavy with the costs of lawyers and the funding of "educational programs." These programs virtually never work. The public will never believe that the industry is funding a campaign to discourage young people from smoking. And a public that thinks the solution to preventing kids from beginning to smoke is to ban sales or forbid signage within a mile of a school is just as silly. Kids don't start to smoke because the store that sells cigarettes is convenient to home or school, but that's a subject for another forum. Future marketing, however, will continue to explore ways for tobacco companies to get their products into the hands of people who want them. The laws of supply and demand that drive the market have never been circumvented by laws that are based on the premise that "this stiff will kill you."

When Special Isn't Special to Everyone

One of the most dramatic changes in marketing has been the evolution of the "special interest groups" that target tobacco, fur, pharmaceutical, fast-food, film, TV, clothing, and soft drink companies. Once, marketers decided how a product was packaged, positioned, and promoted. Now groups (or individuals) with time on their hands and questionable intentions want to tell businesses how they must act, using threats of boycotts, demonstrations, and lawsuits. In fairness, some of these groups are well intentioned and do perform a commendable service, for example in pressing companies to remove dangerous toys from the market or raising safety standards for flammability in children's clothing and bedding.

But to maintain that teenagers smoke because the company shows a cartoon camel or penguin smoking in an ad continues to be amusing, yet it's an expensive laugh, since the companies gave in and changed their ads.

So far, no group has come forward with a concern that children may see a Travelers Group ad and try to impale themselves on a cartoon umbrella.

Much of this book has urged that marketing should *not be exclusionary*—that an effort to reach one segment of the market should not insist on limiting itself to that market to such an extent that other segments feel more than "left out," but actually offended. An important change in marketing is the fact that so much of the marketing plan must anticipate what *reaction* the public will have to products and ads that it does not like.

In earlier eras, people simply did not buy a product or support a cause if they did not like or want or need what was being offered. The social and political climate at the recent turn of the century, however, actually encouraged consumer response, even attacks.

Cosmetic companies were one target. Critics actively organized campaigns, wrote letters, bought ads, called talk shows, and demonstrated against not just companies that used animals in the testing of their products but also those that used models in their ads who were too thin and might present a bad example to young girls, perhaps encouraging anorexia or other eating disorders, dangerous diets, or drug use, and were lowering the self-esteem of people who, realistically, could never look the way the models looked.

It didn't end there.

Everyone's a Critic

The existence of so many 24-hour cable news channels and on-line news services, and the desire of each to offer something different from its competitors, has resulted in greater marketing options and, on many occasions, more news programs than there is news.

What does one do in a situation such as this? Make news?

That's not always so easy to do.

Create controversy?

That, on the other hand, is *very* easy.

By simply putting out the call, producers have no difficulty finding someone only too willing to go on national television and criticize the advertising industry, insurance industry, banks, film and TV producers and programmers, gun manufacturers and dealers, drug companies, health-care providers, the music industry, concert promoters, airlines, school system, restaurants that permit smoking, churches, beauty pageants, funeral directors, and makers of motorized vehicles from subcompacts to SUVs.

It has been said that the 1990s suffered from an absence of civility. By 2000, the old adage "If you can't say something nice, don't say anything at all" had totally been abandoned. Such a philosophy did not produce interesting TV or newspaper stories.

When the Special Interests Market Against Marketers

What this means to marketers is that it is not enough to provide a product or service that meets a market need and is of reasonable price and quality. A marketer must understand that the reigning generation of special interests and watchdog groups is not simply protecting consumers from abuses, but has an aggressive agenda to *identify and go after* targets that will generate publicity. It is also the basis of their fund-raising and their continuing existence.

In other words, it has become an industry in itself, and each group has its own publications, websites, press releases, and spokespersons who regularly call press conferences, give interviews, and make the rounds of talk shows so desperate for programming content.

Steve Allen, author, musician, and for many years the host of numerous television shows, has made a late-in-life career of crusading against his old bosses, the television industry. In full-page national newspaper ads, he trashes the TV networks and cable companies for programming material that he does not consider worthwhile. He urges his fellow citizens to rise up and write letters, make phone calls, and send money to pay for more ads. It is an irony that 30 years or so earlier, he featured a character (portrayed by himself) on his TV show who was angry about things he read in the newspaper and regularly engaged in table-pounding rants.

It's Not a Brand; It's an Experience

Marketing also used to be concerned about products and services but now sees entrants to the marketplace in terms of *families of products* and broad reach. Starbucks isn't just a brand of coffee or a coffee shop, but an "experience" fitting a lifestyle with the products and image that convey a certain status. In earlier days, a coffee—Maxwell House, Folgers, Hills Brothers—was a coffee. It was promoted for its premium quality, finest beans, robust taste, wonderful aroma, and satisfying flavor. But it was never positioned "to say something" about the consumer. Private-label coffees were often considered an extra-nice touch to cap off a superb meal at a fine restaurant, but it was the *restaurant*—its menu, decor, ambiance, chef—that was the star, not the coffee.

Starbucks is an example of a 21st-century *brand* that is marketed in a way that presents the brand as more important than any one of its products or stores. The case is also an example of the trend to try to get in there fast and copy what someone else appears to be doing successfully. Riding the wave of Starbucks's success, several others quickly moved to duplicate the model, in some cases simply buying coffee shops and attempting to convert them. None came even close to matching Starbucks's success. What was missing was the Starbucks *marketing* focus. Others managed to produce a respectable cup of coffee and, in some cases, even re-create the atmosphere of a southeastern or southwestern coffee bar, but the effect was similar to the look one gets when trying to dress the way a popular celebrity did on television last night. The best you get is a comment that you look like the celebrity. But *looking* like the celebrity is not the same as *being* the celebrity. The imitators did not capture the essence of the original as a *marketed brand*, not simply a location and an array of products.

Exploding Cigars

Dr. Freud is reported to have said that "Sometimes a cigar is just a cigar." All indications are that he wasn't talking about marketing, but the truism applies to how times have changed when it comes to cigars.

Rarely in 21st-century marketing is anything *just* what it appears to be.

Cigars have had a roller-coaster cycle when it comes to popularity or even public acceptance. The product has historically had an association with men in positions of power—the politicians' "smokefilled rooms" where crucial leadership decisions are made, the private men's clubs where only the most elite need apply. It was also an acquired taste, with an aroma that did not appeal to everyone. And a good cigar, like a fine wine, could cost as much as fine clothes and conveyed the same impression of status.

In the 1960s and '70s, the cigar market burned out. The item had become *too much identified* with the "ruling class" of fat cats and business moguls who were the target of the revolutionaries and other advocates for change. Cigars, like fur coats, seemed to be symbols of the disengaged power structure, out of touch with the masses.

But times and marketing changed. By the mid-1990s, the backlash against political correctness was being felt. The Reagan years changed the tone in America. The fictional character Gordon Gekko from the hit film *Wall Street* spoke for millions when he said, "Greed is good," and the general population seemed to feel that, nobility notwithstanding, the idea of "the good life" seemed not so bad. Lavish parties, good wine, thick steaks, and the look of luxury were back in style. Earth tones and guilt about Styrofoam cups were out. And in the midst of this seemingly overt social reversal, what could be a more fitting accessory—the candle on the cake—than the cigar.

In earlier days, a movie star or business leader commonly would be photographed smoking or holding a cigarette. It was a sign of sophistication. The affectation—how one even *held* the cigarette—was a dramatic gesture that would suggest anything from a relaxed mood to extreme intensity. Cigarette smoking wasn't just a smoking habit; it was symbolic.

In the 1990s, the cigar was used to the same effect. A new generation of movie stars and business leaders went to great lengths to be photographed holding or smoking cigars, often calling special attention to them. And in typical '90s fashion, it would be revealed that the individual didn't simply enjoy a good cigar, but had gone into the cigar business. Actor George Hamilton put his name on a brand and announced that cigar stores under his label would be opened worldwide in every Hyatt Hotel. Actor James Belushi became an importer of cigars and provided them to fellow celebrities, who helped promote them. Arnold Schwarzenegger, Tom Selleck, Kevin Costner, Robert Wagner, David Letterman, and others posed for magazine covers and photographs, holding cigars prominently. President Bill Clinton, in a move that some suggested was a master politician's desire to have it both ways, was often shown with an intentionally *unlit* cigar.

As other products of the '90s expanded into multimarket opportunities or vehicles, the cigar became a reason to subscribe to any number of high-quality, well-distributed glossy magazines aimed at cigar smokers and those who found the product fascinating. Cigars were a reason to create "cigar bars" patterned after elegant private clubs or fun and fantasy speakeasys of another era. Websites, books, lines of clothing, and accessories were developed around cigar themes. The magazine *Cigar Aficionado* even introduced a pricey men's cologne under the same name. The objective was to convey to cigar smokers that they were a part of something almost fraternal with other cigar smokers.

For a time, it succeeded splendidly, but as the turn of the century approached, it appeared that cigar smoking was following the pattern of jogging, aerobics, and disco dancing—a fad turned to trend turned to phenomenon turned to fizzle, with only a group of hard-core loyalists remaining to the end. While many marketers rode the wave and profited, a bit more discipline and orchestration on the part of the tobacco industry might have given the cigar smokers' time in the sun stronger legs. Instead, the rush to cash in while it was hot conveyed a sense that even the major proponents believed the craze was too good to last.

Exploding PCs

Computers have not been around as long as cigars, but they are in no way new to the marketplace. It is interesting to note the explosion of interest in a product and a practice that seems to fit so many of its users like a suit that's either too baggy or too tight. Generation X "gets it," and Generation Y embraces it as the medium of choice. To marketers, however, personal computers are being positioned as the item that will change life as we know it. . . . It's just that no one is exactly sure of how.

Computers have come a long way since UNIVAC—the big metal box that took up most of the room. Modern computers are marketed aggressively on the basis of price, quality, compact size, and functionality, and often on little more than image, since most PCs with the same functions cost about the same. And when it comes to image, the message is combative. PC marketers do not suggest or claim so much that theirs is the superior product as that the competition is little short of laughable. The modern concept of brand loyalty takes the position that "all's fair" and pits one brand against another to the extent of affirming that all brands other than yours should be ridiculed and trashed.

This is not IBM versus Brand X, or a good-natured poke in the ribs that was the "Pepsi Challenge." The message is not that *people think we've got a better product*. Rather, consumers are urged to hold the other brands in contempt, by thinking their "Mac" is so superior that other brands are unworthy of consideration. Dell and Gateway took the marketing approach that price and features are what's most important, but they couldn't resist taking subtle and not-so-subtle shots at each other in their ads.

Hipper than Thou

In times past, the fiercest competitors, such as Ford and Chevrolet, Colgate and Crest, or Mobil and Shell, talked to their own USPs, their unique selling propositions: price, quality, integrity, and why they should be the customer's choice.

At the start of the 21st century, advertising copywriters are of a generation regarded as having "an attitude." It is a description with which they are extremely comfortable. They believe that advertising and marketing should push the limits of acceptable standards and have an edge. Many of them believe that an edge and an attitude are the same thing. They perceive that their market is composed of people like themselves, so to let the attitude come through is a good thing. The evolution of children shouting, "My dog's better than your dog" has become copywriters and creative directors shouting, "My PC can run circles around your PC."

As if marketing were not already a competitive enough field, the attitude aspect has made the competition to show brand superiority very personal.

From Shirts to Boots to "Cream of Nowhere"

For example, an ad for a shirtmaker crossed out the word *shirt* and inserted *trouble* above it, so it read *troublemaker*. The ad's headline declared, "It's not premarital sex if you don't plan on getting married." The accompanying photo was of a teenage boy with a bad haircut, bad teeth, and a pierced eyebrow—hardly the usual model in a fashion layout. It might have seemed pointed if it were an ad for condoms, but will it sell shirts? Is it the advertiser's idea of the best way to build brand awareness or brand equity? The Hathaway shirt man of bygone years probably would find his eye patch spinning in confusion.

Another ad, this one for boots, shows the bottom of a style of boot favored by members of Generation Y, called the Powderhound. The ad's headline reads, "Any Boot Can Repel Water. Ours Will Actually Suck the Sweat Off Your Pinky Toes."

An on-line marketer of sports equipment bought a full-page color ad in national magazines to invite readers to "Spend 80 percent less finding out how much you suck at golf." This ad must presume that the reader (and, one would hope, potential customer) not only has a sense of humor but also has the same sense of humor as the copywriter. Insulting a potential customer in the spirit of good-natured kidding is rather a risky practice for any business, much less one that is not well known. Is this the kind of first impression this company wants to make on the marketplace?

It's true that there is a growing number of young golfers. *Older* golfers, however, are the largest segment of the market. If the creative director or copywriter thinks this ad will appeal to the largest segment of the golf audience, it is reasonable to assume this person has not bothered to research this market at all. It is one thing for a marketer to say that he or she wants to get the young end of the market and grow with it, but it's hardly an astute business strategy to say to the market segment that can put you on the map that you're not really interested in them unless they are hip enough for *you*.

What this approach fails to take into account is that people grow up and, in most cases, lose "the attitude." Even baby boomer icon James Dean probably would have found the "rebel" deal wearing kind of thin by age 50. So, when attitudes change—or just become tiresome—the choice will be, as the research indicates it has pretty much always been, a matter of price, quality, value, and image. At that point, an attitude, especially one that insults the customer with its smugness, gets in the way of marketing.

One day, a particular on-line shopping service may be a household name, but it wasn't at the end of 1999. At that time, it placed a full-page ad in a Sunday national edition of the *New York Times*. The ad's headline appeared in regular type in the center of the page and read, "By the time you read this, our prices will be out of date. (They'll be lower)." No prices were shown. The headline was surrounded by blank white space that took up seven-eighths of the page. The name was in the lower right corner. There was no art in the ad. For an unknown enterprise to run full-page ads in premium media is a serious, bold, and costly strategy.

The assumption here is that people will read the ad, remember it, remember the advertiser, and take action, and that is a huge assumption when (A) the advertiser is unknown to them, (B) the ad contains little information designed to prompt action, and (C) the ad is somewhere between understated and boring. To assume the ad will be read, much less remembered, reflects either arrogance or a failure of the advertiser to research what makes a good ad, what ads get read, and what causes people to remember ads they've seen. This information is elementary stuff to bright people at really good ad agencies, whether they are young or old. Incidentally, as of six months later, the company was no better known and the ads were no longer in the paper.

Three *P*s in a Changing Pod

Overall, the most dramatic changes in marketing are in pricing, promotion, and positioning.

There are thousands of products and thousands of choices, but there have always been a lot of choices in most industries, and categories and competitors have always taken each other seriously. A distinction is that products in the 21st century are presented in a context that makes them appear to be more than they are: a soap must have a companion shampoo, deodorant, conditioner, comb and brush, toothpaste, and compact disc of appropriate music to play while using the products.

Celebrities appearing in ads or as spokespersons used to be larger-than-life stars. In modern times, a lawyer or a professor, a mayor or a judge, or a police officer is a product or issue spokesperson, blurring the lines of show business, reality, and serious marketing.

The marketing plans of earlier generations sought to win friends and influence people. Modern marketing methods seem to favor more of an in-your-face mode. While most auto company and airline ads, for example, tend to be of the mainstream, bland variety, some go for "edgy" by adding a soundtrack of jarring, repetitious drumbeats or soul singers at high volume, sounds predictable enough to have been machine generated. Comical, abrasive ads are among the most notable and memorable, but not necessarily the most effective.

Modern marketing increasingly operates on *assumptions of like-mindedness.* That is, the marketer assumes that anyone watching a particular TV commercial, reading an ad, or listening to a spokesperson is in agreement with the speaker, the marketer, and the message, that the viewer or reader or audience member recognizes and automatically accepts the legitimacy of the claim of superiority of the advertiser and of inferiority of the competition. Making this assumption, the marketer then goes on in a tone that only a confederate would use with another member of his or her own inner circle.

Politicians typically address audiences in this way, assuming everyone agrees with what they are saying. However, when the votes are counted, despite the cheers, the air of confidence, and the self-congratulation, someone loses.

Principles of effective marketing require listening to the market, responding to the concerns of the market, and providing what the market wants. To arrogantly assume the public will believe or buy whatever you put out is to make a potentially very costly assumption.

Summary Points

1. Some of the professional services groups prefer to think of marketing as practice building or business development.

2. Sophisticated methods have evolved to provide for direct marketing, database marketing, telemarketing, on-line marketing, and multilevel marketing.

3. Marketers today must anticipate attacks and criticism from any number of special interests that have become an industry unto themselves.

4. The growing number of 24-hour cable news channels and on-line news services represents both opportunities and risks for marketers as these entities become more desperate for content and controversy.

5. Marketers now think in terms of "families of products," with even unrelated products sharing a name and image.

6. By the mid-1990s, the pendulum had swung the other way, and the mood of the public seemed to be shifting. The effects of politically correct actions were wearing thin, and smoking, nightclubbing, luxury items, and conspicuous signs of the good life were enjoying a resurgence.

7. Whereas older generations emphasized positive elements of their products, younger marketers appear to lead by criticizing competitors.

8. Modern marketers often operate on an *assumption of like-mindedness*, assuming the audience automatically accepts their claim of superiority and disdains competitors as inferior, thus creating an "inner-circle" relationship with members of the audience.

Successful Brand Strategies

Past, Present, and Future

Promise, large promise, is the soul of an advertisement.
—Samuel Johnson

BRANDS DISTINGUISH THINGS from one another. In marketing, essentially anything can be considered a brand, from a pack of gum or a tube of toothpaste to a magazine, a school, an airline, a hospital, or a country. NBC is a brand. So is *Newsweek*. Harvard, as one of the world's most prestigious universities, has done well marketing its brand image and licensing its name for use in a variety of merchandise. When Florida, Mexico, New York, or Paris advertise for tourism, they are positioning these locations as brands, packaged as any other product might be. They are more than names in that as brands, they must convey an image and seek an emotional response. From a marketing perspective, it is useful to note which brands appeal to which generation, or to more than one generation, and ask why this is the case.

It Is What It Is, in Other Words

Coke, Xerox, Kleenex, and Levi's have become so important as brand names that, to millions of people, they are the generic names for products in the categories they represent—a situation that has proved maddening to their respective trademark and patent attorneys.

McDonald's and Kentucky Fried Chicken in many ways created and defined the American fast-food industry and have expanded their market penetration to the capital cities of the world. They did it based not so much on their food as on the image of their brands. It is common to hear people around the world say, "We had McDonald's for lunch." Rarely does a listener hear if the speaker had a Big Mac, a Quarter Pounder, Chicken McNuggets, or a salad. "Having McDonald's" is all the information that is necessary.

In his song "America," Paul Simon sings, "So, we bought a pack of cigarettes and Mrs. Wagner's pies," and the mention of the mass-produced, mass-marketed, cellophanewrapped pies, sold off racks in all-night convenience stores, painted a picture of a young couple, eager and afraid, setting out on a journey of discovery. That's quite a bit of imagery from a small, individually wrapped, preservative-laden piece of pastry. But its imagery would not have been there without the brand. A passing reference to simply *pie* or *apple pie* would not have conveyed the same imagery to people who related to the song. While it can't quite be assumed that Mrs. Wagner had a well-conceived brand strategy in play when that song was heard by several million people, the example does speak to the tremendous power of being a brand name.

And Snickers is the "Official Snack Food of the U.S. Olympic Team."

The late David Ogilvy was one of the most respected figures in advertising. He instructed: "You have to decide what 'image' you want for your brand. Image means *personality*. Products, like people, have personalities, and they can make or break them in the marketplace. The personality of a product is an amalgam of many things—its name, its packaging, its price, the style of its advertising, and, above all, the nature of the product itself."

So, we know that a strong brand is more than a name, but how important is the name to the brand? And is the name one that is intended to have specific generational appeal or to consciously avoid a generational bias?

Brand Name Basics

Common sense, as well as good business sense, would say that a brand's name is extremely important. The most basic rules regarding name selection for a product or company are that the name should (1) have a pleasing sound and be easy to pronounce and spell, (2) translate well visually to logos and signage, (3) allow for the possibility of brand extensions into other products that may or may not have anything in common with the core brand product, and (4) relate in some way to what the company or product is or does. Some of the best examples of this are Instant Print, Minute Rice, Jiffy Lube, Comfort Inn, Whole Foods Market, and in the cyberspace world, CommunicationsResource.com.

Curious Choices

Sometimes, eager marketers go to extremes in personalizing a generic product (Mr. Chicken, Mr. Beef, Mr. Submarine) or seek to establish ownership of parts of the universe (Tile World, Carpet World, Dinette World, World of Hair). A bit closer to the ground, but no less ambitious or territorial, are Computerland, Dairyland, and Movieland.

The images that these names inspire speak for themselves. Many are frivolous, silly, simplistic, or stupid to some people, but they do, nonetheless, lend themselves to a certain imagery. Marketers often cite the strange origins of the name of a quirky Chicago gift store. In an effort to come up with an unusual name, the owner asked employees and friends to put their suggestions on slips of paper, and one would be picked from a hat. The winner was *He Who Eats Mud*. The shop is unusual, and its name gets attention, but it so far has not posed a huge threat to Tiffany.

Remember that the name you give your brand should be one that your customers, clients, and supporters will be pleased, happy, proud, or at least comfortable, acknowledging as *their* brand or place of choice.

But Is It Art?

IBM has become so great a power in business and technology that a diminishing number of people now remember (or care) that the company was once known as International Business Machines. The great success of IBM has, alas, led thousands of companies to unwisely bring their enterprises and brands to the marketplace identified with letters instead of names, and the results have benefited neither the public nor the brands. Is that reference to MCA meant to indicate the motion picture and recording company (originally incorporated as the Music Corporation of America but never called that) or the Museum of Contemporary Art? Neither, of course, will accommodate the other by agreeing not to insist on going by its acronym, even in ads, so the public has to deal with the confusion.

Is it important?

Ask their investors.

And what exactly *is* a TRW anyway?

AARP announced in 1999 that it would thereafter be designated as such and not by its original name, the American Association of Retired Persons. While it's true that the original name was a bit of a mouthful and did not always technically describe the actual makeup of the group, it *did* suggest both *what* it was and *who* it was. AARP does not, and in time, fewer people will remember the group's original name or its purpose.

Planned Parenthood, for example, would not likely receive the attention and level of support it is able to generate if it announced that it wished to be known as simply PP.

Businesses help themselves when they help the public know who and what they are and what they do without making people first read a brochure and a mission statement. Most of the public is not inclined to indulge a company or a cause to that degree.

Charles Schwab, founder of one of the most successful discount brokerage firms in America, is reported to have said that one of his smarter moves was to put his photograph in his ads and his name on the door. He believed that people want to know who it is that they are allowing to handle their money. Perhaps that is why so many of the most successful financial firms have followed this formula, among them Merrill Lynch, Dean Witter, Smith Barney, Paine Webber, and Morgan Stanley.

Beating the Odds of Survival

The odds against new products, brands, and companies succeeding are—and always have been—great. Still, each year, the market is flooded with new entries. Those that survive bring a product, service, or message that people want or need, whether they realize it or not.

Staying Hot, from Soup to Lug Nuts

In *Advertising in America*, Charles Goodrum and Helen Dalrymple trace the history of a number of brands that have not only found success but have also outlived competitors and remained strong through generations. Consider the images evoked by the following names and brands from ads created during the last two centuries for products that are still leaders in their categories:

Smith Brothers	From	1847
Arrow		1851
Campbell		1869
Levi's		1880

Ivory	1882
Dr. Pepper	1885
Coca-Cola	1886
Kodak	1888
Sears, Roebuck & Company	1888
Maxwell House	1892
Hires	1892
Quaker	1897
Goodyear	1898
Cadillac	1903
Gillette	1905
Travelers	1912
Camel	1915
Listerine	1915

If the main ingredient in making a business successful is to give the public what it wants, these brands and companies did, and they continue to do so, whether the core product was tomato soup, oatmeal, life insurance, or tires. The products in every case had not been abandoned or pushed into the background in favor of something "hotter."

Certainly the products changed with the times. Gillette has improved upon the quality of each generation of shaving blades and does a substantial business in disposable razors for both men and women. Today's products are not the products of 1905. Travelers has enlarged upon its catalog of insurance products far beyond anything its founders could have envisioned in 1912.

Maxwell House has added premium blends, flavors, and decaffeinated varieties, making an effort to maintain its position as a leading brand, while Starbucks, Seattle's Best, and Millstone, to name a few, try to convince consumers that they are the brands of the future. But Maxwell House is still a company that, trends notwithstanding, wants to keep its core brand image tied to its reputation as the "good to the last drop" coffee that was introduced at the Maxwell House Hotel in 1892.

And Cadillac has definitely added a few models to its line and made some design changes to the product that appeared in ads in 1903. If brands are to appeal to members of the next generation, they must be careful about being too closely identified with the last generation. Neither, however, should a brand abandon the customers who helped it become successful.

At the end of the day, and the century, the brands remained true to what their customers expected of them—consistently—over the years.

Back in Style?

Playboy was more than a successful men's magazine; it literally redefined the category. The company's foray into the hotel business, nightclubs, and the recording industry failed, diluting the brand's equity by its identification with so many unprofitable ventures. This all came at a time when a changing cultural landscape made it appear that the whole *Playboy* concept might well be passé.

Its comeback strategy involved returning its emphasis to what the customers wanted. If *Playboy*'s readers wanted beautiful women, as shown each month in the magazine, then give them beautiful women, in settings like those in the magazine. By refocusing on the magazines, spinning out single-subject issues featuring the most popular women, and adding home video, cable TV, and on-line versions, plus calendars and photo books expanding both the most popular issues and photographs, *Playboy* returned to the niche it had created and had veered away from. In the 21st century, the company sees E-commerce—selling merchandise on its website—as a big part of its future.

Real estate mogul and erstwhile celebrity Donald Trump did very well in property development, but Trump Airlines and a syndicated TV game show were high-profile failures.

Brut was one of America's most popular men's fragrance lines, but the company went nowhere with an expanded line of personal-care products and the series of albums it released on the Brut Records label. Its return to success was a return to its roots—high-visibility advertising for a consistently popular fragrance.

Once a brand is well known, its managers sometimes develop an arrogance about it, believing that its imprint on virtually any product will turn it to gold. Life Savers gum failed. So did Pepsi Clear and Pepsi AM. The lesson here is that a brand's becoming known as excellent in one area does not mean the public will give it a pass and make a market success out of anything else that bears that brand's name (unless the brand is *Elvis*, which has found eager customers waiting in line to buy anything that bears the name and likeness of the late King of Rock 'n' Roll, from musical telephones to gym shorts; still, it is a matter of giving his public what it wants—mainly, a wide array of souvenirs).

In the booming 1960s, well-nigh any company with a name ending in "tronics" was hotter than a firecracker with investors and Wall Street analysts. But by the '70s, the firecrackers had got wet enough that most of them no longer lit and had to be thrown out. The rush to share in the momentum of a trend can make marketers forget that success involves more than being there with a name. It takes giving the public what it wants.

With Slogans, It Ain't Over till It's Over

In 1999, Career Press assembled what it called "a highly subjective list of the pieces of our past that won't survive the century change" and included 50 advertising slogans and jingles, many of which were the essence of brand positioning strategies used for decades. These were the *bites* that marketers hoped would become synonymous with products, brands, and companies. While most are now ensconced in the dusty archives of advertising, the Career Press designation may have been premature. Thanks to the popularity of nostalgia and the appeal of "retro" ad campaigns to certain generations, many of these lines can still register in the 21st century. If a memory or image of a product, or even of a particular ad, commercial spot, or campaign, can be called up in a person's mind, then the lines are far from dead. They managed to "survive the century change" very well. This association validates the message as a marketing device, showing that it worked and that it *continues* to work decades later.

Here are those iffy 50. As a study of some classic positioning strategies of brands (or just for fun), test yourself on what product or company put its image on the line with lines like these (answers follow):

1. Plop, plop, fizz, fizz, oh what a relief it is!
2. It's the *slow* ketchup
3. You can trust your car to the man who wears the star
4. The quicker picker-upper
5. When you care enough to send the very best
6. Good to the last drop
7. The Uncola
8. A little dab'll do ya
9. Mmm, mmm good

10. You're soaking in it now!
11. Double your pleasure, double your fun
12. Reach out and touch someone
13. Look how good you look now!
14. We bring good things to life
15. With nooks and crannies to hold the butter
16. Melts in your mouth, not in your hand
17. Can't pinch an inch!
18. Ho, ho, ho!
19. We'll leave the light on for you
20. Bring out the best!
21. When it rains, it pours
22. The great American chocolate bar
23. You deserve a break today
24. We do chicken right!
25. Look, Ma, no cavities!
26. Mikey likes it—he hates everything!
27. Something special in the air
28. Snap! Crackle! Pop!
29. Don't leave home without it!
30. I'm the loneliest guy in town
31. Just for the taste of it!
32. It's one-quarter cleansing cream
33. Breakfast of champions
34. Fast, fast, fast relief
35. Have it your way
36. Does she . . . or doesn't she? Only her hairdresser knows for sure.
37. Diamonds are forever
38. I'd rather fight than switch!
39. 99 and 44/100 percent pure
40. I'd like to teach the world to sing in perfect harmony
41. Ring around the collar
42. Takes a licking and keeps on ticking
43. Where's the beef?
44. The beer that made Milwaukee famous
45. Two scoops of raisins in every box
46. Leave the driving to us
47. You'll wonder where the yellow went

48. Let your fingers do the walking
49. Always a bridesmaid, but never a bride
50. Bet you can't eat just one!

(The answers)

1. Alka-Seltzer
2. Heinz Ketchup
3. Texaco
4. Bounty paper towels
5. Hallmark cards
6. Maxwell House coffee
7. 7-Up
8. Brylcreem hair cream
9. Campbell's soups
10. Palmolive dish-washing liquid
11. Wrigley's Doublemint gum
12. AT&T
13. Avon personal-care products
14. General Electric
15. Thomas' English muffins
16. M&Ms chocolate candies
17. Special K cereal
18. Green Giant
19. Motel 6
20. Hellmann's mayonnaise
21. Morton salt
22. Hershey's
23. McDonald's
24. Kentucky Fried Chicken
25. Crest toothpaste
26. Life breakfast cereal
27. American Airlines
28. Rice Krispies
29. American Express
30. Maytag appliances
31. Diet Coke
32. Dove soap
33. Wheaties
34. Anacin
35. Burger King
36. Clairol hair color
37. DeBeers
38. Tareyton cigarettes
39. Ivory soap
40. Coca-Cola
41. Wisk laundry detergent
42. Timex watches
43. Wendy's fast-food restaurants
44. Schlitz
45. Post raisin bran
46. Greyhound bus lines
47. Pepsodent toothpaste
48. Yellow Pages phone directory
49. Listerine
50. Lay's potato chips

Reach In, Reach Out

In some cases, the brand strategy was a bit of Advertising 101—find the USP, the unique selling proposition that distinguishes products that seem indistinguishable from one another. And when there appears not to be one? Use your imagination. *Reach.*

Heinz ketchup was so thick that it seemed to take forever for it to drip, much less pour, out of the bottle. It was the *slow* ketchup—and that was good. Add a background of Carly Simon's hit song "Anticipation," and the bottle of ketchup becomes the lead in a pop-culture melodrama.

What can you say about a Hershey's chocolate bar—the candy bar that America grew up with, that GIs during World War II reportedly shared with children across Europe in acts of kindness and generosity, that went to school in lunch boxes for decades? You could say it was "Hershey's—the great American chocolate bar," and you could almost see the flag waving.

And what's so different about one chocolate or another? In the case of M&Ms, it's the candy shell, so that the chocolate "melts in your mouth, not in your hand." The line was popular, and so was the candy. While chocolate-smeared hands were in fact a nuisance, the line lingered in people's minds longer than the ad campaign that brought it to their attention. The fact was that when and where it melts was not as important to people as how the chocolate tastes. Candy lovers have to be so enticed and seduced by images of taste and enjoyment that they can't wait to find the store or vending machine to satisfy the craving. Functionality in this instance made a memorable line, but it did not sell as much candy as did visions of people enjoying it. While generationally and economically candy makers have sought distinctions (upscale Godiva versus supermarket bulk-rate barrels), the major brands have tried to appeal to kids, while appealing to "the kid in all of us."

It was nice to be reminded that Campbell's soups were "Mmm, mmm good" and that Diet Coke was a good drink "just for the taste of it," but these well-advertised lines didn't tip the balance of whether or not to buy the product. The decision to buy came from the saturation media and the heavy exposure that continually reinforced the presence and availability of the product.

Grand Motel

One positioning line that did make a difference was reportedly a lucky accident (or a great story the company's PR man thought up to impress the media).

Motel 6 was one of America's largest chains of low-end, low-cost motels. It was known as a no-frills, bed-and-bathroom situation for long-distance truckers and others in need of a bed and not much else for a little money. That was the image Motel 6 wanted to change. Marketers knew that the properties as they were—inside and out—did not exactly lend themselves to color magazine ads or TV commercials of the Marriott or Hilton variety. So, how does one create an image without pictures?

Radio. The "theater of the mind." Orson Welles had scared an entire country with verbal images of a *War of the Worlds*, and legendary comedian Stan Freberg had people visualizing acrobats, chorus lines, and giant marshmallows being dropped into a sea of hot chocolate. For Motel 6, the room the audience might picture was very likely nicer than the basic simplicity the company had to show. Tom Bodett, a National Public Radio essayist and humorist from faraway Homer, Alaska, was known for contributing folksy, funny short pieces in the style of Will Rogers and Garrison Keillor. With the help of Motel 6's very competent ad agency, he delivered the chain's spots, accompanied by an easygoing guitar picker.

Bodett's relaxed drawl and comfortable patter suggested images of Andy and Barney and the nice folks in Mayberry, at a motel where there was "nothin' fancy like at those places that cost a lot." At the conclusion of the spot, Bodett is reported to have improvised the line "We'll leave the light on for you."

Whether it was in fact his own idea or that of a very bright copywriter, it was inspired. Almost immediately, the image of the absolute simplicity of Motel 6 made it a choice of senior citizens and others traveling on a budget. People *felt* better about choosing Motel 6 because it was a good place for *plain* folks, and besides, they'd "leave the light on for you." What could sound more welcoming than that? Seniors liked its "folksy" sound, while appreciating lower prices. Younger generations caught the humor and didn't mind saving money either.

Every Dot-Com Will Have Its Day

At the recent turn of the century, any new company with a "dot-com" in its name was noticed. As one example, in the Super Bowl game played in 2000, some 17 television commercials for dot-com companies were more talked about in the days before and after the game than was the game itself. The public, the emerging generations, and the media were moving from complacency to a brave new universe that reflected vision, promised opportunity, and maybe even some excitement. It was ironic that the charge into the future—at least in cyberspace—would be led by people who looked and acted like the most unstylish kids in the class. They were the *nerds*, but they were the smart ones.

The marketplace would determine which of the new Web-based enterprises had quality, value, and image at a good price. The survivors would then compete at the next level, to demonstrate that they could get noticed, become accepted, and win loyalty. Despite how it might have appeared, just existing and being on-line wasn't enough.

For marketers, this was the most dramatic opportunity in decades: to help clients learn how to market what they had in a new marketplace that had no decaying real estate and no parking problems or rude shoppers ahead of you, and that was open 24 hours a day, seven days a week. Service was about as personal as it could get, whether it was a retail consumer transaction or a business-to-business arrangement. Maybe you didn't get a smile, but the welcoming greetings and expressions of gratitude on the computer were more than a lot of people remembered getting on that last trip to the mall.

Ad agencies, PR agencies, and marketing consulting firms began reengineering and retraining their operations to become brand marketing firms, such as CommunicationsResource.com, BrandEra.com, and Upshot.com. They could provide services to agencies or perform the agency functions themselves—creative development, strategic marketing, website design—at significantly less cost than agencies of old.

(In the interest of full disclosure, the publisher acknowledges that the author of this work is a consulting partner in CommunicationsResource.com, a content provider for marketing communications on the Internet.)

Pretty much every business wanted a website, even if the companies didn't know what to do with it or how it would benefit them—or even *if* it would benefit them.

The future had arrived. Things were changing dramatically. Some companies would continue to do business as they had always done it and would be fine, if they had a solid brand marketing strategy. Others would not be just a part of the change; they would lead it. Most marketers would realize that not everyone gathered around the TV set on Monday night to watch *I Love Lucy*, nor did everyone wait at the family PC to get on-line. Different generations are more than ever before wanting to have things their own way and marketers need to understand that.

Summary Points

1. To be successful, brands must convey a unique image and seek an emotional response from the consumer.

2. Products have their own personalities that can define them in the marketplace and help them to become successful.

3. Brand names should be easy to say and spell, translate well visually, and allow for the possibility of brand extensions or spin-off products. Ideally, names should clearly relate in some way to the product, its uses, or its benefits.

4. Over the years, the brands that have succeeded (and continue to succeed) have managed to establish a reputation for giving their target audiences what they want, while improving or adapting core products and at all times maintaining the perception of value.

5. Major brand failures, such as Coca-Cola's line of clothing or the Playboy Hotels, occurred because the companies stopped listening to the voice of the market and permitted their names to be used on products that had little or nothing to do with their brands or the reason people liked their brands. The value in a brand name must be protected by extending it only to products that make sense to consumers.

6. The emerging on-line market may be innovative in its technology, but the same rules of marketing apply. A product or service must be perceived to have value. Just being "hi-tech" isn't enough.

The Future Marketing Casebook

Amazon.com, Barnes & Noble,
Barbie, American Girl, Beanie Babies,
HBO, IKEA, Starbucks

HERE ARE SOME successful brand histories and strategies, with a prediction for how each one is likely to reflect a sense of future marketing.

Amazon.com

As the year 2000 dawned, *Time* magazine and *Advertising Age* named Amazon.com their choice for Company of the Year and Marketer of the Year, respectively. Many others thought the company was a publicity machine that had been oversold, overhyped, and certainly overreported, and cries of "Enough!" could be heard echoing throughout the cybervillage and beyond. Still, with all that's been said and written, Amazon.com remains the most often cited example of the innovative marketing that set the tone for much future marketing.

In the fall of 1999, *Business Week* reported: "With a brand already recognized by 188 million U.S. adults, (CEO Jeffrey) Bezos wants Amazon.com to be the place for consumers to find almost anything they want—whether Amazon itself sells the products or simply takes a cut from other merchants selling on its website. If he is successful, the conventional description of Amazon as the Wal-Mart of the Web will prove too limited. Says Bezos, 'We want to build something the world has never seen.'"

The beginnings of Amazon.com sound like folklore. Jeff Bezos started his business not in a log cabin, but in the garage of his home in a suburb of

Seattle. From there, he created the first Internet superstore, on its way to becoming a mall. Projections for 1999 were a volume of some $1.4 billion worth of books, CDs, toys, and other merchandise sold to more than 10 million customers. It is also estimated that nearly 70 percent of Amazon sales are from repeat customers. That fact has proved to be of no small consideration to securities analysts, whose highly favorable ratings of the cyberspace company during most of its first six years kept its stock prices in the stars.

It was apparent from the start that Bezos both knew his market and was building a business on a premise that contradicted conventional wisdom. That is, he was creating a new business that was strictly on-line, not just an on-line extension of an established retail company, so there was no existing reputation, awareness, or core group of customers.

Second, he was limiting his total "walk-in" clientele to people who (A) had a personal computer and a modem, (B) liked to shop without leaving home to examine the merchandise before buying, and (C) were willing to provide their credit card numbers on-line, when people had growing reservations about doing so.

But perhaps most important, Amazon's core business was being a bookstore—an on-line bookstore—at a time when the largest market segment using the Internet supposedly didn't read much and had even less of an interest in buying books.

Except that, in this instance, they are buying books by the millions and asking for more.

It was another risky decision to go public early on. It was risky because the enterprise not only was not showing a profit, but it did not expect to do so for several years. Securities analysts were being asked to recommend the stock based on its potential and its vision for the future.

Book buyers were indicating their approval of the concept initiated by Barnes & Noble, Borders, and Crown Books to replace the dusty, dark, crowded bookshops with well-appointed "superstores" featuring deep-discount pricing, comfortable furniture, a café, and classical music. Amazon was urging them to stay home and order from a screen.

Amazon plays up its heavily discounted prices, but, alas, there are also those pesky shipping and handling charges. Clearly, Bezos has been counting on his customers' wanting the convenience of shopping from home—browsing through a large selection of books and other merchandise without having to deal with the crowds, parking lots, and hassles too often associated with retail shopping.

It is also said that Bezos "quickly realized the buyer is king of the Web—and set out to build the most customer-centered store anywhere."

Book lovers often don't just love to read books; they also love to read *about* books. An Amazon feature includes reviews written by staff and invites customers and browsers to submit comments, as well as offering the books' authors a chance to comment on their own books or on the comments made about them. The process allows customers and others to become involved with both the book and its presentation to the market in ways never before possible. It shows a respect for customers' opinions—always important in creating brand equity and brand loyalty.

It appears Amazon.com has hit on a winning formula, one that has inspired a seemingly endless number of new "dot-com" retailers to copy it. Note that while Amazon has seemed to shut out the vast number of book lovers and potential customers who prefer not to shop via the Internet, the company nonetheless does not rely on the Internet alone to reach the market it *is* after. Amazon invested millions of dollars in television and print advertising that is as slickly produced as anything for any long-established brand. People are being directed to the Amazon.com site with an aggressive traditional marketing campaign.

While the decision to go public early on was risky, the vote of confidence that Wall Street gave the company became an additional source of revenue, publicity, and an excellent path to success.

By the beginning of 2000, the first tremors on the landscape were being heard. Some stock analysts were growing impatient and wanted to see profit sooner and vision later. If more analysts follow, the chain reaction could suggest that the Amazon brand is in trouble, and even such rumors are bad for business. However, a company that could create such an impact on the vast, open Internet frontier likely has a strategy for responding to that as well.

Future Marketing Prediction

With all the predictions of an inevitable Internet shakeout, Amazon.com has a better chance of surviving the bumpy ride than a lot of others. The downside of being the Internet's first great success story is that the spotlight is turned up so much brighter. Every event will get more attention than it might deserve, especially negative news. A major reason for the company's extraordinary success is that it is an electronic catalog for people who like to catalog shop. Expectations are a lot higher than they would be for a more moderately successful operation. Recommendation: Slow down. Lower expectations (of both investors and customers). The goal of being the great mall of the universe is commendable in its ambition, but it puts off a large part of the market that doesn't care and is nonsupportive of companies that get "too big." Isn't there a saying about "The bigger they are . . . "? Amazon's core customers are baby boomers and Generation Xers. Seniors are slow to change and will likely stay with the shop around the corner, which will probably be gone by the time the members of Generation Y (and Generation "Next" coming up behind them) are seniors.

Barnes & Noble

In the summer of 1999, the chairman and chief executive of Barnes & Noble, Leonard Riggio, told *New York* magazine: "I see connections between books and bookstores and networks.

"If a network is cool, like XYZ discount store, there isn't an endearing relationship between the client and the network. But when the network gets hot, the customers bond with the store strongly, almost endearingly. That is why the great retailers' bags become fashion accessories. At its best, a chain becomes a network, so that people who participate in Barnes & Noble activities, which include shopping, feel something in common with people in faraway places who share the same activity."

Uh, OK. That theoretical, philosophical, very flawed statement sounds more like "boardroom thinking" than market research.

People toting a particular shopping bag—Tiffany, Neiman-Marcus, Saks Fifth Avenue—may well impress fellow shoppers by their purchasing power and their choice of a store with a reputation for attracting the more discriminating shoppers. But carrying a Barnes & Noble travel mug does not create a bond of commonality with other Barnes & Noble customers, most of whom do not interact with each other any more than shoppers at Sears, Target, or 7-Eleven interact. On-site reading groups, children's story time, and author signings and readings tend to foster customer interaction and comaraderie under the retailer's roof more than even 10 matching shopping bags in the same elevator would.

The *New York* magazine piece describes how Barnes & Noble superstores succeed because they create a more comfortable—even if it is a more commercial—way to buy books.

Riggio adds, noting the challenge that Barnes & Noble faces from on-line retailers, "The Internet affords you the opportunity to do the kind of hand selling that you logistically can't do in a bookstore."

And the rent is less in cyberspace than it is for three square blocks of prime real estate, not including the parking lot.

On-line, a customer may see a long and varied list of reviews and comments about a single book—repeated for thousands of titles—that could not practically be displayed in a store setting. Riggio has good reason to be interested in the distinctions between on-site and on-line shopping; the tremendous success of Amazon.com doubtless has stolen much of the retail superstore's thunder, not to mention more than a few customers. Some observers have suggested that on-line retailing is so much the wave of the future that, just as Barnes & Noble was attacked for forcing smaller, independent booksellers out of business, it is itself seriously threatened with the possibility of extinction—or at least with the loss of market dominance and, with that, the loss of industry clout—by on-line businesses.

The vast technical capabilities for marketing and warehousing on-line make the on-site superstores look like mom-and-pop businesses, totally unable to compete.

Maybe. But, as noted in the Amazon.com case study, on-line shopping is not quite the oversimplified process it is often represented to be. True, it can be accomplished from the comfort of one's home or office without many of the cursed hassles commonly associated with "going out to shop." And it is definitely faster under most circumstances—click on your order and wait for the mail to arrive. It does, however, require a computer, a modem, a credit card, and an inclination to purchase from an unknown, unseen order-taker behind a screen, with greetings, gratitude, and a genial wish to have a nice day conveyed by a computer program—a clerk that doesn't exist. Not to mention the added hassle of returing mechandise.

Do people care? Maybe not. But then again, many thousands of successful businesses tout their "personal service," and still have customers tell market researchers the lack of personal attention and service is what most turns them off about so many businesses.

Even in the 21st century, not everyone has or wants a computer, and much less are people willing to totally alter their shopping or buying habits as a concession to technology. Many businesses emphasizing personal service will continue well into the future, and many customers will reward them with their patronage. A large part of the successful Barnes & Noble strategy has been to market both the reading experience and the highly pleasurable experience of shopping in a fine bookstore. To book lovers or even casual readers, this experience is more than a purchase of a disposable item. Often books remain in a home for years, a part of the decor and a reflection of the tastes of the people who live there.

The superstore concept is built around offering a large selection and heavily discounted prices, but it is also built on presenting the *atmosphere* of the store: well lit, with comfortable chairs and tables, an atmosphere that encourages customers to come in and stay a while, listen to the music, peruse the shelves, have a cup of coffee, and sample the merchandise without cost or obligation. An attitude that welcomes customers is one that keeps them coming back.

Some customers don't like to leave home. They would rather watch television than go out to the movies. Movie studios respond to this by making "made-for-TV" movies and by cycling theater films to TV after their big-screen and video interest declines. Not conceding that on-line segment of the market, Barnes & Noble's strategy is to aggressively promote its Barnes & Noble.com as an alternative to Amazon.com (as well as to the separately operated Barnes & Noble retail locations). But for the book lovers who want to touch the bindings, flip through the pages, have a cup of coffee or tea, and enjoy the bookstore experience, the store offers a place to go to meet authors, to relax surrounded by walls of thousands of handsomely packaged volumes, and to be on the same side of the screen as the printed word.

Future Marketing Prediction

There is a reason that Barnes & Noble has grown so successful among booksellers. It was neither the first bookstore nor the first successful chain of bookstores. It was not the first place where books were offered at discount prices in warm, comfortable surroundings. What it does very well is to put a superb marketing combination together: price, quality, image, courtesy, service, nice atmosphere, hundreds of convenient locations, a mail-order service.... But most important, it watched and listened and gave book lovers what they wanted. There are those who get excited about shopping for anything on-line, and Barnes & Noble is there too. Its future prospects are good if the company stays true to what it does well and does not abandon its loyal base. It got the better of its competitors by offering them more in products and services. As competition increases, it cannot afford to coast. On-site activities (meeting authors, having books signed, participating in reading groups) build brand loyalty. B&N knows this. It just has to remember it.

Barbie

Marketers follow the trends, and when the marketers are very good and very lucky, they *start* trends. Each year, the media turn their attention to "this year's hot toy." Children and toys are of course synonymous. For as far back as anyone can remember, it has been almost ritual at certain stages of life to desperately hope for a bike, skates, a playhouse, a magic set, a chemistry set, a doctor's bag, a musical instrument, sports equipment. . . .

But it is only a recent phenomenon that one particular toy gets the star treatment each year and is the lead story on the evening news during the year-end holiday season. Whatever the designated object, stores run out of it. Morning news shows post listings of places that still have it. Members of the public call the media with information on who may have the item available. People log on to the Internet, putting out a call, pleading, offering to pay double, triple, 10 times (!) the manufacturer's suggested list price for a Cabbage Patch doll, a Mighty Morphin Power Ranger, a Tickle-Me-Elmo, a Furby. . . . And several weeks after the holidays, the search for the next big "this year's hot toy" begins again.

On cue, most marketers rush to their booths at the trade shows, issue their press releases, and dispatch their spokespeople to the media and retail outlets, each chanting enthusiastically about how great the item is and how much kids love it. And then they pray.

Above all this sits Barbie on her pink throne, outfitted to make any starlet at the Academy Awards presentation envious.

In 1999, Barbie turned 40, but she doesn't look it. Every inch of her 12″ plastic body is in perfect shape, trim and curvaceous, at times rendering her the object of scorn by feminist groups, who charged she was *unfit* to serve as the role model of what little girls would look like when they grew up.

Few women look like Barbie, that is true. Barbie's face, figure, wardrobe, and accessories—from her mansion to her beach house, helicopter, airplane, horses, and cars—could upstage the most self-indulgent rock star. Barbie may be the ultimate "material girl in a material world." But through the years, whether she had one outfit or a change for all occasions, little girls all over the world loved her.

Little girls have had favorite dolls for as long as anyone can remember—Tiny Tears, Betsy Wetsy—but Barbie has outlived and outlasted them all, along the way being a brand-extension machine with a seemingly unlimited number of additions and extensions to the line in books, clothes, music, and still more toys. Barbie is a franchise and a fantasy. How did she get there, and more important to marketers, how does she *stay* there?

Barbie was the creation of a mom, who, while watching her young daughter at play, noticed that the child had the most fun dressing and undressing her dolls, putting them in different outfits so they could go to different places and engage in a variety of activities. She thought it was so simple. Kids love to play "dress-up." The child didn't need a new doll for each new moment of make-believe; her doll just needed a new outfit. The same lift that an adult experiences upon buying a new outfit or accessory is what the child experienced when her doll got something new. The delight was often even beyond that of getting something new, since the article *improved upon* a favorite toy.

The strategy has been to offer the doll—"My First Barbie"—at a very low price, affordable to most family budgets. Accessories are then priced at all levels, from inexpensive T-shirts and sporty outfits and equipment to the most elegant, higher-priced, (literally) designer-label clothes. Barbie could mirror each child's own life or fantasy. With the right accessories, she could be a schoolgirl, a rock star, an airline pilot, a dentist, a movie star, a ballerina, a hairdresser, or the owner of a pet shop. The strategy gave the child a friend and a fantasy world and kept on giving. As a child's interests change, Barbie is ready to change with her.

New friends are regularly introduced for Barbie and are representative of various races, ages, and ethnic groups. Yet, the basic strategy has remained the same for more than 40 years. To mark the toy's 40th anniversary, a TV spot showed young girls imagining they could "Be anything—a princess, queen of the ocean, or soccer champion of the universe." The Barbie doll itself appears only briefly in the ad. As a Mattel Toys ad agency spokesperson told *Advertising Age*, "We're trying to show that Barbie is about dreams and empowerment and letting little girls aspire to something."

There is software for kids to design their own Barbie clothes on the family PC and to create the patterns to make them.

The cuddly, lovable, huggable, homely Cabbage Patch Kids, along with Power Rangers and Pokémon, each moved on at the end of the season, but Barbie simply changed her clothes and began a new adventure.

Future Marketing Prediction

With apologies to feminists, Barbie has "legs." Sales may dip from time to time, but this little plastic beauty has shown that she's got staying power. While the basic look of the doll has remained the same for decades, the appeal to several generations of children has been in the fact that Barbie has outfits and accessories to go along with any interest a child may have, from being an astronaut or a gymnast, a rock star or a dentist, to a teacher or a mom. That freshness and versatility have kept the toy from becoming dated. Barbie is on-line for kids with computers and in very inexpensive coloring books and storybooks sold on drugstore magazine racks and aimed at the youngest of children—perhaps even too young for the doll. "Collectible" Barbie dolls (such as Scarlet O'Hara and characters from Broadway shows) are priced high and are being bought by women who received their first Barbie doll decades ago. That marketers have created a Barbie link to various interests, ages, and incomes suggests a strategy that should hold until the first gray-haired Barbie appears around 2039. It is to the brand's credit that it understands each generation of children looks for something a little different, while keeping its core traditions intact. As technology becomes more a part of a child's world, Barbie's great strength is being there to hold.

American Girl

A woman with the pleasant-sounding name Pleasant T. Rowland had an idea. She also had a daughter. The idea that found its market in the late 1980s was this: create a doll that a young girl could *enjoy*. These were not the Barbie escapist fantasies of rock stars, Malibu, or the glamorous life, nor the cuddly, crying baby dolls with bottles and diapers. Rowland's creations would be "American Girls" and as such would have stories as interesting, colorful, meaningful, and rich as America is in a child's eyes.

The first four dolls are each set in a time of great events in America's history, and each has a library of six books that tell her story. Felicity (1774) is

Presenting American Girls and Their Girls

First dolls then doll clothes, accessories, books, buttons, computer software and games, and, ultimately, a line of high-quality children's clothing from bathrobes and pajamas to school clothes, jackets, and caps that allow little girls and their dolls to have matching wardrobes. It's a brand marketing idea based on total involvement and identification between product and consumer, and it's working. (Photograph by Karin Gottschalk Marconi)

the "spunky, spritely colonial girl"; Kirsten (1854) is "a pioneer girl of strength and spirit"; Samantha (1904) is "a bright Victorian beauty"; and Molly (1944) is a wartime "lovable schemer and dreamer." Later, Josephina (1824), "an Hispanic girl of heart and hope," and Addy (1864), a "courageous girl of the Civil War," were added.

Each doll is 18″ high and features a soft cloth body, poseable arms and legs, and a head made of vinyl with hair that seems real. Another doll, the "American Girl of Today," could be chosen with hair color, eyes, and skin tone close to that of the child herself, making the doll look like a little sister or another member of the family.

A doll and a book or series of books is not exactly revolutionary. What makes the American Girl line different is that, at nearly $100 each, the dolls are pricier than those that most children of average-income families would be getting. Also, the "stories" of each of the "girls'" lives are well constructed and educational and provide a vivid history of America in its time. Each doll has its own line of clothes and accessories representative of the period, and matching clothes are available for girls so the child and doll can dress alike.

Rowland describes her philosophy as celebrating a history that links the child to the long, proud tradition of American girls through the generations.

Except for one American Girl retail store, opened in Chicago in 1997, all merchandise is available only by catalog—an elegantly done catalog that offers a child a doll, a fantasy, and a learning experience. And quality.

Soon the line expanded to include backpacks, school supplies, additional lines of books, a monthly magazine, a CD of music, computer software for creating original American Girl plays, stationery sets, a scrapbook of trading cards, and calendars.

Each item reflects the theme, is somehow educational, and looks like fun. As with many other successful products, the American Girl line of merchandise—dolls, clothes, books, accessories—does not promote a single-item, one-time sale, but a catalog of related items that invite a child to become a part of the American Girl experience. It's much like what Disney has done for generations with the Mickey Mouse Club, where a child's enthusiastic acceptance of an invitation to enter that world makes the child receptive to a seemingly endless array of must-have merchandise.

Because the American Girl line includes products of such visibly high quality, safety, and educational merit, every angle makes parents feel better about supporting the child's serious, if slightly expensive, interests. The children's clothing is stylish, also well made, and priced comparable to other quality brands.

In the late 1990s, Mattel (makers of Barbie) bought the Pleasant Company, and many industry observers feared the American Girl brand would slip and become overcommercialized. By the turn of the century, it appeared as though the opposite has happened. Mattel seemed to be retaining the discriminating look and standard of the American Girl brand.

As noted earlier, Walt Disney reportedly said that everything with the Disney name should both educate and entertain. The success of American Girl establishes that such a notion can still exist in the 21st century and, moreover, that a large segment of the public is willing to pay a premium price for it.

Future Marketing Prediction

American Girl has the potential of being to young girls what Brooks Brothers symbolizes in adult clothing: not so much a designer brand, but a quality label that speaks well of its owner. The brand's great strength is in maintaining its position that it is not for everybody, but is stylish, pricey, and educational. As the product matures, a finely targeted and carefully orchestrated campaign to new mothers, recalling the pleasure they experienced from their own American Girl dolls and accessories, seems like a logical strategy. The quality of the merchandise will appeal to generous gift-giving grandparents as well.

Beanie Babies

If you ever doubt that fads are created and do not just develop out of incidental interest, look no further than Ty Inc.'s Beanie Babies. These little palm-size creatures are cuddly, adorable, collectible, valuable, and as spontaneous an occurrence in popular culture as broccoli.

In 1993, one of the toy industries' surprise sensations was launched. From their modest rollout in gift shops, no one could have predicted how enormously popular Beanie Babies would become only a few years later. True, some folks are still scratching their heads in wonder over the success of the hula hoop—the simple plastic ring that, through masterful marketing, created a sensation in 1958. Wham-O manufactured and sold some 25 million units that year, at $1.98 each.

Year after year since then, the toy industry has been watching for something as simple and inexpensive and equally phenomenal.

Beanie Babies come close, looking something like a cross between a simple little beanbag and a sock puppet. The actual "beans" are a mix of fiberfill and polyvinyl chloride pellets. The first characters introduced were cute, colorful, and priced under $5.00 list and came with adorable puppet names such as Chocolate the Moose, Legs the Frog, Patty the Platypus, and Splash the Whale.

Created by Ty Warner, a toy industry veteran, Beanie Babies appeared with no advertising, but that is not to suggest they are not marketed. The "official" line is that the product skyrocketed to popularity on word-of-mouth advertising. This particular form of word of mouth is regularly accompanied by stories pitched to all major media, touting the product as the hottest new product around.

Every media outlet worth its salt is regularly bombarded with such claims for a wide array of undistinguished products. They are mostly ignored. Occasionally, however, one gets through, and someone runs with the story, only to have it take on a life of its own. While each media organization's members like to pretend that they don't even look at the competing media, much less take story ideas from them . . . they do. *All the time.*

It is almost like a chain letter, with a piece on a given subject appearing in either *Newsweek*, *People*, the *Chicago Tribune*, the *New York Times*, or the *Wall Street Journal* and finding its way to one or more of the others fast. And these media got the message that Beanie Babies were hot.

Who put out that message?

Certainly not the manufacturer of Beanie Babies. That would spoil the myth. Quickly a group of suburban homemakers began telling the media how they had gone on-line to trade Beanie Babies around the world and how very collectible they are. The *Today Show*, America's top-rated morning news program, picked up the story, and that was all that was needed to give credibility to the premise that Beanie Babies were the new sensation.

On the Internet, clubs continue trying to keep interest and prices high, as "collectors" plead for certain Beanie Babies that are needed to complete their collections and that could not be ordered from retailers because according to the retailers, (1) Ty is shipping only what it wants to ship—demand has been so strong that special orders are rarely accepted, and phone calls to the company are unanswered, and (2) Ty has "retired" certain of the early Beanie Babies and announced plans to systematically and rapidly retire others, thus increasing their value to collectors.

"Unauthorized" Beanie Babies magazines, price guides, and collector's manuals seem to be everywhere, with about a dozen in print. Favorite-sports-team Beanie Babies, a "Princess Diana" commemorative Beanie Baby, and numerous special limited-issue Beanies have been introduced for a limited time. A "mini" Beanie Baby series was offered exclusively at McDonald's, where customers literally were lined up around the parking lot at many locations, and sales of "Happy Meals," which included the toy, took a healthy spike.

How much of the Beanie Babies sensation is merely an *illusion* of excitement, fueled by the Internet rumors and by calculated announcements of sales of certain Beanie Babies for astronomical amounts, is the subject of some controversy.

More than many other new product launches, Beanie Babies' introduction seemed to be based on "buzz"—the hottest toy for under $5.00 and highly collectible; and certain "retired" Beanie Babies are selling for more than 100 times their original prices. And the consumers, eager for their collections to increase in value, seem to be cheering the company on.

No less impressive a tactic on two accounts was the company's announcement in September 1999 on its website that, on December 31, 1999, at 11:59 P.M. (CST) all Beanies would be retired. It was and is impressive because, first, no one believed the announcement. That a company that was known for virtually nothing else would up and pull the plug on its most important product seemed absurd. Second, customers didn't seem to care that the company was flipping them off.

Ty has successfully marketed Beanie Babies not with advertising, but with the strategic releasing of statements and rumors and coordinating Internet activities to appear as if it were all amateur driven. As the product begins to run out of steam, rather than adding more varied products, advertising, or in any way moving to protect and bolster the company's inventory and assets, Ty simply says, that's it.

Advertising Age summarized the development in an editorial titled "Bad Beanie." It read, in part: "We expected to uncover the stirrings of a consumer backlash to toy maker Ty's brazenly manipulative marketing ploy. Instead analysts and observers were quick to applaud the brilliance of Ty Warner's brief and mysterious announcement . . .

"Savvy consumers instantly identified the announcement as pure marketing, then strangely walked right through the trap. . . . We can't help noting our surprise that Ty's calculated move didn't backfire in its face."

As some would say, the whole thing is "just so '90s."

Greed and cynicism seem to be driving both Ty and its customers. Ty wants to generate greater interest in its products. The public, in this instance,

These Toys Aren't Playing Around

Beanie Babies were originally introduced as toys, but quickly became collectibles and, as such, became more important to acquire and collect than for children to play with. After a highly successful run as the "toy du jour"—a must-have for child and parent alike—prices soared and interest declined, affecting the branded item's staying power as either a plaything or a collectible. A less-contrived campaign to focus on the enjoyment of the product and not its resale value might have extended the life of the brand. (Photograph by Karin Gottschalk Marconi)

is made up of people who have collections and do not want to see them devalued.

The dust has settled somewhat, and the casual collectors have moved on. Those who remain are fiercely loyal to Ty because they have interests to protect.

Without a doubt, Beanie Babies will be regarded as among the most successful new products of the late 1990s. Just as doubtless, they will be relegated to the list of fads that were never regarded as serious products with staying power at any time during their cycle of popularity. The product did, however, achieve significant success in the area of return on investment. It was cheap to make, and little was invested in its marketing. It is noteworthy for having been introduced as a toy that was virtually never played with but that quickly became a success as a collectible. This is a time in popular culture when "collectibles" become collectible unto themselves. Stamp collectors and coin collectors really want the stamps and coins, but many collectors of Beanie Babies seem to be interested more in amassing the entire collection or specific-named issues than in having what the individual item represents.

Ty Inc. also distinguishes itself as a savvy manufacturer and marketer that subscribes to the take-the-money-and-run philosophy, angering retailers and showing an overt indifference to customers. The company's attempts at goodwill quickly fell apart as its invitation to join a "Beanie Baby Club" resulted in months of delay in processing requests. The company does, however, now have a database of die-hard toy collectors. It is reasonable to assume that these people will be receiving something soon in the mail.

Beanie Babies are a huge success, but many who have been touched by the experience would not be disappointed if they did not have to deal with Ty Inc. ever again.

Future Marketing Prediction

It is possible for lightning to strike twice in the same place. A "Beanie Babies—Back by Popular Demand!" event can easily serve as a relaunch, and Internet-fueled rumors of high collector's prices could well give the brand a second life. The product, however, having plummeted in interest since its apparent peak in 1998, doesn't have legs, and the customers, while they of course care about the value of their collections, have no loyalty to the product or the company. What will continue to fascinate is the example set here of a manufacturer so blatantly trying to manipulate both its customers and its product's resale value, while customers reacted with indifference. If this becomes the rule and not the exception, marketers are going to have to rethink all they thought they knew about principles of good marketing. As marketing case histories go, this one can be compared to a child's trip to the circus. The child might not have enjoyed it much, but if the drum is loud enough and the popcorn smells fresh, the kid may go back again.

HBO

Cable television operators face a mighty challenge. Research indicates that the public at large believes there is precious little on TV that is worth watching. Cable operators must persuade those same people to pay a monthly fee to receive even *more* channels of programs they think they don't want to see.

And for an *additional* fee on top of that, they can receive a premium channel, such as HBO.

HBO stands for "Home Box Office." Arguably the best known of cable TV's premium channels, it was originally positioned and pitched to be the viewer's home box office—the location on the TV remote where major motion pictures could be seen uncut, without commercials, without interruptions. As time went by, however, it became more difficult to interest the public in seeing major motion pictures on HBO for $7 or $8 per month when a video of the same film could be rented for a dollar.

The answer? Supplement the uncut, uninterrupted films with *original* movies and programs of a type that "free TV" would never program, such as uncut comedy specials in which anything could be said or done, free of both commercials and censorship; top performers in concert; and exclusive championship sports events. It worked.

Cable subscribers pay additional monthly fees to get the uncut movies, along with award-winning shows starring "cutting-edge" creative performers such as Tracey Ullman and Garry Shandling, popular dramatic series such as *The Sopranos* (a series that was reportedly turned down by major broadcast networks, which regarded it as "too hot"), championship boxing, and, for kids, episodes of *Dear America*, a series based on the bestselling children's books.

Presenting material regarded as "too hot" or "too arty" or "too intellectual" for the TV networks is a solid point of differentiation—a reason, according to HBO publicists, why people should be willing or prepared to "pay extra" for "premium" entertainment.

And then, there is that great slogan and positioning statement all in one: "It's not TV. It's HBO."

The public watches a lot of TV, so give the public what it wants. But the public tells the researchers that it doesn't feel good about TV, so call what you're giving people something else, and play up the aspects of it that they have told you they like. The HBO line is arrogant or deceptive only if the public perceives that what was promised is not what is delivered. Based on the numbers, the public is satisfied with what it's getting from HBO, whether it is TV or not.

Future Marketing Prediction

As the competition gets tougher and every channel becomes more familiar, HBO will come to be regarded as TV again. It is probably a mistake that the brand is being fragmented to expand to at least four channels. A mansion becomes less special when three others just like it rise up on the same block. As long as it can accentuate programming that is on the "creative edge," it can maintain its niche. As other cable channels begin to copy the success-ful strategies of the winners, HBO stays ahead with innovative program-ming. NBC, after all, didn't fully own Thursday-night TV audiences and call itself "Must-see TV" until it had been on the air for 50 years. Despite offer-ing some children's programming and some sports (mostly big-event box-ing), HBO has targeted baby boomers. As the boomers age, the channel risks erosion of its largest audience segment. Generationally, its movie schedule is likely to draw the same audience demographic it attracted in movie theaters.

IKEA

Right from the start, IKEA has been something of a maverick brand by American standards. Its innovations are handled with such an air of casual dispatch as to be worth noticing. Not many giant U.S. retailers provide free child care while its customers shop.

As for marketing, the company broke a guiding rule early on: its name is awkward to pronounce, as well as being a newly minted word. In addi-tion, it sounds Japanese to at least a segment of the market. It's not. It's Swedish. The problem isn't one of attitudes about nationalism, but rather one of tastes; IKEA is in the business of home furnishing and accessories, in which Swedish and Japanese styles reflect distinctly different tastes.

While these irregularities can be overcome by good marketing, it means that two obstacles have been placed in the path of the brand even before the journey begins.

In fairness, these are considered marketing missteps from the American perspective only. IKEA operates more than 150 stores in some 29 countries, and the hitch is not a serious one on a global level, since foreign companies are expected to have foreign sounding names. Yet, it illustrates the challenge that a company or brand faces as it moves into markets where it may be regarded as distinctly foreign. Does the company emphasize the distinction, exploit it, and *market* it, or does it go in the opposite direction of generic, mainstream simplicity?

The answer depends on the company and the brand. French wine or perfume, Swiss chocolate or watches, German automobiles, and numerous other products have benefited from being synonymous with a history of innovation or quality.

IKEA's position is much like the one that dealers in luxury automobiles have held for years. That is, once the prospective customer sits in the car, the sale is almost made. Customers in IKEA stores experience a sense of amazement, wonder, and for the most part, approval. The challenge is in getting people into the stores, one not uncommon in retailing. To accomplish this, the brand's strategy must become more of a "from-the-outside-in" effort, rather than "marketing from the inside out."

Most members of the general public in America, if they know IKEA at all, know it as a very large store . . . sort of.

But what *kind* of a store? A furniture store . . . that has day care . . . and serves Swedish meatballs.

IKEA strongly reflects the persona of its founder, Ingvar Kamprad, a man of strong opinions and vision, whose mission was to create "a better everyday life for the majority of people." The *I* and the *K* in the company's name represent its founder's initials; the *E* is for Elmtaryd, the farm in Sweden where he was born, and the *A* is for the village of Agunnaryd, where he grew up. Such a highly personalized brand identification would be worthy of Donald Trump. To a marketer, it is an area of some distinction: each IKEA store is a huge place, yet tied to the personal sense and vision of its founder and to a visible concern for the environment.

A description of the 411,000-square-foot facility outside of Chicago offers that the store is so large that it "could hold 961 million Swedish meatballs, 576 million ABBA CDs, and 8 million pairs of Nike Air Jordans."

The lighter touch is a friendly, welcoming message to present to new customers.

Getting down to serious business, IKEA says its aim is to be more than a giant furniture store. Gallery owner and design historian Jim Walrod called its designs "exactly what modernist furniture is supposed to be about—introducing good design into everyone's life, not just the rich." He added, "These principles have been in place since the Bauhaus movement but don't always work out due to the high costs of manufacturing. IKEA is the only mass-market company who figured out how to make it work."

With design experts telling its story and helping to set it apart from its competition, IKEA positions its message to consumers of discriminating tastes at a variety of price levels.

Beginning as a mail-order operation, IKEA opened its first warehouse showroom in Sweden in 1953, and growth has been steady. The company has become more closely identified with its products' sense of style and design at affordable prices. But IKEA has distinguished itself by successfully marketing what it describes as "an *attitude*, a mix of free spirit individualism, while operating out of a vast warehouse/showroom and catering to the masses."

In most situations, an attitude is not good for business. Here, it seems to work to the advantage of the company and the brand.

The very fact that a brand would attempt to project an image that is almost a contradiction in terms seemed to connect with the public in the 1990s. Unlike other retailers, the sheer size of its typical facility precludes a master plan for an IKEA store in every mall, but that also is clearly to the brand's advantage. Part of its appeal is being worth the trip of perhaps some distance to see and experience an IKEA property.

An Internet presence seems to be a requirement of the times, but visiting a website cannot replicate the feeling a customer gets by being in the actual facility. The ambience is upbeat. Additionally, no other retailer as yet has managed to master serving Swedish meatballs in the quantities IKEA delivers from its in-store restaurants. It will be a while before that happens on-line . . . at least, while they're still hot.

Future Marketing Prediction

IKEA's strength is that it is a nontraditional retail store, not the typical furniture store, nor a mainstream department store, at a time when the

Pages of Life and Home

Putting a contemporary brand image on a variation of the traditional "women's magazine," IKEA introduced a full-color, oversized magazine to explain, promote, and share its message of finely designed furnishings for the home, environmental concern . . . and appreciation of Swedish meatballs. It's virtually a newsstand version of a catalog, brand-oriented, yet stylish enough to find an audience. (Copyright 1999 IKEA Systems BV) market environment favors mavericks and outsiders. Usually, retailers get into problems when they become so big (Sears, Wal-Mart) that they lose their connection to their base and can no longer feel the pulse of their core customers. IKEA can remain successful as long as it stays in touch with that base, maintaining its uniqueness and not trying to be everybody's store for everything . . . with the possible exception of the Swedish meatballs. The marketing advantage has been IKEA's "outside of the mainstream" image. Such a position is difficult to maintain as success grows.

Starbucks

Starbucks is another in the familiar handful of examples (Microsoft, Amazon.com, Martha Stewart) that the marketplace holds up as displaying "outside-the-box" innovation and image marketing. It is one of a small number of brands that, from its launch, has been represented almost more as an experience than as a product. The company literally repositions an extremely common core product and offers it as the centerpiece of a lifestyle image that extends well beyond coffee.

Of course, the idea of "having coffee together" has long been associated with socializing as well as with some of life's more meaningful moments. This is central to the Starbucks image. The coffee bar is a place to go for a conversation, after a walk or a date, or just to meet or to meditate. It is less beverage, more experience, and the more significant the moment, the greater the importance of having Starbucks and its products as a part of the moment.

Marketers who start with coffee might be expected to have as a goal taking away market share from Folgers, Maxwell House, or Taster's Choice. Not this time. In fact, the Starbucks name didn't make its first appearance among those other brands on store shelves until more than a quarter century after its introduction. Rather, Starbucks was to become to coffee what *Playboy* was to magazines: a new version of a product that created a place in its class so distinctive that it has become a class unto itself.

While Starbucks's introduction was in 1971, the company's serious marketing strategy didn't evolve for a dozen years or so. The coffee bars that offered unique blends of very strong coffee (at about three times the average price of a cup) in an atmosphere designed with young upscale urban professionals in mind, had grown to 17 stores in 1987. By the end of 2000, the company's goal was appropriately 2,000 locations.

One might ask if the brand's success led or followed the cultural revolution. Members of both the baby boomer generation (at each end of its long spectrum) and Generation X were ready to enjoy the finer things: fine wines, fine clothes, fine homes and cars in which style and status are equal to functionality. In that environment, the idea of a special type of meeting place or a "stopping" place seems right.

More important, if that place sends a message that the person stopping could afford the price of a very special premium-grade cup of coffee, so much the better. The distinctive paper cup with the bright, artful green Starbucks logo carries the message along.

It is the right premium product at the right premium price at a time when a particular group of consumers need help in defining themselves.

Taking home a pound of beans to grind and serve to guests later—with a nod and a mention, "It's Starbucks"—extends the brand and the point, as well as the image. Later, coffee mugs, biscotti, even a CD of music selected on the basis of sophistication and demographic appeal, were added as a nice (and very profitable) accompaniment. These items are brand extensions that help to set the tone, even among non–coffee drinkers. It is a tribute to Starbucks's creativity that virtually every added branded product is an *existing* product that has simply been repositioned within the brand's own image field.

In 1999, the first issue of *Joe*, the company's lifestyle magazine, debuted to good notices and very good sales. Starbucks, the image-lifestyle coffee, now had a slick coffee-table magazine that could be visible all the time, even while the coffeemaker and mugs are being rinsed, keeping the image and the brand out front. Alas, customers didn't like having to pay for the "house magazine" and the publication folded after a few issues. The concept was solid enough that the book will likely return in a more modest format.

A cold coffee beverage, Frappuccino, was introduced and marketed through supermarkets as a way of putting the Starbucks brand and image in homes and lives during the hot days of summer, when coffee consumption throughout the day is down. It is no surprise that the product did not receive a warm response (sorry). The Starbucks *experience* isn't the same when a bottled beverage is taken from the refrigerator. A separate line of beans and ground coffee (not the same varieties sold in the Starbucks coffee bar locations) has done better in supermarket sales because, when the coffee is prepared at home, the brand's image is transferable, albeit seriously lacking the carefully considered surroundings that the coffee bar provides.

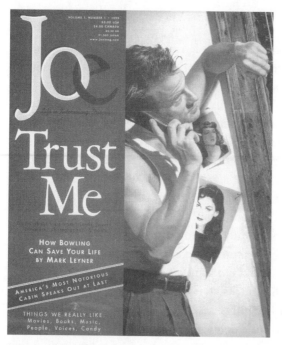

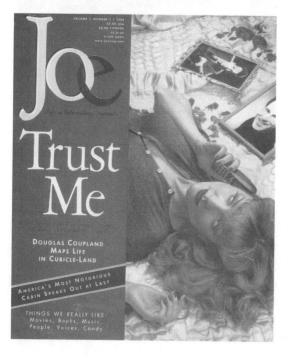

Words to Set the Style

The first issue of Star-bucks's coffee-table maga-zine *Joe* came with a choice of covers—one pic-tured a woman, one pic-tured a man. Both sold very well in the company's coffee house locations. Starbucks created a new market with pricey designer coffees, serving pieces, rich desserts, and "upscale fast food," all pro-moting the brand, as much a symbol of a young, good life as it was of coffee. The magazine was simply a wrap-around packaging for the total brand image. Although well-received, it was discontinued after only a few issues. Customers seemed to think it should have been "free to read" with coffee, as other mag-azines are available in wait-ing rooms. It is likely a vehicle this smart will reap-pear in some form. (*Joe* is copyrighted 1999 Starbucks Coffee Company and Time Inc. Custom Publishing)

The serving and consumption is a Starbucks *moment,* or *experience.* No one was interested in having an at-home "Frappuccino experience."

Starbucks CEO Howard Schultz has indicated his hope to use the Internet for Starbucks to create the "premier lifestyle portal on the Internet—a place that offers a feeling of romance and relaxation" and, according to a *Newsweek* report, "an amalgam of storefronts at which to buy not just overpriced coffee, but overpriced kitchenware, home furnishings, and gourmet food."

This is where the strategy may get a little shaky. The success that Starbucks enjoys has come from its ability to extend the value of its own brand and image in a line of related items that have no comparable brand in the marketplace. To enter areas where others are already recognized as the standard of quality has it "coattailing" the image of another established brand. The market is heavy with E-retailers and merchandisers. Buying a coffee table from Starbucks on the Internet somehow doesn't have the same magical ring.

Future Marketing Prediction

There are a lot of products that Starbucks can add to its menu that are logical extensions of its successful core products and extend the Starbucks experience. As in the IKEA example, on-site or on-line, it can be a great specialty store or a mediocre department store. A certain arrogance comes with success. People don't go to an ice cream parlor to buy carpeting. So, when asking customers what they would like to see added or what else they would like, it's a good idea to keep it within the scope of reason, or at least within the brand's own image-identity range. Starbucks can offer accessories for entertaining and a line of specialty foods. As a lifestyle experience, it doesn't need to redo the closets or the garage. By sticking to what it does best, it has the strongest chance of growing and holding its base. It must also be sensitive to the aging of its core customer base. As boomers and Gen Xers grow older, will they still be drinking so much Tall Mocha Cappacino? Tracking tastes trends as generations age will have a lot to do with Starbucks's future.

Summary Points

1. Marketers must not only be tuned in to the latest (or emerging) trends but also to market *cycles*. The future will produce many new flavors-of-the-month, but those that survive to become the choice of the next generation will do so because of solid research and planning—of providing steak with the sizzle—and because they listened to the voice of the market.

2. In the 1960s almost any company with "tronics" on the end of its name was considered hot. In the '90s, anything with "dot-com" looked like a winner. It takes more than that to succeed.

3. All of the casebook examples have experienced being hot, but as trends fade and cycles change, the brands that position their core products and services as having the *perception of quality and value* will survive to see the next cycle. Those that simply exploit the trend of the moment or that expand into product lines that aren't logical extensions of what they do, will not.

4. To date, the big on-line success stories in retailing are the companies that would have enjoyed success through traditional direct marketing methods. The Internet is a great electronic catalog of products, services, and features for persons who prefer to shop or otherwise do business without leaving their desks.

5. Whether on-line or on-site, businesses and brands that present a warm and welcoming image will more likely win brand loyalty in the 21st century, much as brands did in centuries past. Time and technology haven't changed the principles of what works in business.

6. There have always been (and probably always will be) novelty items that break out from the pack and are hugely successful beyond all expectations. They take advantage of their moment in the spotlight with little regard for creating goodwill in the marketplace or real brand loyalty. If your objective is to have a hot product and then take the money and run, it still can happen in certain circumstances. But brand equity and brand loyalty continue to result from providing both value and the *perception* of value. That usually means demonstrating a concern for your customers and your market.

7. A good marketing plan with a strong image message can convince some people that a cup of coffee (Starbucks) or a doll (American Girl) is worth many times the cost of apparently similar products offered by hundreds of competitors. Such occurrences support the case for creating a strong brand image.

8. It is important in maintaining the uniqueness of a brand's image that it not "oversaturate." HBO is unique for what it offers among cable television networks. Four separate HBO channels, offering basically the same content, is not unique and diminishes the power of the brand.

12

21st-Century Media

How the Internet, Cable and Satellite TV, Specialty Print, and Direct Marketing Have Changed the Media and Changed the Rules

The Cybernaut generation is intrinsically anarchistic, endlessly antiauthoritarian and hates corporate America.
Therefore, this is not an ad for Coke.
We repeat, this is not an ad for Coke.
—a 1996 ad for Coke

A WORD THAT marketers like to use nearly as often as *change* is *revolution*. Hyperbole is among the biggest and most used hammers in the marketing toolbox. So we have the technology revolution, the marketing revolution, the media revolution, and a couple of others that the Beatles hadn't anticipated in their hit song—which has been licensed for use in a number of commercials.

Would the so-called revolution in marketing and media not have taken place without the millennium? It just seemed like such a natural link—a perfect fit. Some people may even suspect that marketers actually created the millennium as a marketing opportunity. But to phrase the question differently, could such dramatic changes have occurred in 1994? Or *1984*?

Of course. And some *did*.

In marketing, the old expression that "timing is everything" is just that: *an old expression*. When the big idea comes, it is rushed to market—alas, sometimes before it is fully matured. An exciting new product such as Apple Computer's Newton, the powerbook that was supposed to do practically everything but the dinner dishes, was overpromoted, overpromised, and born prematurely. Hence, it was dismissed as being too light.

In another case, the richest man in the world's first public presentation and demonstration of Windows 98 software brought to mind images of a high school kid from the AV Club who could never seem to get the movie projector to work. Likewise, countless TV programs have gone on the air before they were ready and looked like it. To pull a show for "some tinkering" or "retooling" after much hype should make some people feel very ashamed, if they are not already beyond that.

Ready, Steady, Go

The fact is that by the year 2000, the market and the public were ready: they wanted *something revolutionary*. Technology had been promising something big for a long time and so far had gotten only about as far as freeze-dried coffee and microwave ovens (which were being used largely for reheating leftovers). Over the years various combinations were tested, using telephones and computers, phone lines and cable TV, satellites, fax machines, pagers, and cameras. The Internet had been around for more than a decade before there seemed to be enough personal computers, modems, sites, and more specifically, *interest*, to justify calling it an "Internet explosion."

Great old magazines that had become American institutions, such as *Look* and the *Post*, folded for lack of interest. By 2000, specialty or "custom" magazines captured the attention of the public as companion products to computers, cigars, coffee, and, not just toys, but *specific* toys.

Once again, the magazine business is flourishing. Publishers are not trying to reach everyone, but only those with very particular interests, who are themselves of interest to very particular advertisers, publicists, and marketers. Similar vehicles had been launched decades earlier and went largely unnoticed. Was the presentation not as good then, or was the market simply not ready for it—not preconditioned enough? No one can say for sure.

Direct marketing is no longer junk mail—it is both serious and respectable.

Cable and satellite TV, after a clumsy, much-hyped introduction, have changed the way people watch television. After decades of telling researchers how much they detest commercials, millions of people sit watching the Home Shopping Network—24 hours of uninterrupted advertising—until they go to their phones to order the merchandise before it vanishes from the screen.

Infomercials—program-length commercials running as faux game shows, newscasts, or talk shows—draw larger audiences than many "real" programs.

Again, it is a matter of convergence. The audience is ready, the technology is ready, the start of the 21st century meant the marketplace is ready for a change, and . . . the revolution has begun.

What this means and will continue to mean to marketers is channels, pages, and mailboxes full of opportunities. It also means realistic expectations. There is a reason why a commercial minute on Bravo costs less than a minute on CBS during any day part. There is a reason an ad in *ESPN the Magazine* costs less than an ad in *Sports Illustrated*. And there is a reason why your publicist can get your expert opinions on almost any program on MSNBC more easily than on *Good Morning America* or the *Today Show* or on *Oprah*.

The reason is audience size and demographic makeup. What is important to recognize, however, is that if your product is jeans or skin-care treatments for teens, MTV or VH-1 may be not only a more targeted buy but also a far less expensive one than most broadcast networks in the same day part.

This information has not escaped the TV networks, independent stations, other cable channels, and pretty much all other media. Rate wars and combination buys are more frequent and only likely to be more so in the foreseeable future.

And as combinations go, practically no video venue ends a program without a pitch to "check out our website," from ABC to C-SPAN. Practically none of the sites are adfree, and most are hungry for fresh contact. Publicists who used to wine and dine producers and editors for a placement now find a welcome parking space on the information superhighway. The challenge there is getting people to stop for a look. And to seasoned marketers, *challenge* is another word for *opportunity*.

TV: Turning On the Big Knob

For years, the three major U.S. television networks had been warned that cable would change things. They would not have a monopoly for long. Ratings and ad rates would change. And, as was the case in other industries, where giants such as Xerox, IBM, and General Motors refused to take aggressive upstart challengers seriously, the networks slept. As with other giants noted, this proved to be a mistake. What should have sounded a warning bell to the networks was the success of VCRs in the mid-1970s—the home videocassette recorders that provided people the ability to tape a show for later viewing at their own convenience (and then fast-forward, skipping the commercials).

Then came the creation of a fourth TV network, the Fox Network, by Rupert Murdoch's News Corporation, which found almost instant success in the 1980s by programming almost exclusively to a younger, niche audience. After a couple of shaky seasons, the young network began attracting and keeping younger viewers. The critics who had earlier dismissed Fox as a long shot now acknowledge that it just might have found a niche with younger, "edgier" comedy shows and programs such as *A Current Affair*, an early and highly popular tabloid program.

This should have sent the broadcast networks a message that the public was willing and ready to change its television viewing rituals if alternatives were offered. And offered they were.

Cable TV's Optimists Club

By no means an instant hit, except for the fact that audiences liked having both recent and classic movies uncut and uninterrupted by commercials, cable TV subscribers began coming on board. In most areas, franchises were awarded, and there was no competition, so if a customer was unhappy with cable service, the only alternative was to cancel and go without it.

Audiences also agree that television programming was (and *is*) largely unsatisfying, but they would be willing to pay, on average, $50 per month to get news, information, and entertainment. People who would pay that much like CNN's all-news format, ESPN's all-sports, the Weather Channel, and movies. The much anticipated 500 channels of the information superhighway included a long list of both local and esoteric channels that the vast majority of the public don't want to watch for free, much less pay to see.

Still, ever optimistic, new cable subscribers come on board each month. Often they are driven by events, such as the trial of O. J. Simpson, coverage of the impeachment of President Clinton, a natural disaster, a shooting spree, or hot new must-see series or made-for-cable movies.

CNN, Court TV, and CNBC all have been told that it would be a struggle to find and hold an audience for material that historically earns only a single digit (or less) in ratings. No one had anticipated that current events would create an appetite for more information and discussion than broadcast networks ever would have thought of providing.

The big lesson that marketers learned from this, if they had not known it already, is that small, dedicated niche audiences are willing to keep coming back for more, and advertisers who want to reach these audiences could be persuaded to shift dollars from other ad buys, particularly broadcast TV.

A Niche in Time

Publicists find cable TV to be a new frontier for promoting books on every subject from collecting to coping with grief, dieting, cooking, and the history of railroads. Suddenly the demand for content brings out lawyers, therapists, doctors, financial advisers, and consultants to every industry imaginable. The proliferation of 24-hour "news and information" channels has created a need for content that publicists and marketers of every stripe are stepping forward to fill. What used to be a brief segment on "the morning shows" has opened up to a new catalog of promotional opportunities.

Innovative marketers find greater potential in cable TV than in just waiting for a breaking news story on which they may be able to capitalize. The idea of a niche audience for television once made sense only in fringe times (predawn and after midnight), when lower operating costs justified deliberately programming to more esoteric tastes. Cable changed that.

Because of their smaller audiences, cable channels operate similar to local TV stations, paying talent and production staff less, operating on lower budgets, and charging less for advertising. But in developing a rate card for ads, cable would often position itself as comparable to a magazine's "special edition" or "special section" on a particular subject or industry. The idea behind these "specials" is to get businesses that have never advertised before—or have not advertised in that venue—to believe that people interested in the subject will be especially drawn to the issue and that any businesses not represented in it would be conspicuous by their absence among competitors. Through this means, FNN (the Financial News Network), which became the daytime network of CNBC, was able to attract numerous financial services companies and securities firms as both advertisers and contributors of information and commentary.

Other niche subjects have generated such appealing marketing show-cases as the Food Network, Travel Channel, Discovery Health Channel, Learning Channel, History Channel, and BET (Black Entertainment Television), among literally dozens of others. Whether the draw is religion, spiritualism, capitalism, or aerobic exercise, cable has a channel, and that channel is open to advertisers, contributors, and content providers.

Marketers' Surfing Safari

Marketers have a variety of choices. For an advertiser, there are the standard 10-, 15-, 30-, and 60-second spots in either selected programs or run-of-schedule (which is a far less random buy on these venues, since all the programming deals with a single subject). There are opportunities for infomercials—the controversial, but nonetheless effective, format in which a 30-minute commercial is produced to look like a newscast, quiz show, talk show, or magazine program.

Programs frequently have multiple marketing angles. For example, handyman Bob Vila, best known as the host of the PBS series *This Old House*, left that show to develop a cable program for Sears to be shown on the Learning Channel. The giant retailer became the primary sponsor of *Bob Vila's Home Again*, shown several times each week on TLC and other cable channels. On the show, Vila, who also appears in Sears commercial spots, demonstrates how to rebuild, remodel, and restore a home, using materials available at Sears. The program is promoted in Sears stores at point-of-sale displays bearing Vila's photograph.

On the Food Network, a variety of chefs serve as program hosts. All of them are authors of cookbooks, most are paid endorsers of various foods and kitchen appliances, and program sponsors are . . . food product companies. Assume that the placement of a particular brand of blender, frying pan, or knife sharpener on the set is not inadvertent.

The Travel Channel, in a paid ad in *Advertising Age*, was described as "the only network specifically programmed for active upscale viewers with plenty of spending power." A part of the group of "Discovery Networks," the Travel Channel is a logical showcase for ads, features, promotions, and events involving resorts, hotels, airlines, cruise lines, and festivals. Every tourism board from the smallest hamlet to the most emerging countries should be aware of the marketing opportunities in this venue, which is available to some 30 million cable-subscribed homes, especially since people only watch this channel if they are already interested in travel destinations.

By the year 2000, more than 40 members of the Cabletelevision Advertising Bureau were identified as single-focus cable networks. Multiply that by the number of hours in a day, and that's a significant amount of opportunities for marketers to present their message to potentially millions of viewers around the world.

It doesn't take a genius to see quickly that a marketer of sports equipment or products of interest to sports fans has some potent opportunities in television besides *Monday Night Football*. ESPN and Fox Sports Net are only two cable outlets where viewership is unlikely to include a person waiting for the *I Love Lucy* reruns to begin. This is a highly targeted audience and a very efficient and cost-effective media choice.

Pick your category—from health to home and garden—and cable most surely has a channel that will reach at least a significant segment of that market.

Infomercials' Wild Pitches

Cable television has succeeded in areas by programming contradictions. For example, all research says the public is annoyed at the level of commercials in general and is put off by the sheer number of them. Yet, cable channels such as the Home Shopping Network and the numerous variations of that concept attract and hold audiences, who watch and hear nonstop product pitches (some of them pretty shrill) and call to order merchandise that some people would pass up at a flea market.

Infomercials, while a dubious form, sell literally millions of dollars worth of music collections, real estate courses, and self-help programs and a list of specialty products too numerous to mention. While those who study marketing ethics may award some of the infomercial spokespeople low marks, the fact is that people are watching and buying, which confirms the impact of marketing and the power of television, even if it is to a smaller, more selective segment of the market.

How far can it go? How long can it last? One indication is that telethons to raise money for muscular dystrophy, the Children's Miracle Network, and other charities continue to play well and raise millions of dollars annually. PBS on-air "pledge drives" went from annually to quarterly and are still going strong. This seems to support the old sales department wisdom that says, if you want your prospect to give you money, *ask for it*. At any rate, there is no reason to suppose that in the future, this outlook will not be sustained.

Satellite Versus Goliath

Satellite television's distinguishing characteristic is that it carries more channels than the usual cable system provides. Programming is largely developed by content providers, so the distinction between cable and satellite is that of the delivery system, and the fact that most people rate the picture quality of satellite transmission to be superior.

At the turn of the century, marketers of satellite systems were David to cable's Goliath. They were having a difficult time making their case to the public. A major reason is that giants such as AT&T and Time Warner put their considerable muscle behind cable as a product of choice. One day the balance may shift. Meantime, for marketers who are placing advertising or promoting an image, a message, or a cause, contact with a program's segment producer or a news director is still the recommended choice.

Direct Marketing: It's Not Junk Mail Anymore and It Never Was

For years, *direct marketing* has been synonymous with *direct mail* and *direct mail* has been synonymous with *junk mail*. The people on the outside can be forgiven for not keeping industry terminology straight, but marketers should know better. For a few testimonials, ask the folks at K-tel or Lands' End or Laura Ashley or Lillian Vernon. The Sears catalog, the best known of the "dream books" for nearly a century, was once a wonderful example of direct marketing. We've come a long way since then.

Direct marketing is a connection between the marketer and the customer, bypassing (or eliminating) sales reps and retail outlets. Beyond that, the same degree of market research and creative effort is applied that drives any other type of marketing campaign.

When direct marketing was only print, business was largely mail—the catalog or "junk mail" packet—with a call to action by return mail, later by phone and fax, and, of course, currently by E-mail or fax. The term *junk mail* had less to do with the offer as with the presentation. Bulky envelopes with piles of inserts in different sizes, different colors, and different typefaces, with bold banner headlines that screamed for attention prompted enough people to ask, "What is all this junk?" that the label was deserved. And speaking of labels . . .

Volumes have been written on the subjects of how to create direct-mail and direct-marketing campaigns. The instructions vary from one text to another. Some actually recommend loud colors, big bold type, and a bulky envelope of material that few people can actually be expected to read. Others take a more understated, dignified route. The correct formula depends on the product, the company, the offer, and the image and objective of the product or company, both long-term and short-term.

Think "List"

What everyone agrees on, no matter what, is the *list*. It is generally accepted that in direct mail, the list is everything, and no one as yet has mounted a convincing argument to the contrary. How current and accurate a list is and how well qualified it is by gender, age, income, education, geographical area, ethnicity, and politics determine if the list is worth anything at all. The next determinant is whether or not the list has been overused. People who regularly receive large amounts of unsolicited, unwanted mail tend to dispose of all or much of it . . . unopened. For this reason, it is imperative that the list be both current and not overused. How can a marketer know, despite assurances from a list broker, that this is the case? The short answer is that one cannot always be sure, but there are some steps that can be taken.

First, work with a qualified list broker. There are several very reputable brokers that have been in business for decades and serve demanding clients who will not tolerate second-class service, even in third-class mail. Second, whether dealing with an established or known broker or a less-known company, split the list among brokers. That is, if the project calls for a 20,000-piece mailing, secure lists from more than one vendor, and include codes or tracking numbers that will provide information as to which list was more effective. A common question is, if lists of prospects of a particular profile are acquired, isn't there likely to be a great amount of duplication?

The answer is sometimes yes, but that is not always a bad thing. People who receive the same piece of mail more than once will frequently respond to the later mailing. Sometimes, the first piece has created awareness of a name or offer, and a second mailing is more favorably received; it could also be just a matter of timing. Comparing duplicate names on a list also can help in evaluating the level of list quality between brokers—note any similarities and differences at each price level.

The number of "returns" from each broker's list is indicative as well. It is not unreasonable to set a number for returns that is acceptable; a return rate in excess of a certain percentage indicates that the list may not be current and a rebate may be in order. Make certain such a point is clear in the list purchase agreement.

Zamfir, Master of Direct-Response TV

Like *marketing* itself, *direct marketing* is a term that even many professionals interpret differently. For example, to some, the term still pretty much refers to mail, which it literally is, in that one doesn't market more directly to a person than by sending him or her a letter or, more dramatically, an entire envelope full of colorful promotional material. To others, it includes *direct-response TV*, which is usually in the form of a 30- or 60-second spot with a "special TV offer," a hard-sell message, a toll-free phone number, and an urgent call to action. Usually this offering includes a "bonus" as an incentive to respond immediately.

Over the years, these spots have proved memorable and amazing. Few people had ever heard of "Zamfir, Master of the Pan Flute," or even the pan flute itself. Yet, the spot sold millions of albums. Likewise for Slim Whitman, described in the commercials as one of the bestselling recording artists of all time, though few people seemed to have ever heard of him before. The claim in the spot might have been a bit of an exaggeration before it hit TV, but the resulting orders for Whitman's interesting program of cowboy and yodeling selections made the claim true. The singer (and the product) became a smash in England as well as the United States, making it an international direct marketing success.

Infomercials are direct marketing in that they are merely long-form versions of direct-response TV spots.

Theoretically Accounting for Taste

What is it that has made direct-response spots, infomercials, and even home shopping networks so successful after years of consumer and audience resistance?

The question is as much one for psychologists and sociologists as it is for marketers.

There are a number of theories. One explanation offered is that, even with TV remote controls, people still often choose not to exert or inconvenience themselves by turning off or turning away from ads. In a similar vein, other viewers may merely indulge advertisers, when engrossed in a particular program, and accept that commercial interruptions are the price of receiving the entertainment. Also, for some people, television is a companion, regardless of what happens to be on the screen. More likely, though, is the theory that the public has simply accepted the fact that it will be bombarded with advertising messages hundreds of times each day—from TV, radio, magazines, newspapers, billboards, and most significantly, almost every item in homes, offices, schools, and elsewhere, in the form of logos, nameplates, and packaging on everything with which human beings are likely to come in contact. Labels and logos in clothing and on the coffeemaker, TV set, refrigerator door, briefcase handle, computer monitor, cell phone, desk phone, wall phone, milk carton, and eyeglass case all present us with a reminder of who made or sold all that is around us.

So, the TV spots shown within two minutes for three different makes of cars may or may not register. There is a certain amount of what *Chicago Tribune* marketing columnist George Lazarus terms "marketing immunity," in which the spot runs from beginning to end in the consumer's presence without having been seen or heard. But when something does prove to grab the eye or ear, whether it is because it features an attractive model, an adorable child, a dog, several dogs, the loud revving of a motorcycle, a catchy old Beach Boys song, or something else, it gets noticed, and awareness is the first step toward acceptance.

Some of the direct-response ads and infomercials are produced on such modest budgets that they look cheap, cheesy, and awkward, and some marketing professionals believe it is that very element that gets the audience's attention. In a time of slickly produced spots with fine actors and beautiful models looking their professional best, an ill-at-ease person who looks like anyone the consumer might see in an elevator gets attention. While this is largely a by-product of a tight budget, the technique is not foreign to big names and big budgets. Bartles & Jaymes and Calvin Klein are two brands that have spent a lot on making some of their commercials look cheap. Regardless of the budget or the length of the commercial, ads should be interesting and should emphasize *what's in it for the viewer*. That's where the *direct* in direct marketing comes in.

More Vehicles in the Lot

Catalogs qualify as direct-marketing vehicles whether they are mailed, hand delivered, or distributed at designated locations. An increasingly popular variation on the catalog is the "magalog," a catalog in magazine format with feature articles, interviews, and puzzles separating merchandise presentations. They are a good deal more costly to produce and mail than standard direct-mail pieces (or packets), but they have at least three enormous benefts. First, if it is done well, a magalog can have a virtually unlimited shelf life or life span, while a standard direct-mail piece may last minutes unless it is heavy with coupons; second, it can have a pass-along or shared element, increasing its potential reach and value; and third, it can help to create, define, maintain, enhance, or change the image of the company, product, or brand that is producing it.

Newsletters are another form of direct marketing. They are less costly to produce than catalogs or magalogs and are typically more effective than brochures or standard promotional mailings to certain types of audiences. A newsletter has a look of authority and credibility that is typically missing from a brochure or mailer and, again, has a longer life and greater pass-along potential.

Some professionals categorize *telemarketing* as an area of direct marketing because it doesn't require a showroom or retail location or, in most situations, even demand that the telemarketer maintain an inventory or even an office. Telemarketers, thus, are strictly the marketers in the sense that they are facilitating business. As direct marketing, it is a bit of a stretch. Telemarketers are often trained and encouraged to be (or are by nature) persistent and aggressive, as is often the case with a high-power sales force. They also typically are pushed to make quotas. In contrast, direct marketing's uniqueness in the marketing mix is in its presentation of the message in a way that permits the consumer to react and respond in his or her own way.

Some direct marketers prefer the term *one-on-one* marketing. Some marketers also seem to think they are not demonstrating their creativity if they don't rename what they do every couple of years.

Magazines: Out of Vogue? Hardly

In the center of the Internet Revolution, consider this: there have never been so many new magazines launched—aimed at literally every demographic segment—with multiple titles on subjects from A to Z. Magazines are excellent marketing vehicles and are perhaps the most taken-for-granted segment of the media mix, although for years a number of radio reps have claimed that distinction for their own medium.

The reason for magazines' being so largely overlooked is that each season, the emphasis on finding "the next new thing" or "the next big thing" aims for something totally unexpected and seemingly innovative, not merely what looks like a variation of something familiar. Internet marketing will likely be the darling of the industry for a decade or so because there will be new planets to discover in cyberspace.

In previous seasons, the thing du jour ran to working promotional messages into places where the audience could not escape: on ATM screens while waiting for the cash to pop out, on movie screens sandwiched in between the preview trailers for new films and the feature attraction, from the voice that tells you what you're missing by not pressing "seven" to sign up now while you are "on hold" waiting for someone to take your call, on rented videocassettes . . .

These were some of the "breakthrough" ideas during the years when *breakthrough ideas* was the industry's term for *vogue.*

People buy newspapers for news and check TV to catch up on what's happened since the newspapers were printed. Generation X checks the Internet for the news that TV doesn't want them to see. But magazines are what people buy to read on the plane, with as much thought as a pack of gum or a candy bar. Magazines are what people order to enter the sweepstakes or to help the junior high kids with their fund-raising.

People is to magazines what McDonald's is to hamburgers: a weekly, enjoyable portion that sustains without nutrients; *Time* gets inside the Pentagon, city hall, the boardroom, and the prison and reveals who is corrupt; *The Weekly Standard* extolls the virtues of political conservatism; while *The Nation* warns people to watch out for those political conservatives.

Before television, *Life, Look, Post, Collier's* and a handful of others provided the stories and pictures that TV provides today. TV has made them obsolete, and they are all gone (except for *Life*, which Time Warner continues to keep on life support as a monthly, seemingly for sentimental reasons).

Evolving and Multiplying—over Lunch

That magazines are excellent marketing vehicles is true. Magazines as a medium have evolved into showcases for advertisers and for those who retain publicists.

The people whose homes are featured in *Architectural Digest* have had their publicists or their decorators (or their decorator's publicists) bring the various properties to the magazine's attention so that the world may know about these grand properties . . . and their talented and successful owners. Much of what the major business magazines know about the companies they profile is as a result of the companies' having called and told them. *Vogue, Vanity Fair,* and dozens of bridal magazines are read as much for their elegant ads showing the latest styles as for the articles used to separate the ads.

Underscoring the recent wave of new titles, a *New York Times* piece reported that "launches of the computer magazines were at an all-time high, with 54 new titles in 1998 alone. The crafts, games, hobbies, and models magazines have also been on a steady rise, from 21 launched in 1990 to the 67 launched (in 1998)."

Why all these new magazines when people are supposed to be reading less? Why the variety of subjects when it seems the whole world cares only about websites?

First, most, if not all, publications—old and new—*have* websites. Not everyone out there, however, has (or wants to have) a computer. And most people (even computer lovers) find a magazine easier to read on a subway or bus or over a sandwich at lunchtime. A magazine is also easier to share with a friend or to mail.

Increasingly, magazines are being used as companions and "feeders" to websites and cable TV channels, with promises that more information awaits. Advertisers are usually offered a menu rate card: advertise in the magazine at one rate, on-line at another, or get a combination deal and reach, potentially, two separate, yet highly qualified, demographic audiences who have gone to the magazine and/or website by choice and have paid to do so.

Self-Promotion Gets Smarter with Age

There have always been special interest magazines for various sports and hobbies, as well as those created around personalities from Elvis to the

Backstreet Boys and the Spice Girls. The same practice has been extended to promote brands. In the year 2000, marketers could say, "You've bought the toy, seen the TV channel, loved the fragrance, worn the clothes . . . now buy the magazine . . ."

Among the more popular and widely circulated:

American Girl
Barbie Bazaar
Beanie Mania
Bloomberg
Channel
Colors (Benetton)
Crayola Kids
Disney Adventures
ebay
ESPN
IKEA Space
Joe (Starbucks)
Martha Stewart Living
Mature Outlook (Sears)
Microsoft
Momentum (Mercedes-Benz)
Nickelodeon
Nick Jr.
Philip Morris
Pokémon
Sesame Street
Sony Style
Target
Unlimited (Philip Morris)
Yahoo! Internet Life

These are only some of the magazines that have been created to cross-promote and sell a variety of brands and products (while also selling ads and attempting to generate revenue). The 25 titles noted and others would not exist if a particular product or brand did not exist. Their specific purpose is to interest the consumer in something specific. *Colors*, the magazine of Benetton, promotes the social causes with which the clothing designer

Sense of Style

Sony has been a well-known and respected brand in electronics for decades, but its expansion into recorded music and motion pictures have operated under the names Columbia and Tri-Star. The challenge is to make the name Sony Entertainment widely known without diminishing the equity of the acquired brands. A good first step is the publication of a magazine, *Sony Style*, to showcase all the company's products, from digital audio and video to talent, and to promote a cross-sell halo effect. If the magazine's content remains fresh and varied, it should be effective. It can't become simply a catalog if it is to present the desired image. (Copyright 1999 Sony Electronics. Sony Style is a trademark of Sony Corporation. *Sony Style* is published by Time Inc. Custom Publishing.)

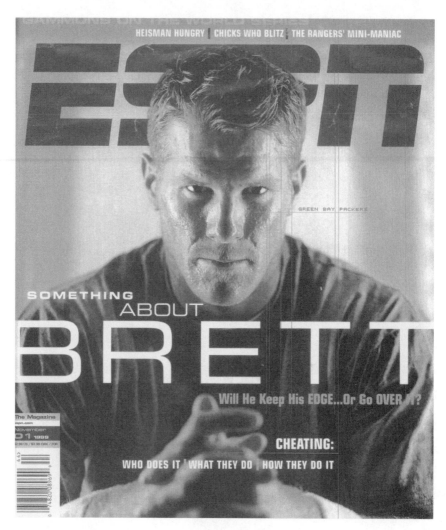

Something New in the Sports Pages

ESPN The Magazine tries to be different from other sports magazines as the hugely successful ESPN cable TV network is from traditional TV Sportscasts. It's big, colorful, slick, and stylish—sports with an attitude—to build synergy and bring the brand to the attention of sports fans who may not regularly remember the channel or who like their sports "to go." It's a good fit. (Copyright 1999 ESPN Inc.)

An On-Line Audience Gets an Off-Line Life

As the Internet becomes more crowded, Yahoo!, the Net's leading search engine, seeks to appeal to wider audiences—who supposedly don't read—with a highly successful newsstand presence through this printed edition. As a brand strategy, it helps set the company apart from other search engines in a more authoritative environment. It also may serve to convert "nontech" readers by introducing them to what Yahoo! has to offer. [*Yahoo! Internet Life* Copyright 1999 ZD Inc., a Softbank Co. Yahoo! is a trademark of Yahoo! Inc.]

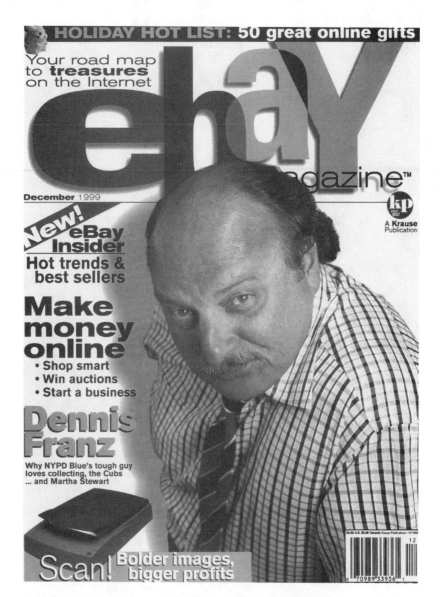

Something for Everyone in a Crowded Auction Market

EBay quickly established itself as the Internet's premium auction market. A news-stand presence helps to raise the brand's profile with a non-Internet audience in an appealing way that its brief TV spots can't convey. The magazine is colorful, irreverent, and packed with celebrity photos, ingredients that would likely make it popular even without its powerful Internet connection it is supposed to promote.

(*Ebay Magazine* Copyright 1999 by Krause Publications Inc.)

and retailer tries to identify itself, hoping that people of like minds will notice and buy the company's sweaters. As was noted in the case study in an earlier chapter, *Joe* is Starbucks' magazine and reflected the image that the purveyor of expensive coffee seeks to present in its stores, brands, and products. The magazine was short-lived, but will likely be back.

Unlimited looks exactly like a men's rugged, outdoor magazine, which is exactly how its underwriter, Philip Morris Companies, wants it to look. *Momentum* is the magazine of Mercedes-Benz, and *Mature Outlook* is for older folks . . . from Sears. The objective is that readers of these magazines will, if only unconsciously, form a connection or a bond with the brand that will manifest itself in greater awareness, a perception of value, and brand loyalty.

A marketer interested in communicating with business audiences is on safe ground with an ad or a story in *Forbes* or *Business Week*, which can be reprinted or referenced for years. The credibility that comes with an appearance in a respected publication, even a city magazine (such as *Boston*, *Chicago*, *Los Angeles*, or *New York*), can often have the effect of a third-party endorsement and of importance among competitors. That was true in 1950 and remained true in 2000. But the emergence of publications that would have once been dismissed as vanity magazines or promotional vehicles is now considered smart marketing. It is artfully allocating and controlling message space and presenting a story the way a marketer wants it presented.

Self-published books, once regarded as irrelevant exercises in vanity publishing, are frequently hitting the bestseller lists. Internet "publishing" has enabled kitchen-table entrepreneurs to have the look and presence, if not always the depth, of large, established publishing organizations. And it is acceptable.

As major magazines were long appreciated for in-depth, behind-the-scenes articles that provide the "back story" on corporations, executives, political leaders, and entertainers, the public now comfortably accepts the fact that those subjects are putting out their own stories and no longer are waiting to be called.

A company or a brand that has the ability and resources to produce its own magazine is providing yet another testament to its position of prominence within its category.

In part, a decline in the public's trust of established institutions and the mainstream media has enhanced the marketer's ability to tell a subject's side of the story and not have it rejected out of hand as self-serving. It is offered as the subject's point of view *for the record*, a term the media take seriously, even if it appears in a fully subsidized format.

And for more information on that story, they can always "check out the website."

The Internet: Very Much Ado

There is no question but the world experienced an "Internet explosion." As with many explosions, it is important to know how much of the excitement is justified and how much is just smoke.

Over time, marketing folklore will surely include stories that will amuse, amaze, and distort the reality of the situation. About a dozen people all claim to be the inventor of the music video; the Internet's success is certain to be the subject of greater debate and misinformation.

Around 1970, the U.S. Department of Defense created the network so that academic and military researchers could remain in contact and continue doing government work even if any part of the network were taken out. As it grew, human nature being what it is, scientists and others with access to the Internet found uses for it beyond work and began sending personal communications to one another. Graduate students constructed elaborate fantasy games, and as it continued to grow, the Internet almost took on a life of its own. It is the closest thing resembling the heralded information superhighway of the future.

It quite naturally followed that marketers would try to find a way to use the Internet for commercial purposes. Newspapers, radio, television, movies, videos, telephones, and microphones had all become tools for people to try to influence other people, so why not the Internet?

Into the Great Unknown

Why not indeed?

It has a language all its own.

Few companies, associations, products, brands, or individuals do not have a "dot-com" or "dot-org" after their names anymore.

People truly believe they are traveling the information superhighway when they are surfing the Net and Microsoft asks, "Where do you want to go today?" Rarely a week passes that a major newspaper, magazine, or TV program doesn't lead with an Internet story—about E-commerce, E-business, or E-tailing.

The "E" of course means *electronic*, and the media would all but have the public believe that all other forms of life will virtually cease to exist and that an event didn't happen if it didn't happen on-line . . . in cyberspace.

A story in the media publication *Brill's Content* asked, "How many? How much? Who knows?" It lamented, "Analysts tell us how many people are on-line and how much they spend there, but research methods vary widely and no one knows which—if any—analysts are right."

That's more than a small problem. While that particular article estimates that electronic retailing will top $17.4 billion in 2001, another source indicated the number could be $37.5 billion in 2002. Clearly, the methodology here is scientific, mathematical, serious, and the conclusions are pretty much all guesswork.

The Christmas season of 1998 was the first year that marketers looked seriously at Internet numbers. That had much to do with 1998 being the year the Internet seemed to turn the corner into undisputed acceptability as a viable marketing venue. Every business, trade association, political candidate, cause, school, and church had a website, and it was considered as necessary as a telephone if one hoped to be in business.

The record Internet sales were impressive, but many analysts said the numbers fell short of projections. There was no reason to either celebrate or mourn, however, because "record" numbers in a medium so young are to be expected (the U.S. economy was also very strong at the time), and falling short of projections is a nonevent for the same reason. "Projections" at an early stage are arbitrary and virtually meaningless.

Hype and a Grain of Salt

What is *not* meaningless is the hype. Millions of personal computers have been sold on assurances from the media and marketers that, like it or not, the Internet is the future.

In one of *Newsweek's* frequent Internet cover stories, the message was hardly equivocal: "E-life—How the Internet Is Changing America" the cover text shouted in letters more than 2" high.

As the end of the century approached, a *New York Times* special section on E-commerce used the headline "A Feeding Frenzy Made for Consumers." It reported that "so many Internet companies, and their investors, are so desperate to get big fast that they are almost willing to bribe people to shop with them. So the savvy cyberconsumer can find sites selling all sorts of items at or below cost, or with free shipping or all sorts of other giveaways or promotions."

Reports of heavy discounts—prices of 40 percent or more below suggested retail levels—were common on E-commerce and, to many marketeers, nothing more than aggressive promotion and even the age-old "loss-leader" idea (bring in customers by offering prices so far below the market that the merchandiser actually loses money on the sale, but use the opportunity to expose the customer to other items and recoup the loss). The story behind the story was less positive. One CEO of an on-line company said directly, "I need to establish and maintain our position of leadership, because whoever gets the lead is in the best position to keep the lead."

At first reading, that may seem like a sound conclusion, but it's not. The reason is that in an industry (E-commerce) that has no history, there can be no truisms. At various times, various corporate giants have held the top spot in their respective industries. They were the undisputed leaders. Then they all lost the top spot. Whether it was because they rested on their laurels, got stale, were outmaneuvered by a more aggressive competitor, or name another reason or combination, it doesn't matter.

What matters for marketers is understanding that in a young industry, every year will be a "record" year, and whoever is the category leader may be little more than the flavor of the month. The very fact that a new industry is able to succeed in changing people's shopping and buying habits is proof that the public is willing to shift loyalties and patronage without sending a condolence card to its former product, brand, or service.

It also means, for the same reason, that the Internet can be a place rich in opportunities.

Sites for Sore Eyes

A media and marketing special report by *Advertising Age*, which evaluated 524 Internet companies, put it well: "Dot-com's $7.4 Billion Advertising Explosion—Boom or Bust? The ad landscape is saturated with Internet business. Call it a state of (very) temporary insanity."

The reference is to the fact that a momentum had begun that professional marketers watched gather strength, and while they were only too delighted to take advantage of it, there was a certain craziness about it. Many of the best-known Internet businesses had gone public, put millions in the pockets of their founders, and ridden optimistic predictions of securities analysts. Yet, after several years, none was showing a profit. In fact, most were still posting huge *losses* . . . while the stock traded high.

The sense was that optimism could take a company only so far. Additionally, some market observers fear that the excitement that developed so quickly could fade just as fast. The Internet was truly a phenomenon, but so much about it was unknown.

And *that* created still more opportunities on two fronts. First, virtually every company or brand believed it needed an Internet presence to be competitive, and that meant that a whole new industry was born: creating Web pages and marketing sites on the Net.

Second, small businesses and huge corporations knew they were going into uncharted territory and big reputations were at stake. Thus, a second new industry was born to coach agencies and companies of all sizes, regardless of their experience: how to market on the Internet.

After millions of dollars had been invested in creating dazzling websites, much of the industry realized that it had taken a "Field of Dreams" approach to Web pages (believing simply, "If we build it, they will come"). So, the sites were built, and the realization hit that a website was *another ad destination*.

The radio spot that for years included the phrases "check out our ad in this Sunday's paper for details" or "watch your mail for more information" or the simple formality "call our toll-free number to hear how you can benefit" now needed to say, "check out our website."

Every ad that ran everywhere had to include the Web address both to direct people to the site and to convey the important message that the advertiser *had* a site and was therefore a player in the modern marketplace.

"I've been in new business for 15 years, and I've never seen anything like this," the chief marketing officer of a major agency told *Advertising Age*. The situation analysis was that Madison Avenue had gone truly mad, with the prognosis being a major shakeout in which hundreds of dubious dot-coms would disappear, fewer new dot-coms would be launched (selectively), and only the strong would survive.

In other words, the Internet will have to go through the cycle that other pioneers have experienced when conquering new frontiers, suffering casualties along the way. On the upside for marketers, something *big* could be accomplished for a lot less money on-line—than on site. That is, just as Matt Drudge, sitting in his Los Angeles apartment, could create his newsletter

"The Drudge Report" and become a national celebrity taken seriously by many established and credible media entities, so too could any individual company or service manage to create a website and both *look good* and *look big* for relatively little money.

How to Market a Website

The next step is marketing the website—getting people to it and encouraging what is being offered—and following through on the service aspect. A business can set up in cyberspace for a lot less rent than in a building on the mall. But once the customer has asked for service, the service must be forthcoming, just as it has to be administered by the clerk in the retail location. A failure to follow through and deliver what a website promises will contribute to the "shakeout" referenced earlier.

How are successful marketers marketing their websites?

Rev Up the Search Engines The most common answer is through networks of search engines, the Internet connection that is supposed to find the user whatever he or she wants. They're great. But according to a 1999 *Chicago Tribune* report, only some 16 percent of the Internet's content is ever indexed.

Steve Jareo, writing in "Sharp Marbles," the newsletter of his Chicago ad agency Jareo, did the math and published the results: As of the fall of 1999, the Internet had an estimated 800 million pages with 180 million images and "tends to double in size approximately every 18 months."

Relating these numbers to the estimated 16 percent being indexed, and even allowing that system enhancements and upgrades improve by 100 percent, there will still be only about one-third of Internet sites indexed.

The most efficient way for a marketer to ensure that his or her website is part of the search engine's referencing system is to make the contact with search engine firms, pay a fee to the search engine operator or one of the several feeder companies that service search engines, and follow the listing, checking where and how the website appears when the key words are entered and making certain it is accessible.

In the early years of the Internet, it seemed to be just assumed that some type of directory would exist to help people find what they were looking for. In fairness to operators of search engines, they have come a long way and are among the most efficient technology segments, handling literally millions of pages of material. The job is awesome.

Good Ol' Old Media The other way marketers are making the public aware of their sites is through what can be described as traditional media.

Crain's New York Business declared in July 1999, "Old media gets a boost from new media ads—Internet firms find traditional venues best to reach customers." Reporter Valerie Block pointed out that "in 1998, dot-coms spent $597 million on television, radio, newspapers, and magazine ads, a 77 percent increase over 1997." The chief marketer of a large on-line financial company added, "Advertising in (traditional media) provides the realness that people don't get when you just advertise on the Net."

Presumably that comment refers to the theory that, to a great degree, advertising an Internet service on the Internet itself is a bit like preaching to the choir. The Net audience may be assumed to have a sense of who's on board and who isn't. But even that is a stretch. People tend to not know all the other tenants in their own building without some highly visible listing, and the average building is not housing 800-million-plus tenants.

Getting people to a website is the same as marketing any other product or service. How do marketers get people to come to a museum? Or a theater? Or a shopping mall? Or get them to tune in to a particular television network between the hours of 8:00 and 11:00? There is a need to first create an awareness before anything else can happen. Second, people need a *reason* to go to a commercial, political, or educational location or event.

The tremendous attention given the Internet can sometimes distort one's perspective about it. For example, in 1998, only 37 percent of U.S. homes were on-line, according to the consulting firm Jupiter Communications. It has been projected that by 2003, some 63 percent of households will be on-line. If all forecasts prove true, with less than two-thirds of the United States on-line in 2003 and a projected 2.4 billion Web pages, that is enough of a crowd to qualify as *dense.*

Further, sites such as Amazon.com are quick to point out how many of their customers are repeat customers. Statistics are sketchy across the board. What of the customer that goes on-line directly to a particular site and *only* that site. How does *that* customer know who and what else is there?

The answer is provided by checking any major media on any given day, from TV and newspapers to radio and highway signs, and note the glut of ads for dot-coms. These ads are not being placed because on-line businesses believe their audiences are hooked on computers to the exclusion of all other media. Far from it. For all the "check out our website" messages, the numbers are great but they are not expected to be as large as those that serious prospects delivered by the more established media over the years.

People typically pass the same places each day on their way to and from work, school, home, and shopping. All that "passing" exposes them to marketing opportunities in the form of all the businesses and brands that become familiar. On the Internet, consumers do not pass the same familiar merchants. The names of products, brands, and companies must be brought to the locations that they *do* pass via the daily paper, a favorite magazine, radio, or TV. The Internet is a great opportunity, but it will need to go through a maturing process to come fully of age in the costly media mix.

Put Your Money Where . . . ?

Determining where the marketing dollars should go is tricky. Remember, to bring people to an on-line site to receive information or to execute an interactive transaction requires that the target market members all have computers and modems and are inclined to do business that way. Much of the market still doesn't have on-line capability, and even many who do require a certain amount of preconditioning to become familiar enough and comfortable enough to do business and offer a credit card number amid horror stories about computer "hackers" violating the security barriers and obtaining credit card data and other confidential information.

Marketers inevitably raise the question of whether or not an "on-line-*only*" business is a good business. An old-school marketer would answer that it is *not* a good approach, that it is exclusionary in closing out perhaps as much as one-half to two-thirds of the public who, for whatever reason, do not do business on-line. This position is quite valid.

Other marketers offer another perspective that is equally valid. Segmentation and target marketing dictate that if the largest market is on-line, it is unquestionably the best place to be. Some products that are cyberspace-, Internet-, or simply computer-related may well find a far more receptive audience on-line, as the prospective buyer may feel a bond or connection with companies or brands that think the way he or she does. Also, an argument can be made that a retailer placing a facility in an out-of-the-way place, where it is inaccessible to much of the public, is being just as exclusionary as a retailer or a marketer who chooses to work on-line only.

This again makes the case for target marketing and for knowing all that can be known about the market before committing dollars to it. From such information, tactics can be developed that are more likely to produce the desired results.

Everybody Pays to Play

To many prognosticators, it would appear that Barnes & Noble's BN.com is a better bet as a bookseller than Amazon.com over the long run because it offers the public choices of on-line shopping in addition to hundreds of retail outlet locations and a mail-order option as well. The company must still come to terms with its on-again/off-again positioning of the on-line and off-line sites as separate or combined. But Barnes & Noble's overhead is enormous in comparison with Amazon's, so regarding return on investment, the story may be quite different. In addition, the Barnes & Noble's on-line and retail divisions are operated independently of one another, so a customer should expect service levels to be uneven. To paraphrase the Microsoft slogan, marketers must ask themselves what business they want to be in today.

Internet marketing is the future for much of the market, but it is not the future for the *entire* market. Levi Strauss thought the Internet was the obvious place to concentrate on selling its jeans, in light of its demographic base, the huge amount of media hype, and the on-line success of brands such as Lands' End, but the experience proved both disappointing and costly. By 2000, the company had gone back to using largely conventional media. This was discouraging for a brand that not only was very well known but had a high degree of brand equity and loyalty. Who or what was to blame for the failed on-line venture will be debated for some time to come. The hard-knocks lesson is that established brands should not abandon the methods that helped make them successful just for the sake of being part of what so many people have called the way of the future.

Agencies in a Strange Land

On the agency side, both advertising and PR agencies have long been accused of inventing the concept of smoke and mirrors, creating *illusions* of excitement where none existed. That is to say, much of what they told the public was not believed or taken very seriously. The arrival of the Internet explosion was to many ad agencies as if a spacecraft had landed in the middle of a new car showroom. The dealers thought it was nice but not what the customer needed. Many customers agreed, until they noticed how many of their neighbors had spacecrafts, including a number of upstarts of which no one had ever heard.

Ad Age warned practitioners that "waiting too long to develop Internet capabilities may turn agencies into bystanders." A marketing executive concluded, "Clearly the interactive shops continue to eat their [the traditional agencies'] lunch and continue to dominate the marketplace."

Another executive remarked, "They've never put resources into the technology to understand what the technology can do. . . . Until you can do that, you can put pretty pictures on a computer screen, but you can't build a powerful on-line identity for a client."

Many of the hot, emerging Web shops have sought to distance themselves from traditional ad agencies, presenting themselves as *talent*, not ad agencies. The CEO of one such shop has said, "I wouldn't call website development an advertising endeavor. What we do is more than advertising."

Another critic charges, "Ad agencies and traditional media buyers are so caught up in where their agencies have been that their eyes are caught in the headlights."

If these individuals believe their own words (and no one doubts that they do), they have violated at least one firm rule of marketing and, not incidentally, have provided some insight into why so many Web pages look so dazzling—while also looking dizzying and difficult to follow. The major violation here is *Don't get so full of yourself that you forget what you were hired to do*: help create awareness and get business for the client. Too many of the "hot shops" on-line are dedicated to getting attention for *themselves* and their work and winning praise from fellow creative techies, rather than business for clients. In such cases, it appears to be not the old geezers at the ad agencies who've taken their eye off the ball, but the self-satisfied, self-aggrandizing newcomer who, after a thoughtful pause, asks, "What ball?"

Experience and research are important, as well as talent. A problem with arrogance at any level of the marketing process is that it deafens the ear to the sound of the market, and when that sound cannot be heard, success is a matter of luck.

Websites are different from other forms of advertising the way TV ads are different from billboards, radio from direct marketing, and point-of-sale from telemarketing. A good ad agency knows and understands the differences—always conscious of the fact that the brand and the client's interest come first. The "talent" is supposed to be working on the client's behalf, not working to reeducate the client on electronic art.

Is There a Web Doctor in the House? Because the Internet's success is still so new that many experienced marketers don't pretend to understand it, there is a natural willingness to call in a specialist. By itself, that's not a bad idea. Often, however, the specialist's experience is in technology and/or computer graphics and sometimes film or video. That can be great too. But the specialist must also understand marketing, and many do not. Clients come to learn this after having pushed aside their ad agencies and investing the marketing budget in the creation of a really cool website.

They do get a dazzling "Internet presence."

Now what?

It is important to stay fresh and current and check the pulse of the market. It is important to have, whether outside or in-house, a good advertising team that understands websites and Internet marketing. *Or* assemble a creative and account team made up of people with the individual skills to get the job done, working together.

Presence Is the Marketer's Domain

Too often, in their excitement, marketers single out a website they like and ask for "something like this—only better." That can be a good starting point, but the second thought should be to create an Internet presence that achieves the marketing objectives.

Sometimes in the flurry it is easy to forget that the basic rules still should apply, even if they will be applied in cyberspace. Whether a new venture or an extension of an existing business, the *domain name* you use is decisive. As with any business, particularly start-ups, it is helpful for the name to say what the company does, not just be a cool moniker. Of course, people will point to Amazon.com's success and claim that the rule is not universal. A response to that is, instead of rationalizing based on the few who struck gold, check the number that did *not* pan out and ask what might have been done to reduce the obstacles to success.

Internet businesses such as About.com, MyWay.com, MyPoint.com, and MySimon.com spend enormous amounts of money on TV and/or print ads to tell people their names and that they are open for business on the Internet—but, after all that money spent, most people still don't know what they do.

No matter how great-looking the site or how seductive the ads that direct people to it, it is a lot (maybe too much) to expect people to go out of their way to find out what you do because you or your Internet site designers chose not to tell them.

Five Steps to Internet Marketing

Vince Gelormine, a veteran Internet search engine and software developer, believes there are five basic steps to the Internet marketing process:

1. Obtain a domain name
2. Create a website
3. Place the website on a server
4. Promote the website
5. Update the site and give people reasons to return to it

The Right Start Sometimes the domain names are the same as that of the company, and sometimes not. When not, remember that it is useful to have a name that will help market what you do. For example, a florist might try to get the domain name *flowers.com* or *flowersnow.com* or *freshflowers.com* or whatever along those lines might be available. Have several alternatives ready because, with tens of millions of websites, the list of remaining available names can present a new challenge to the creative team. If your company is Todd's Flowers, choosing Todd.com may help you to remember your name, but it won't catch a prospective customer's attention the way Flowersanywhere.com can.

Be clear with your server as to costs. Because so many young people have websites and spend so much time visiting other websites, the assumption is often that everything's free on the Web. It's not. Costs can run to several thousand dollars per month depending on the size bandwidth you request (your dedicated line). Think of the cost structure as similar to that of a rented post office box on the low end and an 800 number on the high end. Then think about what it might cost if you were to receive several thousand calls per month on your 800 number. An active site that gets a lot of "hits" can be a very expensive place to park on the superhighway.

Needle Meets Haystack On the subject of promoting your site, a Microsoft ad puts it well. The headline accompanying photos of people having an office party reads, "Week 12—We've finally got our website up and running." A larger photo of a man we may presume is the company's CEO carries a subhead that reads, "That little voice: How's anyone going to find it?" The ad's body copy explains, "So how are customers going to find your small business on the Web? You know that they look to search engines, but how do you make sure your business is found when they search? At Microsoft bcentral.com, we've made getting listed on hundreds of leading search engines an easy, one-stop process. . . . "

Well, that seems easy enough. Of course, when one pauses to ponder the phrase "hundreds of leading search engines," the sweating starts all over again. There is little doubt that for some people, Microsoft's solution is as simple as the company claims, but alas, marketers are finding that doing business *anywhere* is not that simple . . . or inexpensive. The Microsoft ad, incidently, ran often as a full page in the national edition of the *New York Times* and in other publications. There is no mention as to whether the company tried using its own easy, one-stop service first.

The *New York Times*' Stuart Elliott (on that same day the ad appeared) wrote, "It often seems these days as if dot-com companies are peddling their wares by buying up every moment of commercial time and every inch of advertising space everywhere from matchbooks to cyberspace to the Super Bowl."

Not that everyone thinks Microsoft might have oversimplified the solution, but another Web heavy hitter, excite@home, bought two-page spreads in the advertising trade papers to say, "Web Advertising Truth Number 1: Anyone who says they have all the answers is a liar." The copy cautions: "The Web advertising landscape is cluttered with fast-talking salespeople and fly-by-night start-ups. Keep your guard up. Ask to see case studies. Pose tough questions and don't be satisfied until you fully understand the response. If a solution seems a little too perfect, it's probably smoke."

As established earlier, the enormous interest in the Internet has not only created thousands of new on-line businesses but has also created a role for thousands of new (or reengineered) businesses to advise marketers how to do business on the Net.

Before the name-calling spirals out of control, let's place the marketer's own objectives in context. It is important, all hype notwithstanding, to define the business to be marketed. Is it a new Internet business offering a product or service to other Internet businesses? Or is it an entity with a product, service, or message that now wants to add Internet marketing to its media mix?

In either case, the rules still apply as they would to any new product launch: Define the target market, and determine the market preferences—that is, if an overwhelming percentage prefer on-line reading to traditional media, then by all means, make certain your message is listed with as many search engines as possible, as well as on bulletin boards and banners. If you know that a part of your market looks elsewhere for information, from the daily newspaper or TV news to the yellow pages, respond accordingly.

Remember that people who check the Internet for information are also exposed to many other impressions in many other places. If you are a florist and want business from on-line customers, show yourself on-line, but don't neglect the rest of the market for flowers. Be where the people are.

Two Ways to Go Wrong After all the effort and expense of creating a website, marketers tend to make two common mistakes, perhaps for budgetary reasons, but more likely as a result of lack of thought. First, all too often the content of the website is ads, brochures, or catalogs that have already been seen; in the worst cases, it is the same material that prompted the person to "check out" the website to begin with. It is not a bad idea for this stuff to be on the website, but it should not be *all* there is.

Lead with some original and highly visual material, even if it uses a formula theme such as "a history of . . ." or "a look back at . . ."; you present an *archive* of material that hasn't been seen for a while. This situation is actually a great opportunity for agency creative people (or any number of other associates who profess to be creative) to do some bold things graphically that a typical ad, mailer, or brochure does not allow them to do.

The second mistake is that marketers often treat their websites as if they were highway billboards, where a visual and text are put in place and left there, not to be touched or altered for months (or longer). Keep the site fresh if you hope to keep people coming back. The Internet is supposed to have an edge over other media in its ability to modify, update, or totally change quickly and cost-effectively. The update can be something as simple as a new text from the CEO on a timely matter, a special offer or promotion, or a series of ads that are rotated regularly.

When Brands Think

The Internet is by far the most wide-reaching new development in business and marketing in decades. The opportunity for the broadest possible array of new businesses and for new presentations of established or existing entities is immeasurable. One of the most positive aspects of it all is the wide-open creative possibilities that come along all too rarely. In a young medium, talented people with bold or exciting new ideas tend to be given a wider opening to experiment or express themselves than they are in businesses or other situations where things are done in a prescribed way because that's the way they've always been done.

With this new venue comes the inevitable controversy about what it is (or should be) and how to use it or not. For example, Bob Schmetterer, chairman of EURO RSCG Worldwide, insists, "The Internet isn't just another medium; it's the message itself. It's a four-bell alarm that we're in the midst of a fundamental shift in the way consumers relate to products."

Well, maybe it is a deeply meaningful relationship to *some* people, but to others, it is a catalog with an order form on a computer screen, with romance occurring elsewhere in their lives. Marketers need to be aware of both sides' feelings before a message is targeted, or it may misfire.

There have always been people who feel strongly about one medium over another. People who have done well in TV, direct mail, radio, or magazines advocate for their respective preferences with conviction and enthusiasm. The Internet has its supporters too, but some of them represent its advantages and potential with an evangelistic zeal. They believe it is like nothing that has ever come before and that it is not merely a window to the world, but a portal to the universe and beyond.

There are some indications that the varying levels of passion regarding the Internet are both generational and reflective of personal style. Members of Generation X and Generation Y have developed thousands of new businesses and areas of expertise that remain obscure to baby boomers and seniors. On the Internet, they could create a niche for themselves. E-mail, chat rooms, and links to one another allow for creative expression at a safe distance, role-playing, and exploration. Internet marketers stress the intimacy and personalization of the medium and these are examples of that.

Generating interest, awareness, and support for a product, service, brand, company, or message has always been the job of marketing. The great success of the Internet should be embraced. It should not be intimidating, nor should it mean, as some interpreters contend, that all the proven methods of marketing are obsolete. There will always be those who will not do business with computers, and that's an awfully large segment to simply write off.

The Internet is a medium, a vehicle, and a tool. In some cases, it is itself a product. It plugs into the wall and a phone line. It has batteries. It is not a life or a way of life; it is a place where products, issues, and people go in order for other people to look, learn, and buy, or not. Marketers need to know that and work with it.

Summary Points

1. Among marketers, the term *revolution* gets as much of a workout as the word *change*. The year 2000, the millennium, and technology have been positioned as an "event" and so contributed to creating a marketplace that is ready for a revolution.

2. Magazines are becoming more tailored to segments and introducing more private-label titles linked to brands and companies.

3. Website designers are usually experts on computer graphics, not marketing.

4. Many Web shops consider themselves "talent," not agencies. Know what the people you are working with do and what they *don't* do.

5. The basic steps to Internet marketing are: Obtain a domain name; Create a website; Place the website on a server; Promote the site; and Update it so people will want to return.

6. Choose an Internet domain name that relates to what you have or do.

7. Be sure you understand charges and fees, as an active website can get thousands of hits and prove to be costly.

8. Some people have strong feelings about the Internet and consider it almost a way of life. The attitudes of your market should inform both your message and how you use the Internet to present it.

13

What's Next?

You cannot fight against the future. Time is on our side.
—W. E. Gladstone, 1866

IT IS LIKELY that *technology* will continue to be the magic word for some time to come. Marketers love a word like *technology* because individual people can put their own spin on it and let it mean whatever they want or need it to mean. For marketers, it will likely mean *Internet marketing,* which itself has enough twists and curves to be applied in a variety of ways.

But the future is and will be more than the Internet. All the components that have worked well for marketers will still be around, although the package may look a bit different. It is a matter of both art and commerce. The public votes. If it likes a marketer's product or message, every effort is made to keep giving the public what it wants, albeit with the occasional "new and improved" buffing up.

How New Can You Get?

Since the earliest days of recorded history, people have had a fascination with what's new and with knowing what's coming next. Fads and trends dominate the covers of weekly news magazines. During the last quarter of the 20th century, many of the best-known, most successful corporations paid "trend shops" enormous sums of money to predict what products and interests would capture the public's fancy. Some of their predictions suggested the inevitable results of events already set in motion; others were examples of wishful thinking—sometimes the type of wishful thinking in which companies have a huge equity investment.

In any case, most trend shop predictions don't come true, but people don't seem to mind (except the people who paid the million bucks or so to the trend shops). News cycles are faster and shorter, the hunger for information is insatiable, and looking back at yesterday's story is boring. The number of 24-hour TV news channels and the list of specialty publications have fueled the fire. The better to focus on the hit of the season, the hottest game in town, the flavor of the month, and on revising today's list of what's hot and what's not—what's in and what's out.

As the year 2000 dawned, the most widely publicized scandal in the history of the U.S. government was little more than a year old and seemed all but forgotten, a footnote reference with all the rush-to-market books stacked high on "remainder" tables at $2.99 each. Such is the shelf life of a major scandal and, quite often, of a major success.

Toy makers, desperate for a winner and a big score, were calling Pokémon the year's sensation, with toys, games, clothes, books, trading cards, and a huge movie opening and animated TV show saturating the market in time for Christmas. This was accompanied by the seemingly now-obligatory cover story in a national news weekly. The public dutifully stood in line for hours (with CNN watching, taping, and sending the live feed out to more than 200 countries), only to be told everything had been sold. This validated the marketer's claim of success, or what should more correctly be called the sensation du jour. There were fleeting memories of Furby, Tickle-Me-Elmo, the Cabbage Patch Kids, the Power Rangers . . . all sensations-past and featured at the last garage sale. No one really expects Pokémon to be around long. But no matter. It is more important to the market to have a "hot" item, even if the flames are artificial.

Also in 1999, the long-awaited release of the fourth film in the *Star Wars* series generated more interest and stories about how much the film cost and, more important, how much money everyone was making from it and its merchandising deals, than about the movie itself. The real story was in the grosses and the merchandising. The movie was reviewed as highly forgettable. Hype was more of the story than the story itself. It is expected that the toys and games will remain on the store shelves after the film has had its run at the second-tier cheap theaters.

While Walt Disney Studios seemed to practice merchandising hype earlier and better than anyone else, the first three *Star Wars* films brought the process to new heights and proved what could be done with the right vehicle and some negotiating skills. Since then, few subjects escape the merchandising machine: films and TV shows, the overnight ascent of a "pop star," an airline disaster, the death of a princess, a scandal, and a millennium have all been marked by albums, books, magazines, shirts, caps, videos, websites, and a series of "collector's plastic drinking mugs" from Burger King. Or Tiffany. Or the Franklin Mint.

The public is in on it: *hype rules.*

Credibility Succumbs

Tuning in to see "America's most talked-about new show" is important because, when all the hype dies down, the program will most likely be quickly dropped. The steak will have been totally lost in the sizzle.

So, what's ahead for marketers?

One thing can be counted on for certain: *cynicism.*

Research indicates that people are believing less and less of what they see and hear. A claim of what "nine out of ten doctors recommend . . ." or "people overwhelmingly prefer . . ." is more likely to be dismissed with a shrug and assumed to be untrue, even with "an independent testing laboratory" report or a "seal of approval."

Results of public opinion polls are rejected with comments such as "Well, nobody polled *me*" or with another poll showing the opposite conclusion. The public no longer asks how it is possible for so many things to be the choice of a generation; they simply ignore the claims.

Curiously, among the major entries on most marketers' "To Do" lists, establishing or restoring credibility is missing. The priority is being on the fast track, being *out there,* visible—everywhere—and if the message doesn't connect fast, cut your losses and move on. Shelf space is tight; broadcast and cable space is cluttered with rapid-fire messages and thousands of impressions and thousands of choices.

Market analysts, buyers, retailers, reviewers, and the public have no time for people, products, or causes that cannot register an immediate impact and make them *want* to know more.

It's All a Blur

The lines between *real* and *not quite real* are blurring. The tabloid news shows and the tabloids themselves; "reality" shows; docudramas, programs that look like news or documentaries and feature "recreations of actual events"; *Jerry Springer, Jenny Jones, Maury, Sally, Montel,* and other TV programs showing unlimited hours of human train wrecks stretch the limits of what real people actually say and do and how they live.

Into all this comes the marketer with the products and services that will change your life. A word often used to describe audiences in the 21st century is *numb.*

In the 1999 novel *Turn of the Century,* author Kurt Andersen writes of a company with a plan for "A *New Age* cable channel, although 'New Age' is a non-no. Demi, Deepak, Marianne Williamson, Mars and Venus, Mayans and the Sphinx, gyroscopes, high colonics, homeopathics, chiropractic, yoga, Enya, John Tesh, Dr. Weil, Kenny G, vitamin E, herbs, Travolta, Cruise, lifestyle, feng shui, ginseng, gingko, tofu, emu oil, psychics, ESP, E.T., et cetera, et cetera. Aromatherapy, VH-1 meets Lifetime meets PBS fund-raising specials meets those good-looking morning show doctors meets QVC meets the Food Network . . . and the late night day part, tantric sex."

Anyone for a trend, fad, or flavor of the month?

Andersen shows all the signs of being a first-rate satirist, or does he? Satire loses its edge when the reality of the day's events begins to seem more bizarre than fiction. The concept of the New Age cable channel described seems amusing and includes everything but broccoli. Yet, an hour spent watching daytime TV in the year 2000 left a feeling that the New Age was here and the cable channel description could have been plucked right from the listings in *TV Guide.* Cable channels, in their efforts to top each other, offer outrageous programming that regularly "pushes the envelope" just for the sake of pushing it. Less and less is off-limits in prime time, particularly on HBO, Showtime, and Fox, which base their reputations on taking risks and doing what their competitors won't.

What Happened to Our Standards?

What this means to marketers is a major shift in standards of what's acceptable in all media. While no one openly advocates lowering professional or ethical standards or compromising "family values," the most prestigious newspapers now print stories and photos that less than a decade earlier would have raised eyebrows in the *National Enquirer.*

In an earlier volume, titled *Shock Marketing,* I noted, "Few of us, in or out of marketing, have not at some point seen an ad or a TV commercial or witnessed a promotion of some sort—perhaps even one touted as a major event—that stopped us cold and made us wonder of the advertisers, 'What could they have been thinking when they came up with *that*?' "

The public and the ad industry were questioning whether or not it was appropriate, much less good marketing, to present Calvin Klein ads that critics charged bordered on pornography or Benetton ads that many people found flatly offensive. The questionable material was presented, not discreetly in the back pages of *Playboy* or *Cosmopolitan* or *Hustler* or even on late-night cable TV, but on billboards, on the sides of buses, and on prime-time television.

Ah! But were they *effective*?

The best available data indicate that they were far more effective at generating publicity and controversy—both usually good for brand awareness—than they were at generating sales, brand loyalty, or corporate equity (*not* good for business).

Most marketers operating on limited budgets, at some time or another, must flirt with the idea of doing something outrageous to get attention. Fortunately for the industry and the profession, most of them snap out of it before the media buy is made.

Most, but not all. Some examples . . .

How Many Kinds of Sick . . . ?

In 1999, Budget Rent-A-Car, a global operation with a need to court the business market aggressively, ran a series of TV spots intended to be funny. No doubt, to a certain demographic and, more specifically, to a certain age-group, they were *very* funny. But are these the people who will be renting cars for corporations around the world? The most talked-about spot in the series, to call attention to the fact that Budget rented the popular Ranger sport utility vehicles, showed a bear vomiting on a forest ranger.

Earlier that year, the same ad agency created a campaign for the computer software company Outpost.com that featured gerbils being fired from cannons at the *O* in Outpost. Another spot in the series treated viewers to a high school marching band being attacked by wolves. The agency said it wanted "to establish the brand among hip computer software buyers, and the wilder the better to help navigate the sea of sameness out there in TV land," according to trade press reports.

Uh-huh.

Newsweek, under the headline "Shock Treatment," described how "Nike's arresting new campaign, which spotlights maimed athletes, stokes the debate over the lengths marketers must go to slice through the clutter."

Maimed athletes? That's what they need to slice through the clutter?

Specifically, a rodeo cowboy who'd been gored by a bull and left scarred and blind in one eye, a wrestler with a cauliflower ear, and a hockey player who'd taken his share of sticks to the face.

While it is true that these individuals are athletes, what exactly is the rationale in choosing them for TV spots and in highlighting their injuries? That the creative team at Nike believed this was the way to sell shoes and the company's other products says something about the direction that marketing is taking. It is "edgy" stuff, and Nike has always liked that. But it is also somewhat dark. And it comes at a time when analysts are pointing out that, while still a powerful brand, Nike is steadily losing ground among younger segments of the market. It is regarded as the brand that cuts between baby boomers and Generation X, two groups that are buying athletic shoes and sports-related products at a diminishing rate. It is not likely that this imagery will be very appealing to Nike's core group and just as unlikely that it will find a resonance with the younger market. So, then, who *is* it for?

A guess is that it is one of an increasing number of campaigns that agencies develop more to look interesting on their "new-business reel" than to move a product or enhance an image.

A View from the Pits

Sometimes marketing leads cultural change; other times it reflects it. When *Animal House* launched a series of "slob comedies" in 1977, it was largely accepted that these were fun parodies. After a quarter of a century of consciousness-raising, the pendulum is again swinging away from political correctness. The new century shift has turned up the volume and left much of the marketplace wondering if the blatant "new brutishness" is a gag or if the message really is a return to the image of man-as-caveman.

Both the United States and Britain have rolled out a variety of what have become known as "laddie books"—a dozen or so magazines that include such successes as *Maxim* and *Details* and advance the image of men as beer-drinking party animals whose version of *Masterpiece Theater* is *Baywatch* (the syndicated TV series that is pretty much an hour of buxom young women in bikinis running along a beach).

A very funny campaign that exemplifies this direction is for, appropriately, Brut, a brand of aftershave lotion and deodorant-antiperspirant that was a big name in the 1970s and two decades later had seen its market share in the low single digits. The campaign began with out-of-home signage and limited print ads containing almost teaser messages, such as "Smell better than guys twice as smart" and "Of course I'll respect you. I just won't call."

A TV spot that followed offers a dead-on parody of high-visibility pharmaceutical ads, warning, "Brut should not be used by guys who aren't real men." In a shot of a beautiful, buxom woman wearing a low-cut top and bending over a pool table—a shot designed to emphasize her ample cleavage—as other well-endowed women surround him, a Brut spokesman says soberly, "Brut has been considered an effective treatment for erectile dysfunction." A title card appears on screen with an advisory, "Brut antiperspirant should be applied to armpits only." In the final scene, the spokesman is standing over a hot tub where still more beautiful women indulge themselves as he tells viewers, "A small percentage of men wearing Brut have been stalked by centerfolds."

While there's no doubt that the ads are done in fun, the brand's ad agency CEO admits that, despite the fact that the campaign tested well with both men and women, "certain people might take offense."

Count on it. No doubt the "certain people" would include feminist groups. The culture that commends having a sense of humor shows wildly disparate ideas of what is funny. Further, the image of the sensitive, evolved male and political correctness in general have been experiencing a backlash, often in favor of the lovable, self-indulgent lug who, according to *Advertising Age*, "liked to ogle chicks, make fun of wimps, and generally do guy stuff like leave the seat up."

Former senator Bob Dole appears in intelligent, superbly crafted ads for Viagra, the most popular prescription product used in the treatment of erectile dysfunction. The fact that the product is the subject of a television commercial at all—and that the choice of words is so direct and unself-conscious, is an example of advertising moving light years forward in literally months. A year earlier, that ad would not have made it to TV and certainly not to a network owned by Disney—and been broadcast on Sunday mornings.

Now it is.

And it's parodied by a men's deodorant.

And that's only the beginning. Barriers are falling hard and fast.

Getting Real About the Internet

Marketers have always been sensitive to critical discussions of "perception versus reality." In the future, perception will be a much more dominant force, with reality less obvious and a couple of beats behind.

The attention lavished on the Internet and the World Wide Web has led to their not only dominating but also eclipsing other media and information sources. Even television channels and networks, to which other media have long bowed and stepped aside, encourages—sometimes *pleads* with—viewers of both news and entertainment programming to "check out our website."

What? That was supposed to work the other way. Television was where the mass media and the mass media's audiences met, and the power and ad prices reflected that. If the audience needed more information than the limited time that TV gave a story, that was where newspapers came in. They would have more of the story, perhaps a different perspective, and certainly some different ads.

But wait: the newspaper now *also* directs its readers to check out *its* website for more information.

And nearly every ad on TV and in print includes the same directive, causing audiences who *don't* check out these various websites to wonder what details may have been missed.

As perspectives go, this one is rather blatant. The Web and E-commerce are the new darlings on the cultural landscape and certainly in business and, thus, of marketing.

Here are three messages whose context is relevant to marketers:

"The problem isn't losing your customers to an e-business. It's losing them to someone else's e-business."   (MCI Worldcom in a full-page national newspaper ad)

"net/net: it's not as easy as just putting an e in front of everything." (Oracle software in a national newspaper ad)

"There's a Difference Between Running Banner Ads and Building Partnerships"   (i Village.com ad in a trade magazine)

These ads reflect a trend, a problem, and an aggressive attempt at finding a distinction in a crowded new ocean. Internet companies are aware that with the Internet explosion, the debris that an explosion causes is falling to the ground and leaving a big mess to clean up.

There are so many dot-coms, and so many new ones coming on board each day, that the awareness has come to business that consumers' heads are spinning. The marketplace has become so full so fast—and with such a vast array of new, unknown names—that conventional means (print, TV, billboards, direct mail) are being employed to help shape brand images. The new formula is the old formula. The brand that has the full-page ad is the brand that the target audience sees and develops a greater awareness of. The more times the ad runs, the greater the awareness.

Despite the attempts of many Internet marketers to convince businesses that the Internet is the only tool they need, it is not.

Search engines, billboards, and banners on-line are fine for the people who see them, but there is still a universe larger than the cyberuniverse *until everyone is on-line.* Every prospective client, customer, and constituent does not go first to the Internet to find an Internet company. Some do, but not all. The awareness of dot-com names will continue to come from *outside* the Internet community, and that's where the brand-building emphasis will be.

It is largely obligatory for all businesses and other entities with a message they wish to have known to have an Internet presence. But the great expectations of what the Net can do cannot be realized until the world finds, sees, and responds to a particular site.

Whether or not "getting there is half the fun," it is still more than half the requirement. *Getting* people to the site is the first challenge that marketers must overcome.

This, like all revolutions, will end, and dot-com fever will subside. In the future, the Internet will resemble the cyber–shopping malls that so many businesses have sought to create. And like other malls, some will be crowded and busy all year long, while others will look like rows of abandoned buildings, barely visible from the highway.

Spinning and Partnering: Isn't That Convenient?

In the world beyond the Internet, brand extensions and an unwavering commitment to maintaining visibility and presence will still be a major means of enhancing brand equity. This will be as true for new flavors of Cheerios as it will be for uses of Reese's peanut butter and new divisions of Andersen Consultants.

Time magazine spun off *People,* and *People* spun off *In Style,* both to great success. But *Time* has also recognized the equity in the *People* brand and introduced *Teen People* (dedicated to the teen market), *People Profiles* (with each issue profiling a single celebrity), and several foreign-language editions. Such successes don't go unnoticed, and other popular titles will broaden the markets not with the "special edition" of old days, but with companion editions and sister publications. This format offers marketers the added advantage of more finely targeted, specific demographics for advertising and PR possibilities.

Partnering also will be an increasingly more attractive option for marketers. While there will continue to be mergers and megamergers and acquisitions, business is identifying *relationships of convenience* that stop short of marriage, such as that of Microsoft and NBC television to create the cable TV network MSNBC, as well as Microsoft and R. R. Donnelley & Sons Company, in creating E-books—books that are available for reading on screens that don't strain the readers' eyes. Disney–MGM Studio tours is another such joint venture.

Candie's shoes and *Rolling Stone* magazine struck a deal under which the popular brand of teen shoes agreed to carry selected articles and music reviews from *Rolling Stone* on its website as a way of attracting greater interest in the site. Candie's had been a longtime advertiser in the pages of *Rolling Stone* and continued to be.

In another case, the giant magazine publisher Ziff-Davis launched *ZD Internet Life* in 1995, but after one test issue, the book was modified to reflect the company's agreement to partner with the popular search engine Yahoo! The magazine, *Yahoo! Internet Life,* was relaunched to great success.

Corporate marriages have not gone totally out of style, however. America Online's merger-acquisition deal with Time Warner will have the market watching for synergies to arise from mergers between Disney and Somebody Big, between Microsoft and Somebody Bigger, and between Rupert Murdoch's News Corporation and Whoever Is Left.

Generation X Marks the Spot

Tastes and trends in advertising are showing more of a generational bias. As members of Generation X come more fully into their own and assume the

The Franklin Mint

Treasures for a New Age of Faith

And Now for Something a Little Unusual

The Franklin Mint has developed a reputation as a purveyor of collectible items, mostly replicas of highly desirable statuaries, jewelry, and memorabilia from guns to literary treasures. This catalog allows the company to showcase its diversified offerings in rich four-color and broaden its base. The name "Franklin Mint" as a brand has emerged more prominently than any of the items it sells. Despite the "on-line revolution" the company's largest demographic group finds this traditional direct-mail catalog format, focusing specifically on religious items, very well suited to its tastes. (Copyright 1999 The Franklin Mint) roles of program directors, creative directors, head copywriters, commercial directors, and producers, the sense of humor and sensibilities of that generation will become more reflected in their work. Ads and campaigns are less about promoting a message or a product and are more about projecting a *brand attitude*. The distinction between *image* and *attitude* is insignificant: Image is about how people think of you, while attitude is a deeper coloration, a suggestion that the advertiser almost *doesn't care* what the audience thinks, though, of course, that's not the case. It's a more *agressive* approach. Here are three examples of brand attitude large and small:

- A full-page national newspaper ad left the upper four-fifths of the page blank, except for a single sentence in small type reading, "In the spirit of the season, we're donating $150 to your favorite charity. You." The bottom of the page provided the details: "Get $150 when you sign up for Covad DSL Today." Attitude.
- A full-page ad in advertising trade papers showed a rough marker drawing of a frowning face—the reverse of the classic "happy face" symbol. The headline: "The client wants his wife in the ad. Singing. A jingle."

   The subhead: "Your priorities might be different if you had AIDS."

   The ad was for a fund-raising event to benefit the USA-Federation of New York AIDS Initiative and the American Foundation for AIDS Research. The name of the event was the Madison Avenue Sellout. Fund-raising for causes is a tough and extremely competitive exercise. In light of that, some people might question whether or not it was wise to offer an ad that might be viewed as smug, elitist, arrogant, a bit too in-your-face, or at least off-putting. In any case, it's the attitude.
- An ad that appeared in national magazines and newspapers showed actor Pierce Brosnan all dressed in black. The copy is not attributed to him, and if the reader is not a fan or is unfamiliar with his work, the only reference to his identity is a lower-left-corner line in microscopic type which reads, "Pierce Brosnan photo donated by Greg Gorman." Why is Pierce Brosnan in the ad? It doesn't say. What the ad *does* say, in three paragraphs of reverse-out text—white on black background—in type smaller than the warning on an aspirin bottle, will go unknown to at least a couple of generations of readers. It's unreadable. The headline is "words are not enough," and the logo is a draw-

words are not enough

Everyone knows that actions speak louder than words. And conserving the world's forests requires action. Yours. Mine. Everyone's. Now there's something new that we can do. We can look for the Forest Stewardship Council label when we buy furniture, flooring, lumber and other household goods made out of wood.

The FSC label guarantees that the forest a product came from is managed to protect clean water, wildlife habitat and recreation. That's why World Wildlife Fund, The Wilderness Society, Rainforest Alliance and Natural Resources Defense Council are all proud and active supporters of the nonprofit Forest Stewardship Council.

You don't have to be a movie star to be an action hero. Help conserve the world's forests. Look for and purchase products carrying the FSC label. For more information visit www.fscus.org/trees or call toll-free 1-877-FSC-LOGO

FSC Forest Stewardship Council
Global Leaders in Responsible Forestry

Pierce Brosnan photo donated by Greg Gorman.

Words in the Dark

The Forest Stewardship Council sounds like an environmentally friendly organization. To be effective, it might follow the lead of socially conscious groups that developed themselves according to formula methods of creating brand awareness. In this widely published ad featuring a photograph of actor Pierce Brosnan, the group's identity and mission are lost in small, hard-to-read text. Clearly this ad attempted to convey strength and dignity. The audience shouldn't have to work hard to "get" the advertiser's message, particularly in instances of social consciousness. Simplicity may have had a more dramatic effect. (FSC trademark copyright 1996 Forest Stewardship Council. Pierce Brosnan photograph donated to the advertiser by Greg Gorman)

ing that looks like a tree above the letters *FSC*. Next to that are the words "Forest Stewardship Council." Below are two lines too small to be read. Presumably this is a good cause about the environment (or maybe only about forests), and Brosnan and Gorman thought they were doing a good thing by lending their photograph and image, but this ad is so heavy with a sense of self-importance that whatever the message is supposed to be is lost. Instead, it's attitude.

These print ads are very different in content from the TV spots for Brut and Outpost.com (they are not suggesting they are joking), but they are alike in reflecting a similar sense of smug, self-assured righteousness, of the advertiser's (and its agency's) affecting a posture of superiority. This approach is in marked contrast to traditional ads and marketing campaigns that invite the audience in and ask (sometimes desperately) to be liked. While the idea of breaking with tradition in advertising is often regarded as laudable, this approach *dares* the audience not to accept a message on its terms. The ads challenge the audience and this practice is to be seen as a good thing. Sorry. Certainly the funny spots take a bit of the edge off (the audience doesn't know how much of it to take seriously, if any), but this is still the reflection of a generation of marketing that will not be accused of sucking up to the market, and that means that pretty much anything goes.

Saturday Night Live and *Mad TV* push the limits of comedy and satire on network TV, including a number of outrageous commercial parodies per show. Some are tasteless, others merely loud. This is an exercise in giving the audience what you think it wants. Cable TV dropped the barriers in all types of programming, including documentaries. Radio personalities, such as Howard Stern, continue trying to see how far they can go each day, and they keep going further (in Stern's case, in radio, TV, movies, books, and on-line). Televised congressional investigations of President Clinton gave the public explicit testimony and dialogue that would not have been allowed in any regular programming. After that, where are the media to go? The public wants more hard-hitting, uncensored information and programming, and there is no turning back.

Marketers with a finger on the pulse understand that the public is in a period of uncertainty, cynicism toward established institutions, and frustration with hypocrisy—and yet, in good economic times, opportunities are great. If marketers have something to say, it is time to take their best shot. Words and pictures that tell a story in the most aggressive and graphic way are being permitted and are being judged differently by audiences of different generations. There will be more shots fired before it stops.

The Byword and the Buzzwords

Relationship marketing, a.k.a. *one-on-one marketing*, will occupy marketers' attention, and with good reason. Marketers who are infatuated with the Internet can use it to develop personal and personalized connections to customers, clients, and prospects cost-effectively, reflecting specific areas of interest and building loyalty. Marketers who prefer a more traditional, less technology-driven arena will use phones, mailboxes, and personal contacts to the extent that each method works for them, but pursuing a more personal connection to customers and supporters will be the rule.

Whether the approach, contact, and response are interactive through technology or a postage stamp, future marketers will have greater latitude. More than before, the limits are set high enough to accommodate whatever works.

Some future marketers will also have a larger vocabulary. The buzzwords are coming . . . although the term *buzzword* is already somewhat passé. So, the practice may well be described another way, but it will still amount to not so much reinventing a product, service, brand, or company as repositioning and repackaging it. It could be called the "Julia Child Method." The great American French chef was credited with saying, "If the meal doesn't turn out the way it was supposed to, serve it anyway, but call it something else."

An example of this is the firm formerly known as Arnell Group Brand Consulting, which announced it wanted to be called AG. But that wasn't all. The agency also doesn't want to handle production for the ads it creates and wants what it does to be called "market making." It wanted it so badly, in fact, that it trademarked the term.

A number of other agencies have decided they would rather be called brand agencies than ad agencies. One firm no longer has "specialists" in certain disciplines, it has "competency groups." Agencies are recognizing the need (yet again) to do for themselves what they've been doing for clients for years: differentiate themselves from other agencies. It's a perfectly fine strategy; however, it comes dangerously close to violating an important rule: Don't take yourself too seriously. The light is always to stay on the product, brand, or message, not on the ad agency (or market maker, as the case may be).

Stunts, Sponsors, and Stand-Alones

In a case of family values getting covered over by its popular "Big Shirt," Abercrombie & Fitch has decided that its attempts to attract younger customers have done well, so it's time for sex. The grand old retailer has developed a catalog that contains mostly close-to-nude photographs and an interview with a porn star. The catalog also sells for $6. A&F has warned that due to mature subject matter, customers must be 18 years of age or older to buy this catalog. A logical question is, why would such a respected, established retailer resort to what appears to be a gratuitous publicity stunt?

One reason is that it works. Within days of the catalog's publication, it was being talked about on NBC's morning network show. Millions of people who will never see the catalog got the message that the store is out to change its image to that of a livelier, sexier, *younger* store.

Is putting out a sexy catalog the market trend?

Maybe. More likely, a catalog, a fashion layout in *Vanity Fair,* a controversial celebrity endorser—whatever gets the network news spot and the story on the AP wire that says "This company is not what you thought it was, so look again"—is the next trend. A lawsuit, a gift to make a dream come true . . . the old-fashioned publicity stunt is back, and even old-line, conservative businesses aren't above rolling the dice to cut through the clutter and be noticed.

Speaking of clutter . . .

"This evening's performance is brought to you by . . ."—Hey, wait! If I just paid full price for these tickets, where does this sponsorship business come in?

It comes in to the legitimate theater, which used to be too proud, too sophisticated, and too lacking in marketing savvy to make the deal. Most plays attract a specific demographic that advertisers like to reach and impress with their willingness to support the arts and, by the way, slip in a product message. Belatedly, the arts are learning what organized sports learned decades earlier: that appreciative fans, supporters, and spectators, because they paid for their tickets, need not be placed in a marketing-free environment.

Buy a ticket and look for an ad—on the ticket itself, as well as on the ticket envelope. Be shown to your seat by an usher who gives you a playbill with the usual amount of advertising in it, but with a new addition, a richly printed insert featuring a special welcome from a sponsor. Some theater programs appear to be on their way to looking like Sunday newspapers, filled with "supplements" and promotional messages.

We may soon come upon an insert that reads, "In tonight's performance, the part of Maria will be played by an unknown actress, but she was brought to the theater in a new Lexus—how about you?"

And speaking of newspapers, selling ads has always been a matter of circulation, demographics, ad size, and cost: the factors that determine who's in, who's out, and who couldn't afford the media buy, no matter how much sense it seemed to make. But what if there were a more affordable, more targeted format with much of the impact of the newspaper's prestige, less clutter, and a longer shelf life?

That could work, and one example of it is *Mature Adult,* a digest-size guide to hundreds of assisted-living and care facilities. This is a market of growing importance to seniors and their families. Most facilities don't have ad budgets, and very few can advertise in daily newspapers, such as the *Chicago Tribune,* at all, much less on a regular basis. The guide is put together through the resources of the newspaper and carries its masthead on its cover, but it is not part of the paper itself. It is distributed at shopping centers, commuter stations, and strategic drop points, where it is available free of charge. Participants get a longer run than a daily paper provides and the halo effect of the paper's reputation.

Summary Points

1. For marketers, much of the attention in the future will be on technology and Internet marketing, yet the principles of marketing that have proved true (and worked very well) over time will be no less important.
2. The great demand for content, created by the sprawling, 24-hour, multimedia machine of cable TV stations, specialty magazines, and the Internet, will force marketers to continually "refresh" and refashion messages to keep brands and products hot.
3. Standards of acceptability in media are changing, but getting attention for brands with "shock marketing" techniques will not create brand equity or brand loyalty any more than such practices did in years past.

4. Marketing can *lead* cultural changes or it can *reflect* cultural changes. Either course offers tremendous opportunities.

5. The "attitude" that was clearly on display in ads that flooded the market in 2000 reflected the Generation X sensibility, cynicism, and sense of humor. The controversy provides a lesson for marketers: be bright, but don't exclude members of other market segments or generations from either the joke or the chance to act on the offer in your message. Some of them may be your target market next season.

What's Wrong?

Earlier, the term *generational bias* crept into this text. Alas, sometimes a particular style or trend will appear to gain momentum when it shouldn't. If that statement seems in itself to reflect a bias, generational or otherwise, consider the principles of effective communication that have been proved worthy enough to justify their continued use. Then consider some all too frequently committed acts that marketers are perpetrating against their own best interests:

- Ads with too much reverse-out text (in some cases, entire brochures). This technique may look bold, dazzling, or arty, but reverse-out text for more than a headline and subhead is hard on the eyes and a strain to read, so it doesn't get read, and the message is never received.
- Printing in colors with poor contrast, such as blue on blue, white on gray, white on yellow, black on dark blue may look artistic, but it all too often can't be read.
- Disjointed, chaotic layouts for print ads, direct mail, and other printed material: micro type in six different fonts, stories within stories, sidebars everywhere. When it's hard to read, it doesn't get read—even if it looks really cool.
- Noisy commercials with people screaming and incessant percussion (drum solos). They get attention and often make an audience not like the advertiser. Although this is not new, it is an increasingly popular method of standing out from a cluster of ad spots. But when more than one advertiser is doing it, no one is standing out. Loud ads are also a poor substitute for creative ads.

Creatively, whether in TV programming, commercials, or print ads, every season and every generation has its style. Successes are copied; style of humor and even layout and design are emulated. Print advertising in 2000 is marked by two distinguishing features that are somewhat opposing. One is the previously referred to mix-and-match of typefaces and hyper-layouts that attempt a print version of the MTV quick cuts or of a computer screen of banners, snipes, rolls, and multiple images in one frame. The other side of this bad penny, also discussed previously, is a heavy use of white space, where the upper half or more of the available message area carries a short centered headline. This is supposed to create impact. The bottom of the page responds to the headline, makes a statement, and closes with a logo.

Either or both of these treatments can be effective if done well and if the offer is attractive or seductive enough. Too often, though, the first approach appears so cluttered, with too much going on at once, that a reader won't go to the trouble of sorting it out. In the other, to devote most of the page to a setup line suspended in a sea of white space, the line had better be good. A glib or cynical setup that assumes a self-important positioning is an invitation to turn the page. The reader is not a captive audience and does not owe the advertiser the investment in seeing where the ad is going. Since readers are mainly interested in what's in the message for them, a self-indulgent ad won't get read and is money poorly spent.

What's Right?

Very much.

This is a period in marketing in which the old rules apply if they still work, *because* they still work.

It is also a time in which creativity is encouraged, and new ideas are blossoming all around.

The Internet is a grand new stage, playing field, and venue that offers opportunities to fit every marketing budget.

Print in magazines, newspapers, direct mail, and out-of-home media has never been more alive and well. Target marketing and demographic segmentation have helped marketers to be more effective more often with less waste and less money. It is often said (especially by people in the printing business) that TV and radio ads, no matter how interesting, are forgotten not long after the pictures and sounds have been replaced by other pictures and sounds, but print stays around to look at again and again. While there is an obvious truth to that, the impact generated by the immediacy sometimes is worth sacrificing the longer shelf life. Both are positive methods.

Cable and satellite TV have brought numerous opportunities for targeted, cost-effective advertising and message placement through PR or event coverage.

It is truly a good time to be a marketer.

It is a golden age . . . on its way to platinum.

The future is a moving target with changes and innovations all the time. This can be a blessing or a curse. Try to think of it as a blessing and work with it.

Bibliography

Advertising Age: "Advertising's trouble starts with its fixation on youth" by Rance Crain, September 13, 1999; "Arnell tries on new moniker, focuses on 'market making'" by Beth Synder; "Bad Beanie," editorial, September 6, 1999; "Barbie gets image ads in time for 40th birthday" by Beth Snyder, February 8, 1999; "Beanie brouhaha" by Laura Petrecca, September 6, 1999; "Bear vomit for your next ads? Sorry, Budget beat you to it" by Rance Crain, October 25, 1999; "Brut ad reeks of bad-boy attitude" by Anthony Vagnoni, October 18, 1999; "Interactive Special Report," November 1, 1999; "Top 100 mega brands" by R. Craig Endicott, July 12, 1999; "Volvo creates a Gen Xer pitchman for Web effort" by Laura Clark Geist, February 15, 1999; "Watching the E-parade" by Patricia Riedman, July 26, 1999; "Web shops savor their differences from ad agencies" by Jennifer Gilbert, July 26, 1999; "*Yahoo! Internet Life* finds real success in virtual world" by Carol Krol, March 8, 1999.

Advertising in America by Charles Goodrum and Helen Dalrymple. New York: Harry N. Abrams Publishing, 1990.

Age Wave: The Challenges and Opportunities of an Aging America by Ken Dychtwald, Ph.D., and Joe Flower. Los Angeles: Jeremy P. Tarcher, Inc., 1989.

American Demographics, "Targets big enough to miss" by Joe Marconi, October 1996.

Beanie Collector, published by Beckett Service Group, Inc., 1997.

Brill's Content, "How many? How much? Who cares?" by Jennifer Greenstein, November 1998.

Business Intelligence by Kirk W. M. Tyson. Lombard, IL: Leading Edge Publications, 1986.

Business Week: "Generation Y" by Ellen Neubourne with Kathleen Kerwin, February 15, 1999; "Masters of the Web universe" by Steve Hamm, September 27, 1999; "The most influential people in the electronic business" by Robert D. Hof, September 27, 1999.

Chicago Tribune: "Boomer consumers" by Ellen Warren, April 17, 1997; "Donnelley, Microsoft hope for E-bookworms" by Rob Kaiser, November 5, 1999.

The Conquest of Cool by Thomas Frank. Chicago: University of Chicago Press, 1997.

Crain's New York Business, "Old media gets a boost from new media ads" by Valerie Block, July 7–13, 1999.

Forbes Critical Mass, "A revolutionary question" by Bob Schmetterer, Fall 1999.

Generation X: Tales for an Accelerated Culture by Douglas Coupland. New York: St. Martin's Press, 1995.

Global Demographics by Judith E. Nichols. Chicago: Bonus Books, 1995.

Hearing the Voice of the Market by Vincent P. Barrabba and Gerald Zaltman. Boston: Harvard Business School Press, 1991.

How to Market to Women by Carol Nelson. Detroit: Visible Ink Press, 1994.

The Late Show by Helen Gurley Brown. New York: William Morrow and Company, 1993.

Marketing Revolution by Kevin J. Clancy and Robert S. Shulman. New York: Harper Business, 1991.

Marketing to Generation X by Karen Ritchie. New York: Free Press, 1995.

Mass Communication by John R. Bittner. New York: Prentice-Hall, 1986.

The Mature Market by Robert S. Menchin. Chicago: Probus Publishing, 1989.

Maxi Marketing by Stan Rapp and Tom Collins. New York: McGraw Hill, 1987.

Megatrends 2000 by Jerry Naisbitt and Patricia Aburdene. New York: William Morrow and Company, 1990.

MTV: The Making of a Revolution by Tom McGrath. Philadelphia, PA: Running Press, 1996.

Newsweek: "Shock treatment" by Adam Bryant, November 1, 1999; "Trouble brewing" by David A. Kaplan, July 19, 1999; "Wired for the bottom line" by Steven Levy, September 20, 1999.

New York, "Barnes & Noble's Jekyll and Hyde" by Daniel D. Kirkpatrick, July 19, 1999.

The New Yorker, "Fast, cheap, and out of control" by Kurt Andersen, July 12, 1999.

New York Times: "Despite appearances, dot-com companies try to spend advertising dollars effectively" by Stuart Elliott, November 9, 1999; "A feeding frenzy made for consumers" by Saul Hansell, September 22, 1999; "Measuring a combined Viacom/CBS against other media giants", September 8, 1999; Advertising supplement, "Playing the numbers, research shows the power of print" by Samir Husni, October 6, 1999; "Research finds consumers worldwide belong to six basic groups that cross national lines" by Stuart Elliott, June 25, 1998; "What's new, pussycat?" by Samir Husni, October 6, 1999; "Where does Generation Y go to shop?" by Sharon R. King, August 28, 1999.

New York Times Magazine, "Brand illusions" by Todd Prugan, September 12, 1999.

New York Times Pocket MBA Series: Sales and Marketing by Michael A. Kamins, Ph.D. New York: Lebhar-Friedman Books, 1999.

Ogilvy on Advertising by David Ogilvy. New York: Crown Publishers, 1983.

The Portable MBA in Marketing by Alexander Hiam and Charles D. Scheve. New York: John Wiley & Sons, 1992.

Relationship Marketing by Regis McKenna. Reading, MA: Addison-Wesley Publishing Company, 1991.

Selling the Invisible by Harry Beckwith. New York: Warner Books, 1997.

Sharp Marbles, "Looking through the Internet" by Steve Jareo, Jareo-Jareo Marketing Communications, 1999.

Shock Marketing by Joe Marconi. Chicago: Bonus Books, 1997.

Silver Linings by Herschell Gordon Lewis. Chicago: Bonus Books, 1996.

Time, "Battle for the soul of the Internet" by Philip Elmer-Dewitt, July 25, 1994.

Turn of the Century by Kurt Andersen. New York: Random House, 1999.

2,001 Things That Won't Make It into the 21st Century, compiled by Career Press, Franklin Lakes, NJ, 2000.

Used and Rare: Travels in the Book World by Lawrence and Nancy Goldstone. New York: Thomas Dunne Books/St. Martin's Press, 1997.

Wall Street Journal, "*Rolling Stone*, shoe firm set unusual deal" by Rebecca Quick, November 4, 1999.

Index

About the Author

JOE MARCONI IS a marketing communications consul-
tant and writer with more than two decades of award-winning work to his
credit. His writing has appeared in the *International Herald Tribune*, the
Chicago Tribune, American Demographics, and *Adweek.* He is the author of
eight books including: *Image Marketing, Crisis Marketing, The Complete
Guide to Publicity,* and *The Brand Marketing Book.* He is also the editor of
the newsletter *Marconi on Marketing.* He is managing principal of Marketing
Communications in Western Springs, Illinois, and a partner in
CommunicationsResource.com in Chicago.

For more information contact:

Joe Marconi Marketing Communications, Inc.

Phone: 708/246-7102

Fax: 708/246-6790

E-mail: casmgt@aol.com

The American Marketing Association is the world's largest and most comprehensive professional association of marketers. With over 45,000 members, the AMA has more than 500 chapters throughout North America. The AMA sponsors 25 major conferences per year, covering topics ranging from the latest trends in customer satisfaction measurement to business-to-business and service marketing, attitude research and sales promotion, and publishes nine major marketing publications.

For further information on the American Marketing Association, call toll free at 800-AMA-1150.

Or write to:

The American Marketing Association
311 South Wacker Drive
Suite 5800
Chicago, IL 60606-2266
Fax: 800-950-0872
URL: http://www.ama.org